The excellence of play

The excellence of play

3rd edition

Edited by Janet Moyles

 Open University Press

Open University Press
McGraw-Hill Education
McGraw-Hill House
Shoppenhangers Road
Maidenhead
Berkshire
England
SL6 2QL

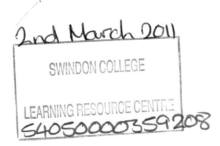

email: enquiries@openup.co.uk
world wide web: www.openup.co.uk

and Two Penn Plaza, New York, NY 10121-2289, USA

First published 1994
Reprinted 1994, 1995 (twice), 1996, 1998, 1999, 2000, 2002, 2003 (twice), 2004, 2005
Second edition 2005
Reprinted 2007, 2008, 2009
First published in this third edition 2010

A catalogue record of this book is available from the British Library

ISBN 13: 978 0 33 524094 4
ISBN 10: 0 33 524094 1

Library of Congress Cataloging-in-Publication Data
CIP data applied for

Typeset by RefineCatch Limited, Bungay, Suffolk
Printed and bound in Great Britain by Bell and Bain Ltd, Glasgow

Mixed Sources
Product group from well-managed forests and other controlled sources
www.fsc.org Cert no. TT-COC-002769
© 1996 Forest Stewardship Council

The **McGraw·Hill** Companies

Contents

Figures and photographs

Figures

Photographs

Notes on the editor and contributors

Angela Anning is currently Emeritus Professor of Early Childhood Education at the University of Leeds and visiting professor at Leeds Metropolitan University. She has a background in teaching early years education at class teacher, headteacher, lecturer and researcher levels. Her current research interests include the curriculum for young children (in particular, art and design education), the professional knowledge of those who work with young children, and multi-agency teamwork in delivering services to young children and their families. She is an investigator within the National Evaluation of Sure Start team based at Birkbeck College. She has a strong belief in the key role of creative play-based activities and high-quality experiential learning in promoting young children's learning at home and in early years group settings. Angela has written widely on early years education.

Pat Broadhead is Professor of Playful Learning at Leeds Metropolitan University, and was formerly an early years and primary teacher. Her main research interest relates to how children become sociable and cooperative through play and the links with learning across the 3–7 age range. She has a number of publications, including: *Early Years Play and Learning: Developing Social Skills and Cooperation* (RoutledgeFalmer 2004), *Children, Families and Communities: Creating and Sustaining Integrated Services* (OUP 2008, with Meleady and Delgado) and, most recently, 'Conflict resolution and children's behaviour: observing and understanding social and cooperative play in early years educational settings' (*Early Years* 29(2): 105–118). She was, until recently, Chair of TACTYC (www.tactyc.org.uk).

Tina Bruce, CBE, is an honorary visiting professor at Roehampton University, having originally trained at the Froebel Educational Institute as a primary teacher (3–13 years) with emphasis on 3–7 years. She was head of the Froebel Research Nursery School in the college and joined the staff, becoming Director of the Centre for Early Childhood. Tina has worked with the British Council in New Zealand and Egypt, and was awarded International Woman Scholar by the University of Virginia Commonwealth, where she has given guest lectures and workshops. She was part of the working groups developing the Early Years

Foundation Stage and has published many books and articles, and given keynote lectures in the UK and abroad.

Tricia David has been extremely fortunate throughout her career in early childhood education and care to learn from so many wonderful people: children, parents, headteachers, teachers, advisers, researchers, lecturers, policy makers, colleagues from other services. Much of that experience has been international, much has been at home over her lifetime with family members of six generations, within different and changing communities. As Emeritus Professor of Education at Canterbury Christ Church University, Tricia continues to be fascinated by young children's learning and the role of play.

Dan Davies is Professor of Science and Technology Education and Director of the Centre for Research in Early Scientific Learning (CRESL) at Bath Spa University. He started his career as a primary and early years teacher in London, spent time as an education officer at the Design Council and lectured in primary science education at Goldsmiths University of London before taking up his present post. He has written extensively on primary science and technology in the early years and primary phases, and is the author of the forthcoming *Teaching Science Creatively* (to be published in 2010).

Bernadette Duffy, CBE, is Head of the Thomas Coram Centre in Camden, one of the first schools to be designated a Children's Centre. Bernadette was part of the working parties that devised the Early Years Foundation Stage Framework and is a member of a number of Department for Children, Schools and Families advisory committees. She has contributed to a range of publications and is the author of *Supporting Creativity and Imagination in the Early Years* (OUP 2006). She is co-editor with Dame Gillian Pugh of *Contemporary Issues in the Early Years* (Sage 2009). Bernadette is Chair of the British Association for Early Childhood Education and was on the advisory committee of the Cambridge University Primary Review.

Aline-Wendy Dunlop is Chair of Childhood and Primary Studies at the University of Strathclyde, Glasgow, where she provides leadership in teaching and learning and in applied educational research. Her current research includes a 14-year longitudinal study of 150 children, which is nearing completion and will allow inferences to be drawn between two major educational transitions: entry to primary education and subsequent entry to secondary education, as well as offering insights into transition trajectories throughout the years of statutory education. She was Principal Investigator for the Positive Behaviour in the Early Years Study (2008) and the Scottish Autism Toolbox Project (2009). She is Vice-President of Early Education.

Hilary Fabian is an education consultant with a long career in education, teaching in primary schools and universities, and researching transitions. Since 1991 she has worked in the university sector, first at the Manchester Metropolitan University where she was course leader for the Early Years Continuing Professional Development programmes, then at the University of Edinburgh. From 2002 to 2009 she was Head of Education and Childhood Studies at Glyndŵr University, Wrexham. Her PhD thesis, books and journal publications reflect her interest in transitions, particularly children starting school, children transferring between schools, and the way in which the induction process for children and adults to new settings is managed.

Jan Georgeson has a background in experimental psychology, and many years of teaching experience supporting children with communication difficulties and their families. Her doctoral study focused on culture and pedagogy in day nurseries and preschool playgroups. She has been involved in a range of research projects related to disability, disadvantage and children's voice, and supporting parents as educators of very young children. She is currently senior lecturer in Early Years Professional Status at the University of Chichester and is also seconded to the research team at the Children's Workforce Development Council, evaluating projects looking at new ways of doing social work.

Kathy Goouch is a lecturer and researcher at Canterbury Christ Church University, following a long teaching career in schools with children from 3 to 13. Her knowledge and experience of teaching and research span the fields of literacy and early years, and her publications reflect these twin interests, with the central theme of play weaving through both. Much of Kathy's research and writing, including her PhD, is now focused on the interactions between teacher and learner, and her current research project is attempting to understand the nature of the relationships in baby rooms in nurseries.

Rose Griffiths is a Senior Lecturer in Education at the University of Leicester, and was awarded a National Teaching Fellowship by the Higher Education Academy in 2009. Starting as a teacher with a particular interest in working with children who find maths difficult, Rose taught in primary, secondary and special schools, and worked with young children and their parents, including through Sure Start. Her publications include many books for children, parents and teachers. Rose's research interests have included counting and early arithmetic, raising the achievement of looked-after children, and childhood bereavement.

Justine Howard is Senior Lecturer in the School of Human and Health Science at Swansea University and the Programme Director of its Masters in

Developmental and Therapeutic Play. She is a Chartered Psychologist and holds a PhD in the psychology of education. Justine has worked as a play specialist alongside children with additional learning needs, and retains close links with practice via research and consultancy. Much of her research is concerned with children's perceptions of their play; she has published extensively on the topic of play and is co-author of *Play and Learning in the Early Years: From Research to Practice* (Sage 2010). She is also the Editor of the *Psychology of Education Review*.

Alan Howe has 25 years' experience of working in the field of education, teaching children, undergraduates, in-service and trainee teachers. He is currently co-programme leader for the undergraduate Education Studies programme at Bath Spa University, and has research interests in science and creativity. He has published widely in the field of early years and primary science and technology.

Helen Jameson is a practising teacher with over 20 years' experience. She has taught throughout the primary age range in both the maintained and independent sectors, working with very able/talented children as well as those with emotional and behavioural difficulties. She developed a special interest in learning through play while involved in research at Homerton College, University of Cambridge. Her paper on 'The effect of play upon oral and written storytelling in able 5 to 7-year-olds' was presented at the Jean Piaget Society 33rd Annual Meeting in Chicago in 2003.

Neil Kitson was previously a Lecturer in Education at the University of Leicester, with special interests in early years development and the role of drama in early childhood learning. He is currently involved with schools development in Northamptonshire. Having started his career working as a primary teacher, his interests in this area were further developed through his work as an advisory teacher for drama. He has lectured extensively, both in the UK and abroad, on the area of drama and its function in early childhood development, and has written books, chapters and articles on drama and other early years and primary issues.

Sara Knight is a Senior Lecturer in Education at Anglia Ruskin University. Originally trained in drama, but with grandparents all keen gardeners, Sara has found working with children in the early years or in playwork an excellent way to combine creativity with a love of the outdoors. She works with the environmental charity, the Green Light Trust, in Suffolk, latterly taking on the launch of Forest School across the eastern region. Sara is now working towards the inclusion of Forest School in all the degree pathways in the Faculty of Education. In 2009, she published *Forest Schools and Outdoor Learning in the*

Early Years (Sage) and is now working on *Forest School: Implementing the Ethos in a Range of Settings*.

Janet Moyles is Professor Emeritus, Anglia Ruskin University, and a play/early years consultant. She has worked as an early years teacher and head, and has written and edited widely, including *Just Playing?* (OUP 1989), *The Excellence of Play* (OUP 2005) and *Effective Leadership and Management in the Early Years* (OUP 2007). She has directed several research projects, including *Jills of All Trades?* (ATL 1996), *Too Busy to Play?* (Esmee Fairbairn Trust/University of Leicester 1997–2000), *SPEEL (Study of Pedagogical Effectiveness in Early Learning)* (DfES 2002) and *Recreating the Reception Year* (ATL 2004). Her PhD was in the area of play, learning and practitioner roles.

Theodora Papatheodorou is Professor of Early Childhood and Director of Research in the Faculty of Education at Anglia Ruskin University. She joined higher education in 1997 and, prior to that, had been a nursery teacher in early years, bilingual and special educational needs settings. Theodora's research is wide ranging and she has an overall interest and focus on pedagogy that is inclusive and offers equality of opportunity to all learners in order to reach their potential. She has published widely in national and international journals, and is the author of *Behaviour Problems in the Early Years* (Routledge 2005) and co-editor (with Janet Moyles) of the book *Learning Together in the Early Years: Exploring Relational Pedagogy* (Routledge 2008).

Rod Parker-Rees worked as a nursery and reception teacher in Bristol before joining the University of Plymouth where he is coordinator of Early Childhood Studies. He has particular interests in playfulness, early forms of communication and the emergence of self-awareness. He has co-edited a four-volume collection of research papers, *Early Years Education (Major Themes in Education)*, for Routledge, and a coursebook, *Early Childhood Studies: An Introduction to the Study of Children's Lives and Children's Worlds* (3rd edn, Routledge 2010), and is co-editor of *Early Years: An International Journal of Research and Development*.

Jane Payler is currently Senior Lecturer in Early Years Education at the University of Winchester. Most recently, she has been researching reactions to the introduction of the Early Years Professional Status in the early years workforce. While at the University of Southampton, she also researched inter-professional education for professionals in Children's Services and the experiences of young children with special educational needs. Her PhD and MPhil research, both funded by the ESRC, studied aspects of learning processes in 4-year-old children, particularly relating to interaction. Jane has previously been a health education officer in inner-city Birmingham, worked as a crèche supervisor for three years, and lectured in colleges of further education over a 14-year period in early years, health and social care.

Linda Pound has a lifelong commitment to young children and their families. She has been deputy head of a primary school, a nursery headteacher and a local authority early years education inspector. She has worked at three universities, most recently at London Metropolitan University, where she was responsible for early childhood courses. She is currently working as an early years consultant – writing, training and supporting practitioners. Her most recent publications include *Thinking and Learning about Mathematics in the Early Years* and *Leadership and Management in the Early Years* (co-written with Caroline Jones) (both OUP 2008). The third in her very popular series entitled *How Children Learn* was published in 2009.

Sacha Powell works at Canterbury Christ Church University in the Centre for Research into Children, Families and Communities – a multi-disciplinary research unit designed to encourage learning through research that crosses traditional disciplinary boundaries. She has worked with children as participants in research projects and with children as researchers. Sacha is an advocate of children's participation in decision making and is a trustee of Kent Children's Fund Network. She has worked with local, national and international organisations to research play opportunities for children and young people. She speaks Mandarin and collaborates regularly with colleagues in Chinese early childhood education and care settings.

Wendy Scott has 18 years' teaching experience, across all sectors. Following headship of a demonstration nursery school, she became senior lecturer in early childhood education, coordinating an advanced diploma in multi-professional studies. After six years as early years and primary inspector in ILEA and Kensington and Chelsea, she led OfSTED inspections across England. As chief executive of the British Association for Early Childhood Education, she was elected chair of the national Early Childhood Forum. Since spending two years as a specialist adviser to the DfES, Wendy has worked abroad with the British Council and UNICEF, and with local authorities nationwide. She is currently President of TACTYC, an organisation concerned with promoting high-quality early education.

David Whitebread is a Senior Lecturer in the Faculty of Education, University of Cambridge, UK. He is a developmental psychologist and early years education specialist (having previously taught children in the 4–8 age range). His research interests are concerned with the development of metacognition and self-regulation in young children, and their impact upon children's learning. He is a governor of his local Children's Centre and Book Reviews Editor for the journal *Early Years*. His publications include *The Psychology of Teaching and Learning in the Primary School* (Routledge 2000), *Teaching and Learning in the Early Years* (Routledge 2008) and *Supporting ICT in the Early Years* (OUP 2004, with John Siraj Blatchford).

Marian Whitehead was formerly a Senior Lecturer in Education at Goldsmiths College, University of London, with responsibility for organising and teaching MA degrees in Language and Literature and Early Childhood Education. She has published extensively on literacy, literature and bilingualism, and was for many years an editor of *Early Years, An International Journal of Research and Development*. She now combines writing with language and early years consultancy work, and is a critical friend of Earlham Early Years Centre, Norwich, where she leads a multi-professional birth-to-3 research group. In recent years, Marian has developed an interest in the abilities and needs of children with autism spectrum disorders.

Foreword

Wendy Scott

The Excellence of Play brings together many well-documented facets of thinking about play, based on research evidence and refined through experience. The References section alone offers plenty to think about: references go back as far as Plato and include established classics as well as very recent research, illuminating a persistent strand of thinking about the nature and purpose of young children's spontaneous play and learning. This third edition provides further convincing support for Froebel's belief that 'play at this time is not trivial, it is highly serious and of deep significance'.

The right to play is enshrined in the United Nations Convention on the Rights of the Child, and the vital importance of play is widely acknowledged. The unstinting efforts of the editor and authors contributing to all three editions of this book have influenced the growing understanding of the central role of playful learning and teaching worldwide, especially throughout the United Kingdom. In Scotland the emphasis is on learning through exploration, creativity and play in the early years, which are seen to extend into the primary school. *Play* is the main vehicle for learning in the *Enriched Curriculum for 4 and 5 year olds in Northern Ireland*. The *Foundation Phase for 3 to 7 year olds in Wales* is designed to help children play, learn and grow. In England, practitioners are encouraged to support children's learning through providing for and extending their spontaneous play both indoors and out in the *Early Years Foundation Stage (EYFS)*.

Two recent reviews of the primary curriculum in England also endorse the value of play to children's learning and development; one, commissioned by the government, states that 'Play is not a trivial pursuit. Drawing on a robust evidence base, the interim report highlighted the importance of learning through play . . . The purposes of play in promoting learning and development should be made explicit and planned opportunities made to fulfil them in the primary curriculum' (Rose 2009: para. 4.49). The final report of the extensively researched *Cambridge Review of the Primary Curriculum* (Alexander 2009) acknowledges the importance of play in learning, notes that this demands a more complex pedagogy than traditional transmission, memorisation and recall, and advocates the continuation of the Foundation Stage up to the age of 6.

Taken together, the chapters in this book provide a powerful rationale for the principles underpinning these developments, and address the implications of what is now known about how body, brain, mind and understanding develop in young children. It is important to emphasise that although children enter school exceptionally early in the UK, this does not mean that formal education should start by 5. In Wales, early years is seen to continue until 7, and both primary reviews in England address the importance of continuity from the reception year into Key Stage 1.

Fisher (2010) explores issues around this transition and shows convincingly that at least up to 7, children are still strongly engaged in play. Her examples illustrate how testing out new skills and understandings in situations over which they have control helps children to make sense of the world around them in a context that has personal relevance and meaning. She points out that there are many skills that are more effectively learned through the trial and error of play rather than direct teaching, and provides evidence of raised levels of motivation and achievement among children in Year 1 who have extended opportunities for play. These improved outcomes are predictable: by definition, children following an adult-initiated activity are constrained by what has been planned whereas there are no limits applied in play. As Fisher says, 'In play, no-one gives boundaries to the learning, so children explore at the very edges of their own experience, reasoning and imagination' (2010). This information, confirmed in inspection reports and local authority data as well as through the evidence reported in this book, needs to be widely disseminated at a time when external demands for intended learning outcomes in the EYFS as well as in Key Stage 1 so often undermine the confidence of staff, and parents too, in the power of learning through play.

Planning for playful experiences may result from well-meant efforts by adults to inject meaning and enjoyment into tasks designed to meet external objectives. Although this has a place, it undermines children's own intentions and sense of agency. As Howard's investigation into children's perceptions of what constitutes play activity in the classroom shows (Chapter 13), play is essentially directed by children. Fortunately, the phrase 'planned purposeful play' in the EYFS has now been clarified in further guidance from the DCSF/ National Strategies (2009), which says clearly that practitioners cannot plan children's play because this would work against the choice and control that are central features of play; rather, they must plan *for* play by creating high-quality learning environments and ensuring uninterrupted periods for children to develop their own purposes through their play.

Although apparently easy going, this approach demands high levels of insight from staff, coupled with deep knowledge of child development and curriculum. It also needs to be informed by self-awareness and sensitivity to individual children and their families, taking account of special needs as well as cultural differences that influence attitudes, expectations and practice in early education and care. This book provides thought-provoking questions for practitioners as well as evidence to support the views expressed in each chapter.

As emphasised throughout the book, sensitive observation reveals the wide range of skills and concepts that children develop through play, and shows it to be a very effective way for them to access and consolidate (or hunt and gather) new skills and knowledge. The art of practitioners is to discern this learning and to identify what might come next. Given the variable levels of qualifications and experience of staff working across the non-maintained sector, there is understandably a gap between pedagogical theory and practice in English preschools. Although there are now training opportunities and plenty of guidance, many staff find it difficult to undertake the kind of detailed observations that enrich planning for play, or know how to identify children's learning across the curriculum, and to share this with parents. Regrettably, there is also tension between rhetoric and reality for practitioners who are expected to implement the EYFS guidance and also be accountable to local authorities and OfSTED for the demands of the National Strategies, which currently require detailed data on particular aspects of children's achievements. This is most marked in relation to the Early Learning Goals for literacy, which mainly affect teachers working in reception classes, although top-down pressures are frequently experienced in nurseries, too.

There are concerns about the situation in too many reception classes, where practice does not match the statutory expectations of the EYFS. Rose (2006), in his accounts of visits to schools involved in the Early Reading Development Pilot, commends the fun and active learning that he witnessed without recognising the constraints the focus on phonics puts on the organisation of time and the overall balance of all six areas of learning. The priority given to group work on a limited and limiting aspect of literacy is manifestly counterproductive for children who cannot keep up with the expected pace of the programme. Although staff may be aware that the programme is not mandatory, and that some children need richer playful experiences across all the areas of learning in order to develop their language and communication skills, the knowledge that OfSTED will judge teaching according to prescriptive criteria means that they do not feel able to exercise their principled professional judgement in the way Rose recommends.

By the time this book is published, there will be a new government in Westminster. The indications are that, apart from the problems implicit in the Early Years Single Funding Formula at a time of financial constraints, there may not be marked change from an early years perspective. However, by then we shall have discovered when, or whether, the EYFS will be reviewed and in what way. We shall find out if those in power respect the right of parents to decide the age at which their children start school and, indeed, choose an approach to match their beliefs. It will become clear whether ministers understand the principles underpinning the EYFS guidance, and are able to relate these, together with lessons from research, to coherent policy. We shall discover if politicians and officers at local as well as central levels prepare well-qualified professionals who understand the vital role of play in early learning and know how to evaluate children's progress through formative assessment. It will be instructive to note the impact of books such as this and a forthcoming volume that makes recommendations for future research, as well as reporting on recent studies and their implications for practice (Broadhead *et al.* 2010). It will be particularly interesting to see whether current expectations in relation to reading are influenced by recent quantitative research showing that children who start formal reading at 5 have no advantage at 11 over those who start at 7 (see Suggate 2010).

It will also become clear whether OfSTED is enabled to develop into an organisation that is in touch with the rounded realities of lived experience that uses its unique position to support professional development generating constructive dialogue and debate. Inspectors could start with their report on a recent survey of 44 secondary schools (HMI 2010), which concludes, among other things:

- creative approaches to learning have a positive impact on pupils' personal development
- pupils who were supported by good teaching that encouraged questioning, debate, experimentation, presentation and critical reflection enjoyed the challenge and had a sense of personal achievement; the confidence they gained encouraged them to develop and present their own ideas with greater imagination and fluency
- all schools should ensure that teachers and support staff have the knowledge, skills and confidence to encourage pupils to be independent and creative learners.

These findings resonate with Bruce's advocacy for learning through play in the early years as a key part of the infrastructure of any civilisation. She argues in Chapter 18 that this approach 'produces adults who are able to problem-solve, persevere, concentrate, be imaginative and creative, make connections, improvise, see things from different points of view, tune in to the thoughts and feelings of other people or situations, thus making a major contribution to the development of individuals and humanity as a whole'.

Our powerful heritage of learner-centred pedagogy persists in thoughtful practice even at a time when dominant concerns lead to a demand for the introduction of knowledge and skills at an ever younger age. The contributors to this book draw on their wide experience and deep thinking to counter some of the prevailing myths and provide strong evidence for the value of play in learning, for adults as much as children. They argue for an approach to teaching young children that integrates what they know, feel, learn and understand.

Because this combines the application of what is known with exploration of what might be, it has lifelong value. Gopnik (2009) affirms that play is the signature of childhood; as adults, we can free children to internalise and extend their learning by protecting, promoting and celebrating the excellence of play.

References and further reading*

Alexander, R. (ed.) (2009) *Children, their World, their Education: Final Report and Recommendations of the Cambridge Primary Review*. London: Routledge.

Broadhead, P., Howard, J. and Wood, E. (eds) (2010) *Play and Learning in the Early Years: From Research to Practice*. London: Sage.

Department for Children, Families and Schools (DCSF)/National Strategies Early Years (2009) *Learning, Playing and Interacting: Good Practice in the Early Years Foundation Stage*. London: DCSF. Available online at: www.nationalstrategies.standards.dcsf.gov.uk/node/242798 (accessed 21 January 2010).

Fisher, J. (2010) *Moving on to Key Stage 1*. Maidenhead: Open University Press.

Gopnik, A. (2009) *The Philosophical Baby: What Children's Minds Tell Us about Truth, Love and the Meaning of Life*. London: Bodley Head.

Her Majesty's Inspectorate (HMI) (2010) Learning: creative approaches that raise standards. London: OfSTED. Available online at: www.ofsted.gov.uk/ Ofsted-home/Publications-and-research/Browse-all-by/Documents-by-type/Thematic-reports/Learning-creative-approaches-that-raise-standards (accessed 25 January 2010).

Rose, J. (2006) *Independent Review of the Teaching of Early Reading*. London: DfES. Available online at: www.standards.dfes.gov.uk/phonics/report.pdf (accessed 22 January 2010).

Rose, J. (2009) *Independent Review of the Primary Curriculum*. London: DCSF. Available online at: www.dcsf.gov.uk/primarycurriculumreview/ (accessed 25 January 2010).

Suggate, S. (2010) Research finds no advantage in learning to read from age five. Available online at: www.otago.ac.nz/news/news/otago006408.html) (p. 4) (accessed 25 January 2010).

* Texts that provide useful further reading are denoted in bold in the 'References and further reading' sections at the end of each chapter.

Introduction

Janet Moyles

Instead of beginning with a cameo of children (as in previous editions), I am handing over the first few paragraphs of this book to practitioners across the early years who have recently written with regard to their experiences of young children and play in educational settings:

> Opportunities for individual learning and discovery are still limited by a structured, staged approach to learning. Formal learning is still introduced too early [in England]. Practitioners are inhibited in providing spontaneous activities by the need to cover topics and prescribed outcomes. Too much paperwork – not enough play!
>
> (Early Childhood Studies lecturer)

> There is a continued dilemma between practitioners' wish to support more play-focused learning and the downward pressures of school leadership and targets. Many children still experience a very adult-directed environment and there is a lack of pedagogical knowledge of child development and play in some early years teachers in schools.
>
> (LEA adviser)

> Reception classes have moved on from opportunities to socialise, learn playfully and engage in new experiences to a preparation for compulsory education . . . an extension of formal schooling. Teachers . . . do not have time for the 'mess' and 'chaos' of sand, water and free play. . . . I have a very able 5-year-old . . . but have noticed that since entering reception he is overly competitive, easily upset, loses confidence very quickly when he doesn't understand something instantly and requires immediate gratification.
>
> (Parent)

It's surprising – and more than a little distressing to me – that, some 15 years on from the first edition of *The Excellence of Play*, and over 20 years since the publication of *Just Playing?* (Moyles 1989) – we should still be questioning the value of play in children's learning, especially since so much has been happening about play in the education and care of young children in the intervening years. The *Early Years Foundation Stage (EYFS)* curriculum (DfES 2007) in England emphasises the value of play for young children up to age 5 years at least. In the *Welsh Foundation Phase Curriculum* (DCELLS 2008) play is seen as a key way to support children's emotional and intellectual growth. Scotland's new *Curriculum for Excellence*, early years phase, specifically mentions opportunities for children's engagement in exploratory and spontaneous play (LTS 2009). With these and other international curriculum initiatives (see Kelvin and Lauchlan 2010) early years and play have both acquired a significant impetus across the world, which has put young children and early years practitioners 'on the map' and offered a status not conceived of just a short time ago. One has only to think of the pedagogical qualities valued in the Reggio Emilia and Te Whäriki approaches to realise the full potential of play-based, child-initiated curricula.

Why is it, then, that we seem so hell bent on preventing children from engaging in play activities that, let's face it, are an integral and essential part of childhood? While the EYFS appears to be securing *a* role for play in children's learning and development, those in reception classes and those over 5 years of age in English primary schools and in 'formal' systems internationally, have increasingly been subjected to fewer and fewer opportunities to play as the practitioners above rue, in part because of such initiatives in England, for example, as the literacy and numeracy requirements – with their emphasis on formal learning and target setting (Adams *et al.* 2004) – and the assessment regimes, the downward effects of which are often felt by under-5s and practitioners (Adams *et al.* 2004; Chapter 1 in this volume).

In the United States, a recent report from the Alliance for Childhood (Miller and Almon 2009) is concerned with the dire consequences of stifling play for kindergarten children, suggesting: 'When children are given a chance to initiate play and exploratory learning, they become highly skilled in the art of self-education and self-regulation . . . [a play-based approach] is the antithesis of the one-size-fits-all model of education' (p. 5).

So how do practitioners feel about the role of play in education? At a recent conference discussion forum (TACTYC 2009), early years practitioners were asked to write down their thoughts on practice in reception classes in England. The responses gave much food for thought, as we saw above. A couple more are worthy of inclusion:

> There is still a lack of understanding and knowledge of how children learn and play: the lack of space, freedom and provision impedes children's natural development. Reception classes tend to be too

formal for the needs and abilities of young children . . . many boys start the system as failures.

(Nursery nurse)

I agree with the principles and most of the content of the EYFS. However, I feel strongly that within reception classes children are being short-changed and that a lack of understanding by teachers of play-based approaches is primarily the cause of this.

(Reception class teacher)

It would seem from many of these comments that practitioners in England at least have been somewhat conditioned by policy requirements and the nature of OfSTED inspections, to engage heavily in adult-directed activities, although these can be shown to limit children's motivation and disposition to learning (Rogers and Evans 2008).

The links between sustained play and learning seem obvious to many practitioners and to some parents. Yet the dilemma still exists as to whether play can provide any kind of 'excellence' in relation to 'real' learning for children, as current and future citizens. The fact that we are still having to justify play's existence in children's cognitive, physical and social development seems incredible and appears to reflect an intransigence – even ignorance – on the part of policy makers and those who regulate the policies. Yet the POST Report in 2000 outlined developmental psychology research indicating that children's main sensory, cognitive and linguistic growth is developed through play, exploration, talk and interaction with others rather than with systematic, group instruction. This, we know, is related to the fact that each young child learns and develops differently, as Siegler (2005) suggests: 'Perhaps the most consistent phenomenon that has emerged in contemporary studies of children's learning is the great variability that exists within the thinking of each individual' (p. 772). These differences are also related to the cultural backgrounds in which children grow and develop (Brooker 2002).

Some of the challenges of play stem from the fact that 'teaching' is perceived by parents, policy makers and practitioners to be a formal activity – and has been for over a century. We need now to think of pedagogy – and playful pedagogy (Moyles 2010) – rather than just 'teaching', and embrace a whole different range of deeper learning and teaching practices if we are to serve twenty-first-century young children (see Whitehead, Chapter 5). These involve practitioners letting go of some long-established values in relation to schooling and recognising what it is that children achieve in deep, meaningful play. Let's face it – learning and education are both far superior to 'schooling'.

Practitioners often express the view that they 'know' or 'feel' that play for children is, or must be, a valuable learning and developmental process; yet they are also aware that this is not often reflected in their curriculum planning or in their classroom management – let alone in the way they think about their roles in teaching and learning (Moyles and Adams 2001). Practitioners unfortunately show their values daily in the way they respond to children's play – 'You can play when you've finished your work'; 'Go out to play now and make sure you come back ready to work' – all give inherent messages about the purposes and processes of play as well as the lack of real value or depth associated with it. Helpful play research is gradually being undertaken, such as that contained in Broadhead *et al.* (2010) and Moyles (2010), which is presented in ways that support links between the findings and day-to-day practice and reflection on practice. As has been emphasised, play is where children are; 'starting from the child' is enshrined in early years philosophy and is linked firmly with the early years play movement (Fisher 2007).

Some of the constraints under which practitioners perceive they work (e.g. OfSTED, assessments, management issues) are very real but others may well be due to possible confusions about play, work and learning. This is where the need for continuing professional development as well as initial practitioner education is vital. As one practitioner asserted: 'EY practitioners are being "trained" to deliver the EYFS but they should be "educated" to understand why play-based learning is crucial, or rather how learning is a result of play.'

There is now strong support from the English government for playful pedagogy. In a recent document produced by the DCSF (2009), it is noted (p. 14):

> Through all activities in the Early Years setting, a playful approach supports learning because:
> - playful children use and apply their knowledge, skills and understanding in different ways and in different contexts;
> - playful practitioners use many different approaches to engaging children in activities that help them to learn and to develop positive dispositions for learning.

This guidance document goes on to say:

> Practitioners cannot plan children's play, because this would work against the choice and control that are central features of play. Practitioners can and should plan for children's play, however, by creating high quality learning environments, and ensuring uninterrupted periods for children to develop their play.
>
> (DCSF 2009: 11)

Clearly, play is now to be taken seriously by all those who deal with young children. But maybe we still need to convince practitioners – and that is part of the role of this book – of the benefits to children's learning and their teaching.

We must acknowledge that grappling with the concept of play can be analogised to trying to seize bubbles, for every time there appears to be something to hold on to, its ephemeral nature disallows it being grasped! But, in my dotage, I am now asking why we need a definition in order to be able to value play? It is obvious when one observes children in almost any context where they are engaged in self-initiated play that they are gaining something 'special' from the experience, even if it can't be quantified (Smith 2005). It makes more sense to consider play as a process that, in itself, will subsume a range of behaviours, dispositions, motivations, opportunities, practices, skills and understandings.

Any observation and analysis of children's self-initiated play will give some clues as to why any curtailment of play in children from birth to the end of the primary years is, in my opinion and those of contributors to this book, misguided. Both individually and collectively, children exhibit cognitive and physical abilities through their play vital for people in the twenty-first century. One observed episode of role play in the home area of a Year R classroom (no need for a cameo as readers will all have seen the type of play I mean) showed children doing the following (examples in brackets):

- making choices (choosing equipment and who to play with)
- generating decisions (deciding on who should play which role)
- negotiating (ensuring that everyone was happy with the assigned role)
- pursuing their own interests (each child showed specific interests in different elements of the role play)
- using their own ideas and imaginations (several children contributed individual ideas that were adopted by the group)
- showing independence in thought and action (sticking by decisions and persuading others into that frame of mind)
- exhibiting intrinsic motivation and persistence (persisting in the play for over an hour and pursuing a specific storyline)
- being physically and intellectually active in a sustained way (children did not stop thinking about the situation and moving themselves and props as relevant)
- operating from a basis of what makes sense to them (children used many experiences from home and previous role play to support their story)
- being confident and prepared for challenges (children were able to argue their viewpoint with others involved in the play)
- experimenting, exploring and investigating ideas and objects (what could be used for bathing the baby)
- setting their own goals and targets (deciding when they would go shopping and what they would buy for dinner)
- operating in an open frame of mind in which everything is possible,

and engaged in 'what if' situations (speculating on whether there might be a ghost in the house – it was near to Halloween)
- learning new behaviours, and practising and consolidating established ones (counting out the knives, forks, spoons, plates and dishes, and offering a running commentary on what they were doing)
- acquiring new skills and interests (developing the theme of the play over several days)
- using skills and knowledge already acquired for different purposes (fetching a book and reading it to the baby, comparing sizes of clothes for 'baby')
- showing themselves, in an age-appropriate way, to be socially adroit and linguistically competent (continually narrating what they were doing together and to practitioners)
- using a range of social and interpersonal skills (sharing, cooperating and turn taking)
- performing in a literate and numerate way (several examples above!)
- functioning symbolically (making one thing represent another), and
- 'working' hard at something they are developing themselves!

As the Action Alliance for Children (2007) states: 'Play is not a break from the curriculum; play is the best way to implement the curriculum' (p. 2). In the same document, it is emphasised that: 'research suggests that over-use of didactic teaching can suppress child-initiated learning and undermine young children's self-confidence and motivation to learn' (p. 3), citing Shonkoff and Phillips (2000) and Singer *et al.* (2006) as evidence.

Brain studies research is extremely complex but it is not difficult to establish at a simple level that the human mind is seen to be a pattern collector, and that young children are natural seekers after pattern and thence meaning. For meaning to be made, children's experiences should relate directly to them, have meaning and involve first-hand experiences, as the basis for lasting learning through brain connections. Recent research also provides evidence that learning is something that happens through the connections made within the brain as a result of external stimuli received through the senses (see e.g. Blakemore and Frith 2005; Geake 2009; Jong *et al.* 2009). Greenfield (2008) stresses the malleability of the brain in the early years and is concerned that the ability of children's brains to make sense of their playful, sensory experiences, may be compromised by the emphasis on 'here and now, fast paced sensory experiences' (p. 48).

This knowledge facilitates thinking about how we unpick the early relationships between play and learning, especially through thought, problem solving and creativity. It also leads to questions about children's perceptions of formal learning contexts and how children begin to make sense of many of the activities presented to them.

It is clear that there is a vast difference for children between 'performance' and 'internalisation' of learning: by the former, I mean being able to 'jump through hoops' (tasks set by practitioners, such as being able to recognise the sounds of letters) and by 'internalisation', the ability of children to take their learning on board and make it their own. The latter requires significant understanding on the part of children, which can be gained only by first-hand, playful experiences and by meaningful experiences. The complexity of children's pretend play, for example, and the connections with early literacy, mathematical thinking and problem solving are evidenced in research by Van Hoorne *et al.* (2007), among others. Roskos and Christie (2000) also give evidence that children's engagement in pretend play significantly and positively correlates with competencies such as text comprehension and metalinguistic awareness, and with an understanding of the purposes of reading and writing.

A plethora of other writing supporting play and curriculum has also been produced in the past ten years or so, much of it included within the various contributions to this edited book so it will not be repeated here. Suffice it to say that, while the links between play, development and curriculum have yet to be established unconditionally through experimental research, there is more than enough evidence of children exhibiting their desire to play and the kinds of skills and abilities they are able to demonstrate in their play. We may still be only at the beginning in understanding what children learn through their play (Elkind 2008; Broadhead *et al.* 2010), but we can clearly see the evidence play offers for powerful expressions of understanding, enjoyment and dispositions to learning. Linked with the concept of child-initiated learning (Moyles 2008), for a majority of academics, writers and practitioners working within early years contexts there is no 'proof' greater than their own ongoing observations and analysis of children's play.

This all suggests that we need to consider a much more playful pedagogy, particularly in the reception year and KS1, if we are to support children effectively.

Playful pedagogies

So, what is pedagogy? In the government-funded SPEEL project (Study of Pedagogical Effectiveness in Early Learning, Moyles *et al.* 2002) we defined pedagogy as:

> . . . both the behaviour of teaching and being able to talk about and reflect on teaching. Pedagogy encompasses both what practitioners actually DO and THINK and the principles, theories, perceptions and challenges that inform and shape it. It connects the relatively

> self-contained act of teaching and being an early years educator, with personal cultural and community values . . . curriculum structures and external influences. Pedagogy in the early years operates from a shared frame of reference . . . between the practitioner, the young children and his/her family.
>
> (2002: 5)

'Practice' we defined as 'all the pedagogue does within the teaching and learning context on a daily, weekly and longer term basis . . . Practice includes planning, evaluating and assessing children's play and other learning experiences both indoors and outdoors' (Moyles *et al.* 2002: 5; Papatheodorou in Chapter 17).

In Stewart and Pugh (2007: 9), pedagogy is defined as:

> the understanding of how children learn and develop, and the practices through which we can enhance that process. It is rooted in values and beliefs about what we want for children, and supported by knowledge, theory and experience.

Herein lies a fundamental issue: how practitioners perceive themselves as 'playful' or otherwise in handling children's play experiences and in being playful pedagogues (Moyles 2010).

Playful pedagogies are essentially those in which the teacher or practitioner interacts in playful ways with the children (Goouch 2008), the intention being to shape curriculum outcomes without 'formal' approaches. The practitioner's style respects and values the children's contributions to their own learning and allows for children's ownership of the activities. Within a playful pedagogy the play may be co-constructed between adults and children, and the adult acts as a sensitive co-player in line with the children's own intentions and meanings. Playful pedagogies are creative and innovative for both teaching and learning. Hirsh-Pasek *et al.* (2009) stress that traditional research on playful pedagogy points continually to better outcomes for young children. While we acknowledge that play is not the only way that children learn, research by Kagan and Lowenstein (2004) suggests that play is the essential pedagogical strategy to develop children's deeper learning.

The intention of this third edition of *The Excellence of Play* is to strengthen, expand and advance the arguments for play and playful pedagogies as a principal means of educating young children in the light of these contemporary developments.

The book – its rationale, structure and contents

The basic tenet of this book, like its predecessors, is that all human beings learn through the multifaceted layers of the range of activities variously subsumed under the heading 'play'. Each chapter is predicated around discussion of the playful nature of children, playful approaches to pedagogy, and effective, playful curriculum practices. The book is intended for all practitioners across the 3- to 8-year-old age range; it constitutes an attempt to relate play theories to current practices in an ongoing, continuous and straightforward way. Those working with older children might also find much of interest. Throughout, examples of specific practices are given – play with the ideas and make them your own! It is possible to dip into the book at almost any point, for each chapter can be read as a discrete unit or viewed as part of a whole, the writers all operating from different but complementary standpoints.

Among other aspects, we will explore how it is possible to play within designated curricular demands and how children in this age group (as well as older children and practitioners) can use a full range of play activities and pedagogies to implement and validate a broad, balanced and relevant education. Assessment of children's abilities, aptitudes and dispositions, through the important processes of observing, documenting and analysing play, are discussed. Various (playful) strategies will be used to provide opportunities for reflecting on, and articulating, play practices. Each chapter starts with a brief summary so that readers can get a feel for what it is about, and most chapters end with a few 'Questions to set you thinking', intended to generate increased reader interaction with the text and allow individual chapters to be used for initial practitioner education and continuing professional development purposes.

The title *The Excellence of Play* in itself indicates the main stance taken by contributors. Each of them, in very individualised ways, gives value to both the concept and reality of play, and examines the concept from several different stances, all drawing on contemporary research to strengthen their views. The result is a very powerful argument for the 'excellence of play', based on firm beliefs that practitioners themselves must advocate strongly in support of a greater understanding of the direct contribution of play to children's development and learning, whatever the prescribed curriculum (as we saw in the earlier comments from EY practitioners). The motivational qualities of play are accentuated throughout this book, as is the concept that play in educational settings should have *learning* consequences. This is what separates play in that context from recreational play – practitioners need to show quite clearly that, and what, children are learning through their self-initiated and adult-enhanced play.

We must all also remember that play can be just fun! But it is also a powerful scaffold for children's learning: it enables metacognition (learning about how to understand one's own learning and play). It allows children to cope with not knowing something long enough in order to know – they can rehearse, practise, revise, replay and re-learn (Moyles 2005): play is a non-threatening way to cope with new learning and still retain one's self-esteem and self-image.

Anyone who has observed play for any length of time will recognise that, for all children, play is a medium for learning, and practitioners who acknowledge and appreciate this can, through provision, interaction and intervention in children's play, enhance progression, differentiation and relevance in the curriculum – and complete their assessments readily! The sense of children as social and active agents in their own play and learning, with a clear 'voice', is a strong feature throughout this third edition, as is the importance of outdoor provision and the role of culture. Meaningful child- and adult-initiated activities are integrated as a vital aspect of an enabling education for all children.

The book, like its predecessor, has 18 chapters, all of which very much reflect current early years curriculum practices and what we know about children's play and pedagogy. The references and further reading (those titles in bold) will guide readers towards more in-depth reading should they wish to extend their thinking or theoretical perspectives.

The chapters are arranged in four parts: the first covers curriculum, work/play issues and children's meaning making. In the second part, we explore play, language and literacy in three chapters, while in the third part there are five chapters discussing other aspects of the curriculum. In the final part, we reflect on play, pedagogy and culture from a range of perspectives.

In Chapter 1, Angela Anning traces the history of early years and national curricula policies in England. Three key dilemmas in relation to play and the legislated curriculum for early years professionals are explored: interpreting theory and research evidence into how children learn through play into practice; how play can be shaped into an appropriate curriculum model and how to implement a pedagogy of play.

In Chapter 2, Jan Georgeson and Jane Payler explore how children read the signs available in early years settings to help them determine what is expected of them. Jan and Jane suggest theoretical concepts helpful to framing and understanding research into how children learn about what to do and explore what is already known about how children perceive different types of activity that could be construed as work or play. They invite early years practitioners to consider how such knowledge may be used to enhance pedagogy with young children.

Research to support ideas for the creation of a pedagogy that is both centred on play and playful is outlined by Kathy Goouch in Chapter 3. She makes clear the importance for all practitioners of increasing their knowledge of play – in particular the potential for play to fulfil children's needs of the moment. Examples are given from research data demonstrating adults drawing from a repertoire of roles.

The final chapter in this section (Chapter 4), by Rod Parker-Rees, suggests that practitioners' understanding of play may be helped if they recognise a distinction between two different kinds of learning that can both be supported by play. One kind can be characterised as 'getting in' information, while the other can be thought of as a form of gathering, of 'picking things up' as we go along and without necessarily knowing in advance what we might come across.

Focusing as it does on language and literacy, the chapters in Part 2 begin with a stimulating chapter by Marian Whitehead, who argues that the current requirements in England mean that early years practitioners must facilitate play-based learning for children and also introduce the systematic teaching of phonics in a fun way. Among other things, she aims to raise awareness of the possible dilemmas in these requirements, to review the relationship between play, literature and literacy and child-initiated play and learning. This is followed by Chapter 6, in which David Whitebread and Helen Jameson argue for the power of playful approaches and activities in stimulating children's storytelling, creative writing and self-regulation. Evidence is presented of the potential benefits of playful approaches being extended to older and more able children. The example is discussed of work using Storysacks and other props to stimulate imaginative oral storytelling and high-quality creative writing.

Neil Kitson raises some very interesting thoughts and ideas about role play in Chapter 7, highlighting the importance of fantasy role play and socio-dramatic play in the cognitive, social and emotional development of young children. He suggests that socio-dramatic play offers great learning potential for those working with young children, and that structuring the play enables practitioners to extend and enhance children's cognitive levels.

Part 3 opens with Bernadette Duffy's well-conceived views on art and young children. In Chapter 8 she explores what is creativity, and why it is important to the child and the wider society. She also explores the development of creativity from birth and how it is expressed in the EYFS framework, and concludes with an examination of the crucial role of knowledgeable and interactive adults in fostering, assessing and recording children's creative development.

Chapter 9 continues the creative theme, with Linda Pound explaining her use of the term 'playing music', and comparing this with the language used to describe other playful and creative experiences. The biological functions of play and music are discussed and their role in learning and development explored as well as the importance of including playful music in the curriculum.

Science and technology feature in Chapter 10, in which Dan Davies and Alan Howe explore ways in which young children learn scientific concepts, attitudes and skills through play, and how science can contribute to a rich early years curriculum. The writers focus on the relevance of recent research on play in science-rich contexts, the role of the practitioner, science in the EYFS, the place of ICT in early science, learning from the environment and how assessment can inform planning of an appropriate play-based curriculum. This is followed in Chapter 11 by a very practical and informative contribution by Rose Griffiths, who outlines the advances to children's mathematical learning of play. She shows how play can increase the child's motivation to learn by providing sensible and enjoyable contexts, and by allowing children to direct their own learning and build confidence.

The final chapter in this part (Chapter 12) introduces a new topic. Sara Knight starts with the premise that there is a move towards the reintroduction of wilder outdoor play but that there is understandable reluctance on the part of some practitioners to engage with this. She stresses that there are many reasons why risk-taking and outdoor play is important for children and playful pedagogies, and describes one initiative for wilder and riskier play: Forest School.

In the final and longest part of this edition, there are six chapters with broad-ranging foci. Chapter 13, by psychologist Justine Howard, argues that education should be concerned with the whole child and not just the development of skills and knowledge. She emphasises that freedom and choice afforded to children in play promotes confidence, esteem and well-being and, as a result, has powerful developmental and therapeutic potential. Through the outcomes of her empirical research, she stresses the need for early years educators to be equipped with a sound understanding as to *why*, and *in what ways*, play is such a powerful medium, thus empowering them to develop informed play practices. This is followed in Chapter 14 with Pat Broadhead's exciting research on the development of friendships as a seldom considered but key aspect of practitioner responsibility in the early years. She examines and illustrates how friendship is linked both to identity development and to high-order intellectual engagements between interacting and cooperating peers in the context of play.

Transitions between different settings can be traumatic for children. In Chapter 15, Hilary Fabian and Aline-Wendy Dunlop consider the importance of play in supporting children during transitions. Questions are raised about the ways in which play may help children in unusual circumstances to take change in their stride and to develop resilience at times of transition.

In Chapter 16, Sacha Powell and Tricia David move the focus to babies, whom they suggest are born with an amazing drive to socialise, observe and become a member of the family and community in which they find themselves. This socio-cultural development of young children is the focus of this chapter, particularly the ways in which different socio-cultural contexts afford babies and children opportunities to play. This is followed in Chapter 17 by Theodora Papatheodorou's well-conceived theories and practical suggestions regarding the uses of play for the early identification and prevention of factors and conditions that may place young children at risk of not achieving their full educational potential. She offers an overview of current policies and their aspirational outcomes for children, and discusses current thinking, ecological and socio-cultural perspectives in understanding children's development and learning and the relevance of carefully conceived documentation.

The final chapter, as in previous editions, affords Tina Bruce the opportunity to explore, in her own inimitable way, issues relating to diversity and inclusion in play. Tina outlines some play theories and stresses the value of cross-cultural aspects of play, and the inclusion of children with complex needs, disabilities and special educational needs. This is followed by a brief Afterword in which I try to draw some of the threads of the book together and explore some issues for the future.

Predictably, there is much more that could and should have been included had space permitted, for that is the divergent and flexible quality, indeed the excellence, of play.

References and further reading

Action Alliance for Children (2007) *Play in the Early Years: Key to School Success. A Policy Brief*. Oakland, CA: Early Childhood Funders.

Adams, S., Alexander, E., Drummond, M.J. and Moyles. J. (2004) *Inside the Foundation Stage. Re-creating the Reception Year*. London: Association of Teachers and Lecturers.

Blakemore, S.-J. and Frith, U. (2005) *The Learning Brain: Lessons for Education*. Oxford: Wiley Blackwell.

Broadhead, P., Howard, J. and Wood, E. (eds) (2010) *Play and Learning in Educational Settings*. London: Sage.

Brooker, L. (2002) *Starting School: Young Children Learning Cultures*. Buckingham: Open University Press.

Department for Children, Education, Lifelong Learning and Skills (DCELLS) (2008) *Revised Curriculum: Foundation Stage*. Available online at: http://wales.gov.uk/topics/educationandskills/curriculumassessment/arevisedcurriculumforwales/foundationphase/?lang=en (accessed 30 December 2009).

Department for Children, Families and Schools (DCFS)/Qualifications and Curriculum Development Agency (QCDA) (2009) *Learning, Playing and Interacting: Good Practice in the Early Years Foundation Stage*. London: DCFS/QCDA. Available for download at: http://downloads.nationalstrategies.co.uk.s3.amazonaws.com/pdf/85679136be4953413879dc59eab23ce0.pdf.

Department for Education and Skills (DfES) (2007) *Early Years Foundation Stage*. London: DfES.

Elkind, D. (2008) *The Power of Play: How Spontaneous, Imaginative Activities Lead to Happier, Healthier Children.* Cambridge, MA: De Capo Lifelong.

Fisher, J. (2007) *Starting from the Child: Teaching and Learning from 3 to 8* (3rd edn). Buckingham: Open University Press.

Geake, J. (2009) *The Brain at School: Educational Neuroscience in the Classroom.* Maidenhead: Open University Press.

Goouch, K. (2008) Understanding playful pedagogies, play narratives and play spaces. *Early Years: An International Journal of Research and Development,* 28(1): 93–102.

Greenfield, S. (2008) Perspectives: who are we becoming? *New Scientist,* 198(2656): 48–49.

Hirsh-Pasek, K., Golinkoff, R., Berk, L. and Singer, D. (2009) *A Mandate for Playful Learning in Preschool: Presenting the Evidence.* NY: Oxford University Press.

Jong, T. de, Gog, T. van, Jenks, K., Manlove, S., Hell, J. van., Jolles, J., Merrienboer, J. van, Leeuwen, T. van and Boschlooo, A. (2009) *Explorations in Learning and the Brain: On the Potential of Cognitive Neuroscience for Educational Science.* New York: Springer.

Kagan, S. and Lowenstein, A. (2004) School readiness and children's play: contemporary oxymoron or compatible option? In E. Zigler, D. Singer and S. Bishop-Josef (eds) *Children's Play: The Roots of Reading.* Washington, DC: Zero-to-Three Press.

Kelvin, K. and Lauchlan, L. (2010) Thinking through transition, pedagogy and play from early childhood education to primary. In J. Moyles (ed.) *Thinking About Play: Developing a Reflective Approach.* Maidenhead: Open University Press.

Learning and Teaching Scotland (2009) *Curriculum for Excellence.* Available online at: www.ltscotland.org.uk/curriculumforexcellence/index.asp (accessed 17 December 2009).

Miller, E. and Almon, J. (2009) *Summary and Recommendations of Crisis in the Kindergarten: Why Children Need to Play in School.* College Park, MD: Alliance for Childhood.

Moyles, J. (1989) *Just Playing? The Role and Status of Play in Early Childhood Education.* Buckingham: Open University Press.

Moyles, J. (ed.) (2005) *The Excellence of Play* (2nd edn). Maidenhead: Open University Press.

Moyles, J. (2008) Empowering children and adults: play and child-initiated learning. In S. Featherstone and P. Featherstone (eds) *Like Bees Not Butterflies: Child-initiated Learning in the Early Years.* Market Bosworth: Featherstone Education.

Moyles, J. (ed.) (2010) *Thinking About Play: Developing a Reflective Approach.* Maidenhead: Open University Press.

Moyles, J. and Adams, S. (2001) *StEPs: Statements of Entitlement to Play.* Buckingham: Open University Press.

Moyles, J., Adams, S. and Musgrove, A. (2002) *SPEEL: Study of Pedagogical Effectiveness in Early Learning.* Research Report 363. London: DfES.

Parliamentary Office of Science and Technology (POST) (2000) *Early Years Learning.* London: House of Commons Education and Employment Select Committee.

Rogers, S. and Evans, J. (2008) *Inside Role-play in Early Childhood Education: Researching Young Children's Perspectives.* London: Routledge.

Roskos, K. and Christie, J.F. (eds) (2000) *Play and Literacy in Early Childhood: Research from Multiple Perspectives.* Mahwah, NJ: Erlbaum.

Shonkoff, J. and Phillips, D. (eds) (2000) *From Neurons to Neighborhoods: The Science of Early Childhood Development.* Washington: National Academy Press.

Siegler, R. (2005) Children's learning. *American Psychologist,* 60(8): 769–778.

Singer, D., Golinkoff, R. and Hirsh-Pasek, K. (eds) (2006) *Play = Learning: How Play Motivates and Enhances Children's Cognitive and Social-emotional Growth.* New York: Oxford University Press.

Smith, P.K. (2005) Play: types and functions in human development. In B. Ellis and D. Bjorklund (eds) *Origins of the Social Mind: Evolutionary Psychology and Child Development.* New York: Guilford Press.

Stewart, N. and Pugh, R. (2007) *Early Years Vision in Focus, Part 2: Exploring Pedagogy.* Shrewsbury: Shropshire County Council.

Training Advancement and Co-operation in Teaching Young Children (TACTYC) (2009) Discussion Forum at TACTYC's Annual Conference, Inspiring Practice in Early Education: Research, Reflection, Debate, Milton Keynes, 6 and 7 November.

Van Hoorn, J., Nourot, P., Scales, B. and Alward, K. (2007) *Play at the Center of the Curriculum* (4th edn). Upper Saddle River, NJ: Merrill/Prentice Hall.

PART 1
Setting the play context

1 Play and legislated curriculum

Angela Anning

Summary

The chapter traces the history of the introduction of a subject-based broad and balanced National Curriculum for 5 to 7 year olds in English and Welsh primary schools in the 1980s, Literacy Hour in 1999, Numeracy Hour in 2000 and Foundation Stage curriculum in 2000 for all early childhood settings. A policy emphasis on raising standards in literacy and numeracy and 'behaviour' sat uneasily with the beliefs of practitioners, particularly reception (for 4–5 year olds) teachers, in the value of play. Three key dilemmas in relation to play and the legislated curriculum for early years professionals are explored: interpreting theory and research evidence into how children learn through play into practice; how play can be shaped into an appropriate curriculum model; and how to implement a pedagogy of play.

Introduction

Policy: the legislated curriculum

Every education system functions within a social context underpinned by a particular set of values and political imperatives. So it has been with the educational reforms in the legislated curriculum for early years education in England for the past three decades.

There was no statutory curriculum for children of any age in England until the 1988 Educational Reform Act (except for the anomaly of statutory religious education). Curriculum content was determined by custom and practice in English primary schools – the basics of literacy and numeracy and topic work. Play with natural materials (sand and water), construction (block play), small figure play and role play, and 'make and do' messy areas – for 'infants'

(5–7 year olds) was mainly unsupervised by teachers around the periphery of classrooms.

In the 1960s, the Plowden Report (CACE 1967: para. 9), underpinned by Piagetian theories of developmental stages, included the seminal statements: 'at the heart of the educational process lies the child' and 'play is the principal means of learning in early childhood' (1967: para. 523). In reality classroom-based research of the period indicated that English primary schools had remained remarkably 'formal' in their teaching and subject delivery, reflecting the elementary school traditions of the previous century and predominantly male-dominated policy of prioritising 'the basics' (Alexander 1984). But, after 20 years of alleged 'child-centred progressivism', a (Labour) British government, bedevilled by financial problems and influenced by negative press coverage and bleak independent reports on the state of schooling, determined to 'get a grip on' the curriculum. The curriculum, not children, was to be at the heart of education. In the 1980s a Conservative government set about formalising a National Curriculum for children aged 5 to 16.

A National Curriculum for 5–11 year olds

The 1988 version of a Primary National Curriculum included 10 foundation subjects, of which three – English, Mathematics and Science – were designated core subjects. Pupil progression in subjects was tracked cumulatively along detailed lists of attainment targets in each subject, and assessed summatively at the end of each Key Stage (at 7 and 11 years). The role of play within subject learning was not an issue of concern for the predominantly secondary-based designers of the National Curriculum.

The ideologies underpinning the National Curriculum model were based on concepts of value for money in a market-led economy, raising 'standards', a return to disciplined behaviour, competence in 'traditional' school subjects and preparation of a workforce that was capable of underpinning economic recovery. The Programmes of Study of the National Curriculum continued to hold sway for the next 30 years, with minor tinkering by the Qualifications and Curriculum Authority (QCA) quango. Some 'policy' non-statutory bolt-ons such as citizenship and personal/social/health education were shoehorned into an already crowded curriculum in response to moral panics about 'bad behaviour' and 'obesity'.

The National Curriculum was designed to be broad and balanced, but teachers of 5–7 year olds (KS1) were initially strongly resistant to a *subject-based* curriculum, despite evidence that showed their habitual way of teaching the curriculum separated literacy and numeracy, music and physical education from 'the rest'. KS1 teachers reluctantly abandoned their preferred cross-curricular, or thematic, approaches to planning curriculum content and delivering the arts and humanities within 'topics'. They learned to deliver the curriculum in subject-based ways. Increasingly, reception class teachers of 4–5 year olds (and therefore of non-statutory school age) were expected by headteachers to deliver the National Curriculum. Initial teacher training programmes for Key Stage 1 were reduced to delivering competencies and standards in subject knowledge.

Yet learning through play remained a significant feature of KSI teachers' espoused theories. They brought with them to teaching the history of the importance of structured learning activities from Montessori and Froebel, of exploratory and dramatic play from Steiner and Isaacs, and of healthy outdoor play from the Macmillan sisters (see Anning 1997). Translating these ideologies into practice was problematic (Bennett *et al.* 1997). The play-based curriculum in waiting was still lurking around the edges of classrooms – sand and water trays, construction kits, wet areas for messy activities, role-play areas (usually domestic play based). But the teachers tended to focus on seated activities – mostly reading, writing and arithmetic based, and defined as 'work' – with groups (usually by ability) of children symbolically in the centre of the classrooms. Nursery nurses were deployed to be responsible for set creative or craft-based tasks or for play activities based on a current topic. Children were in no doubt that whatever Susan Isaacs' views on play being the child's work, their teachers held a different view. They were kept 'busy' using play activities, or were rewarded with some time to play when they had completed their work. Students on school placements found it hard to make sense of the gap between the rhetoric and reality of their teacher/mentors' talk about the centrality of play in young children's learning.

The Primary National Strategies

Despite the optimism of the educational reforms of the 1980s, there were growing concerns about improving standards in primary schools. From the late 1990s Primary National Strategies, funded by successive Conservative and Labour governments and directed by Departments of Education, competed with the QCA for power and influence over practice in primary classrooms. For example, a Literacy Hour (Department for Education and Employment (DfEE) 1998) was introduced in 1999 and a Numeracy Hour (DfEE 1999) in 2000 to all primary school classrooms. The strategies were designed to raise standards. They included guidance on both the content and the prescribed way of delivering the content. So, for the first time, English governments determined not only curriculum content but also the pedagogy of classrooms. Although the strategies were non-statutory, the schedules used by the dreaded inspectors from the Office for Standards in Education (OfSTED) looked for evidence of their implementation. Conforming to the strategies squeezed the time in primary classrooms available to deliver the National Curriculum.

Anxiety about raising standards in reading in particular was sustained by successive education ministers. In 2007 the Primary National Strategy launched a synthetic phonics scheme for all primary classrooms, including pre-National Curriculum reception classes. The added pressure of the publication at school level of results for 7 year olds in Standard Assessment Tasks (SATs) in language and mathematics (tests in science were soon dropped), left teachers of young children in England in no doubt that what mattered was that their pupils progressed in the basics of reading, writing and mathematics. Headteachers, who were mostly Key Stage 2 (i.e. for 7–11 year olds) trained, pressurised reception and Key Stage 1 teachers into prioritising literacy and numeracy. 'Success' in schools was measured by the scores of cohorts of 7 and 11 year olds' results in SATs (published as league tables in national and local newspapers) and by OfSTED judgements of schools as failing, satisfactory, good or outstanding (reports were posted openly on the internet for parents to access). The rhetoric was that 'good' schools would be popular and thrive, and 'bad' schools would be closed down.

By the turn of the century doubts were being raised about the efficacy of the National Curriculum itself. In primary schools the curriculum was seen to be 'overcrowded' (particularly with the 'obligatory' literacy and numeracy strategies to be met also) and fragmented (as teachers struggled to deliver the ever-expanding statutory content). Assessment was perceived to be driving timetables and shaping modes of teaching, with a return to whole-class teaching at Key Stage 1, few practical group activities and a didactic style of pedagogy (Moyles *et al.* 2003). In many primary schools learning through play became sidelined and play resources locked away in storerooms. Children's choice of play-based activities was limited to perhaps a (tongue in cheek) 'golden hour' for the whole class on a Friday afternoon, or snatched ten minutes of playing for individual children when they had finished all their work *and* been 'good'. For many KS1 children, this happy convergence of criteria – of finishing work and being good – in order to be 'allowed' to play never happened.

Starting school at 4

The statutory school starting age in the UK is the term after the child's fifth birthday. Most European countries start formal schooling at 6 and in other international contexts at 7. However, in order to fund 'nursery education' on the cheap, both Conservative and Labour governments promoted the idea of an *early start to school* being beneficial. In practice, well over 50 per cent of children in England now start primary school in Year R, at 4 (DfES 2007), and all local authorities have individual policies on admissions to confuse parents about what are their children's entitlements. Parents expected that children would start 'proper school work' immediately their children entered reception classes and pressurised teachers to do so. A series of reports citing evidence from research questioned the appropriateness of 4 year olds being offered a 'too formal too soon' curriculum, a lack of outdoor space for learning, play and exercise and a high ratio of children to adults in Year R classes (Rogers and Evans 2008). Reception class teachers felt trapped between conflicting imperatives: to focus on teaching 'the basics' of literacy and numeracy, and to deliver a developmentally appropriate and play-based 'nursery education' curriculum.

Rethinking a National Curriculum

In 2004 the National Strategies launched *Excellence and Enjoyment: Learning and Teaching in Primary Schools*. The publication argued for a renewed 'commitment to high standards and excellence within an engaging, broad and rich curriculum' (DfES 2004: 4). A new zeitgeist demanded that learning be 'personalised' to individual learner needs, capabilities and interests.

At the same time, there was renewed interest in play work – in school holiday schemes, and in the after-school 'clubs' designed for childcare for working parents and to extend the interests of children in sports and leisure activities (Department of Culture, Media and Sports (DCMS) 2006), a national play policy was formulated (DCSF/DCMS 2008) and there was growing interest in and commitment to the importance of children learning outdoors (DfES 2006; see also Chapter 12; www.forestschools.com; www.ltl.org.uk).

This interest in broadening children's learning experiences, often beyond the conventions of a school day and prescribed curriculum, reflected a much wider government agenda for the reform of services for children. The new mantra was 'joined-up thinking': to encourage education, health, welfare and family support services to work together in multi-agency teams (Anning *et al.* 2010). A seismic change in conceptualising children's services was under way. In 2004, the Children Act legislated for a new framework (*Every Child Matters*) for all children's services, including schools, catering for children from birth to the end of secondary schooling and taking a holistic view of children's development. Central to the principles of *Every Child Matters* were five outcomes (related to articles within the *United Nations Convention on the Rights of the Child* (UNCRC 1989): being healthy, staying safe, enjoying and achieving, making a positive contribution, and economic well-being. This overarching framework, and the notion of schools hosting 'extended services' including childcare and leisure activities as a way of encouraging parents to work and as a form of social rescue, sat uneasily with pressure on primary schools to drive up standards in 'the basics' and to deliver a demanding subject-based curriculum.

In 2009, an 'independent' (but funded by the Department for Children, Schools and Families: DCSF) Review of the Primary Curriculum was published (Rose 2009). The review advocated reorganising the primary curriculum into six areas of learning mapping onto a subject framework, with literacy, numeracy, and information and communication technologies (ICT) as core skills. The six areas of learning were: understanding English, communication and languages; mathematical understanding; scientific and technological under-standing; historical, geographical and social understanding; understanding physical development, health and well-being; and understanding the arts. The report hinted that the pedagogy of the Foundation Stage should be retained for at least the early stages of transition to KS1, and commended play-based learning, though added rather tetchily 'Good practice does not leave children to do whatever they want. It is practitioners who create the environment, both indoors and outdoors, to further children's learning through play' (Rose 2009: 53). The review also recommended that all children in England should enter primary school reception classes in the September after their fourth birthday. (Many local authorities were still admitting children to school in two cohorts by age: in September and January.) This recommendation had implications for the business plans and sustainability of providers who currently cater for the childcare of under-5s.

A Foundation Stage Curriculum for preschool education and childcare

In a genuine attempt to rationalise preschool education and childcare services, the government introduced a raft of reforms. Reforms included a Ten-year Strategy for Childcare (DfES 2005); universal entitlement for all 3 and 4 year olds to part-time preschool education; a unified set of standards and inspec-tion regime delivered by OfSTED for both childcare and education settings; an ambitious anti-poverty initiative, Sure Start, to deliver integrated services to families with children under 5 in the most deprived communities of England (Anning and Ball 2008); and a roll-out of 1700 Children's Centres by 2008 in the most deprived areas.

In 1996 the unthinkable concept of introducing a statutory curriculum (Foundation Stage: FS) for under-5s in England was launched by the Qualifica-tions and Curriculum Authority/Department for Education and Employment (QCA/DfEE 2000). The idea of a prescribed curriculum is problematic in other national contexts; for example, the influential Italian Reggio Emilia model of curriculum planning uses the concept of *projettare*, basing its curriculum on observing and responding to the interests of a particular group of children and their communities at any one time (Edwards *et al.* 1998). The Foundation Stage consisted of six areas of learning: personal, social and emotional development; communication, language and literacy; mathematical development; know-ledge and understanding of the world; physical development; and creative development. A total of 69 Early Learning Goals were linked to a baseline assessment system to be administered as children entered KS1 at 5 years. Base-line assessment focused on the first three areas of learning. An unwieldy *Foundation Stage Profile* (QCA 2003), designed to record children's progression across all aspects of learning, was introduced in 2003.

All settings (including childminders and childcare group settings – mostly privately funded), preschool playgroups (in the voluntary sector), Year R classes in primary schools, Children's Centres and nursery schools (in the maintained sector) claiming to offer education to 3 and 4 year olds, and thus to qualify for government funding as providers of preschool education, had to demonstrate that they were delivering the FS curriculum. In 2002 a framework to support children under 3, *Birth to Three Matters*, was published by the Sure Start Unit of the DCSF. The framework was organised around the concepts of a strong child, a skilful communicator, a competent learner and a healthy child.

In 2007, as the distinction between preschool education and childcare became increasingly blurred, the two frameworks and the national standards for daycare and childminding for under-8s were combined into a Statutory Framework for the *Early Years Foundation Stage* (EYFS) (DfES 2007). The *Foundation Stage Profile* was modified to include a set of 13 assessment scales in the six areas of learning, each of which had nine points. Judgements about children's attainments were to be based on observations over a period of time, not one-off assessment tasks. The framework included concerns for child welfare, child protection, and health and safety, and set out standards for learning, development and care for children from birth to 5. Concern for children's well-being and learning were at the core of the guidance, which included the statements: 'Play underpins the delivery of all the EYFS. . . . Play underpins all development and learning for young children' (paras 1.16 and 1.17). At last, did we have 'official' permission to place play at the heart of practice in settings for all our children under 5?

Play, curriculum and pedagogy in early childhood education

I have reviewed the role of play in policies governing the education of birth to 7 year olds in England during the past 50 years. I have referred frequently to the tensions felt by practitioners responsible for delivering curricula between their espoused theories about the centrality of play to young children's learning and their theories in action, which reveal deep confusion about how to conform to government policy and implement learning through play (see Moyles in the Introduction). What might be the causes of this confusion?

Learning through play

The first source of confusion is that research into how children learn through play rarely connects with research into how children learn in educational settings.

Our understanding of how children learn has been transformed in the past 10 years. Yet we still have little empirical research on the efficacy of play-based learning in the contexts of classrooms, though authors in this book are among those in the UK building up such evidence. Early years professionals are accused of arguing for the value of play in learning from ideologies rather than evidence base.

There *is* evidence to substantiate their beliefs. Early years educators have argued the case for educating 'the whole child' and for the importance of recognising links between the emotions, the intellect and the body in learning. Recent research into brain development and functions has alerted us to what many early years educators know instinctively – the importance of the biological basis of learning processes (for example, Gopnik *et al.* 1999) – though there are the usual caveats about the application of medical research to classroom contexts (Bruer 1997).

The biological basis for learning

We know that information comes to the brain via the five senses: sight, hearing, touch, smell and taste. Information is taken on board visually, auditorily or kinaesthetically (i.e. physically experienced or related to feelings). For young children, sensory experiences are strong and powerful. You have only to observe an 18 month old's raw responses to unfamiliar tastes and noises to have this confirmed. There is a processing system to prevent information overload, a sort of switchboard system, within the brain. Information that invokes an emotional response, or with content relating to self-preservation, ranks high in the editing process for selective attention (see also Howard, Chapter 13). All information is processed through the left or right hemispheres of the brain. Both are capable of similar functions but they have particular propensities. The left-brain emphasises language, logic, mathematical formulae, linearity and sequencing – in general, analytical aspects of thinking.

The seminal work on multiple intelligences of the American psychologist Howard Gardner (1983) built on these insights. The right hemisphere emphasises forms and patterns, spatial manipulation, images, things of the imagination, rhythm and musical appreciation. The right hemisphere appears to have the capacity to process faster more holistic aspects of thinking and learning. When the right side of the brain is processing data, it triggers pleasurable responses and chemicals are released that give the learner a sense of heightened awareness and well-being. This positive feedback encourages the learner to repeat the action and is a *strong motivation to want to learn*.

Research by neuroscientists and psychologists helps us to understand what we instinctively know about the power of play as a vehicle for young children's learning; but these insights have not legitimated proper attention being paid to resourcing and supporting play-based activities in *educational settings*.

The socio-cultural context of learning

We know that context and societal expectations have a profound impact on how people behave, and that learning is socially mediated by families, communities and cultural mores. This paradigm shift is called socio-cultural research and scholarship (Anning *et al.* 2009). If we view play behaviours through a socio-cultural lens, we have to acknowledge that the formal contexts of many early childhood settings, where priorities are determined by target setting and individual progression through a prescribed curriculum, cannot be conducive to collaborative 'flow state' play.

Socio-dramatic play among groups of children in informal contexts is characterised by fluidity, spontaneity and changes in direction. Constructing narratives in the mind – storying – is a fundamental way for children to make sense of the world and is central to dramatic play (Paley 1986, 2005; see also Whitebread and Jameson, Chapter 6).

Socio-dramatic and rough-and-tumble play offer children opportunities to test out who they are and who they might become; to negotiate turn taking; to self-regulate behaviours; to feel the heady power of groups working in harmony, and to reconcile differences when conflict arises; and to take risks and feel strong emotions. It is also crucial to the development of a 'theory of mind', described by Bailey (2002: 163) as the 'ability to infer mental states in others and ourselves'. When we observe young children engrossed in this kind of play, we know that the experiences they are having are the building blocks of self-regulation and resilience in young adults (essential tools for citizenship). But such play episodes do not fit neatly with a culture of target setting, timetabling and adult control in primary schools, and increasingly in many Foundation Stage settings.

Multi-modality in learning

We are also aware now of the importance of multi-modality in children's representation, symbolic actions and meaning making in their play (Worthington 2007). Kress (1997) used detailed observations of his own children's journeys towards literacy at home to explore their use of drawing, cutting and sticking, making models and marks, gestures and play with everyday materials to make 'worlds' in which to act out complex narratives. He argued that 'children act multi-modally, both in the things they use, the objects they make, and in the engagement of their bodies; there is no separation of body and mind' (p. 97).

Pahl (1999) extended these kinds of detailed observations and analysis of children's meaning making in the context of a nursery class. She was the kind of teacher/researcher who encouraged children to move resources and objects to different spaces and places in the nursery to support their elaborate play narratives (see also Goouch, Chapter 3). Many early years practitioners find such 'spontaneous' play behaviour with objects and artefacts difficult to manage. An emphasis on teaching 'subjects', metaphorically boundaried by the tradition of workshop areas for language and literacy, mathematical development and knowledge, and understanding of the world, discourages this kind of fluidity of meaning making. For practitioners the results of allowing freedom for children to explore such connections over space and time can be quite literally too messy.

A play curriculum in educational contexts

The second source of confusion is how play can be shaped in educational contexts into a curriculum that accommodates both the deep learning potential of young children and the imperatives of schooling.

An important premise is that early years professionals have a grasp of models of play from which they can design curricula appropriate to their settings. One such model is Smilansky's (Smilansky and Sheftaya 1990), but there are others referenced in this book. Smilansky categorised four types of play behaviour: functional (offering opportunities to explore the environment); constructive (exploring and manipulating the material world); dramatic (at early stages exploring pretend and role play, and later involving others in socio-dramatic play); and games with rules (table-top games and physical games – both involving rules and procedures).

The challenge is to translate conceptual models into practical activities. Early years professionals are bound by the imperatives of managing large groups of children in buildings shared with other services or classes. There have to be routines and protocols holding activities together. But taking a model such as Smilansky's, it is possible for adults to structure environments, resources and daily routines so that all children have an entitlement to routine and self-regulated access to (using this model as an example) four types of play for at least part of the day. It would be left to the professional judgement of practitioners to structure this entitlement. The last thing we want is a formal prescription of hourage for typologies of play! The constraints will be access, time, choice, and the pragmatics of noise levels and resource management.

Access

As I have argued in the first half of this chapter, *access* to play activities for many young learners is constrained by adult rules and educational outcomes. For children the switch from a domestic culture of play, based on real-life problem solving, to the 'peculiar' school tasks of worksheets, sorting plastic shapes, and playing in waist-high containers of sand and water, can be traumatic, particularly where children's cultural norms of learning may be profoundly different from 'educational' versions (Brooker 2002; see also Powell and David, Chapter 16). Teachers are often so socialised into perceiving these school-based activities as 'the norm' that they neglect to explain to children their purposes, or to involve them in the reasoning behind and negotiations about what are 'fair' and 'safe' practices.

Time

The amount of time adults and children spend on activities indicates how much they value them. Currently in FS settings there is confusion about a 'mythical' split of 80 per cent of children's time being spent on 'child-initiated' activities and 20 per cent on 'adult-initiated' tasks. This confusion seems to have arisen from QCA/DFSC guidance about making judgements on children's levels of attainments on early learning goals. The *Researching Effective Pedagogy in the Early Years* (REPEY) project (Siraj-Blatchford *et al.* 2002) argued that, in effective FS settings, adult- and child-initiated activities are split 50/50 in terms of time (but this is heavily challenged by Goouch, see Chapter 3). Proficient early years professionals make pragmatic judgements about a strategic mixture of 'free flow' (where children move seamlessly through spaces, including outdoors, engaged in self-chosen activities) and drawing together small groups for particular purposes for adult-directed activities; but in many Year R classes bored 4 year olds spend too much time seated at tables doing adult-directed tasks and squatting uncomfortably on carpets in front of whiteboards. Even so, Year 1 teachers grumble that Year R teachers are not 'getting them ready' for the start of formal schooling.

Choice

Children's *choice* of play activities demands equal sensitivity. It is unrealistic to argue that education contexts can offer the same freedoms to children's play behaviours as in home or out-of-school settings/contexts. But the shaping of children's self-initiated play into 'sanitised' versions for educational purposes is not helpful. As discussed elsewhere in this book, children's play scripts reflect their cultural and gendered preferences, and children are skilled in subverting the overt purposes of 'educational' play to their own agendas (Skelton and Hall 2001; see also Bruce, Chapter 18). A predominantly female workforce comes into conflict with boys' choices of play content. Banning boys from superhero and conflict play is not helpful; it generates ill feeling between boys and authority figures right at the start of their education.

The strategy of using 'play outdoors' as a safety valve for boisterous, physical play for girls and boys is increasingly being used; but I worry that outdoor play, overseen by teaching assistants, is in danger of becoming a 'dumping ground' for therapeutic and energetic play, when for me the outdoor spaces for learning should be integral to all areas of experience, and valued and resourced by teachers, parents and children for their learning potential (Garrick 2004; see also Knight, Chapter 12).

A pedagogy of play

A third source of confusion is that adults are unsure about their role in supporting children's play.

A Vygotskian model of teaching and learning implies an interventionist model of pedagogy whereby adult scaffolding supports the child's progression through his or her zone of proximal development, 'the distance between the actual developmental level as determined by independent problem-solving and the level of potential development as determined through problem-solving under adult guidance or in collaboration with more capable peers' (Vygotsky 1978: 86).

The holy grail of early years education is to construct 'a pedagogy of play'. Contributors to this book, the Effective Provision of Pre-School Education (EPPE) project with its central notion of 'sustained shared thinking' (Siraj-Blatchford *et al.* 2002) and the QCA in *Continuing the Learning Journey* (2005) have made significant contributions to the debate. But for me there are fundamental problems yet to be unpicked. The discourse about a pedagogy of play often foregrounds cognitive gains (particularly in language and mathematical development) as 'potentially instructive play', and sidelines physical, social and affective outcomes of play. Time-consuming and detailed observations of play on Post-it notes are often at a superficial level and frequently do not feed back into reflective practice or inform curriculum planning. Finally, adults are flummoxed when they intervene inappropriately in children's play episodes and cause them to grind to a halt.

Wood (2010) argues that we need to differentiate between distinct but complementary pedagogic roles and know when best to deploy them. Four complementary and equally valid adult pedagogic roles in promoting learning through play are as follows.

1   *Engaging playfully with learners:* adults adopting spontaneous playful interactions and dialogue with children in episodes such as functional play and games with rules.
2   *Modelling play and learning behaviours:* adults teaching skills such as using appropriate cutting and sticking techniques in constructing puppets, and how to structure language for a puppet show.
3   *Observing and reflecting on play:* adults tuning into evidence of deep and meaningful learning evidenced in children's self-initiated and socio-dramatic play as the basis for reflection and planning.

4   *Becoming a play partner:* adults negotiating entry into play episodes with individual or groups of children. (Examples are given in Goouch, Chapter 3.)

Conclusion

Early years professionals in England have fought long and hard to try to hold on to cherished beliefs about the importance of play in children's learning. Some settings for children under 5 – for example, increasingly in Early Years Units for 3–5 year olds in schools and in effective nursery schools (including some run by the private sector) – are offering their children exemplary play-based learning. But many 4 year olds in reception classes and 5 year olds at the start of statutory schooling have few opportunities for self-initiated and sustained play. We need well-trained early years professionals to demonstrate high-quality learning through play to policy makers and parents. We need them to argue with clarity about how children learn through play, how educational and childcare settings support such learning, and how adults intervene appropriately (or not) in promoting learning through play.

Questions to set you thinking

1   What were the processes by which a *National Curriculum* and *Foundation Stage* were introduced into early years settings?
2   How did these central government initiatives impact on your setting or classroom?
3   Did the initiatives change the way children learned through play in your setting or school?
4   How might a new understanding of how young children learn influence the way you promote learning through play in your setting?
5   What might a robust pedagogy of play in early childhood education look like?
6   How would you get parents to understand the importance of learning through play?

References and further reading

Alexander, R.J. (1984) *Primary Teaching*. Eastbourne: Holt, Rinehart and Winston.
Anning, A. (1997) *The First Years at School* (2nd edn). Buckingham: Open University Press.

Anning, A. and Ball, M. (2008) *Improving Services for Young Children: From Sure Start to Children's Centres*. London: Sage.

Anning, A., Cottrell, D.J., Frost, N., Green, J. and Robinson, M. (2010) *Developing Multi-professional Teamwork for Integrated Children's Services* (2nd edn). Maidenhead: Open University Press.

Anning, A., Cullen, J. and Fleer, M. (2009) *Early Childhood Education: Society and Culture* (2nd edn). London: Sage Publications.

Bailey, R. (2002) Playing social chess – social play and social intelligence. *Early Years*, 22(2): 163–173.

Bennett, N., Wood, E. and Rogers, S. (1997) *Teaching Through Play: Teachers' Thinking and Classroom Practice*. Buckingham: Open University Press.

Brooker, L. (2002) *Young Children Learning Cultures*. Buckingham: Open University Press.

Bruer, J. (1997) Education and the brain: a step too far? *Educational Researcher*, 26(8): 4–16.

CACE (1967) *Children and their Primary Schools* (The Plowden Report). London: HMSO.

DCSF/DCMS (2008) *Fair Play: A Consultation on the National Play Strategy*. Available online at: www.dcms.gov.uk (accessed 4 January 2009).

Department for Education and Employment (DfEE) (1998) *The National Literacy Strategy: A Framework for Teaching*. London: DfEE.

DfEE (1999) *The National Numeracy Strategy: A Framework for Teaching Mathematics from Reception to Year 6*. London: DfEE.

Department for Education and Skills (DfES) (2004) *Excellence and Enjoyment: Learning and Teaching in the Primary Years*. London: DfES.

DfES (2005) *Ten Year Strategy for Childcare*. London: HMSO.

DfES (2006) *Learning Outside the Classroom*. London: HMSO.

DfES (2007) *The Early Years Foundation Stage: Setting the Standards for Learning, Development and Care in Children from Birth to Five*. London: DfES. Available online at: www.standards.dfes.gov.uk/eyfs/.

Department of Culture, Media and Sports (DCMS) (2006) *Time to Play*. Available online at: www.dcms.gov.uk.

Edwards, C., Gandini, L. and Forman, G. (1998) *The Hundred Languages of Children: The Reggio Emilia Approach – Advanced Reflections* (2nd edn). Westport, CN and London: Ablex Publishing.

Gardner, H. (1983) *Frames of Mind: The Theory of Multiple Intelligences*. New York: Basic Books.

Garrick, R. (2004) *Playing Outdoors in the Early Years*. London: Continuum.

Gopnik, A., Melzoff, A. and Kuhl, P. (1999) *How Babies Think: The Science of Childhood*. London: Weidenfeld and Nicolson.

Kress, G. (1997) *Before Writing: Rethinking the Paths to Literacy*. London: Routledge.

Moyles, J., Hargreaves, L., Merry, R., Paterson, A. and Esarte-Sarries, V. (2003)

Interactive Teaching in the Primary School: Digging Deeper into Meanings. Maidenhead: Open University Press.

Pahl, K. (1999) *Transformations: Meaning Making in Nursery Education.* Stoke-on-Trent: Trentham Books.

Paley, V.S. (1986) On listening to what children say. *Harvard Educational Review,* 56: 122–130.

Paley, V.S. (2005) *A Child's Work: The Importance of Fantasy Play.* Chicago: Chicago University Press.

Qualifications and Curriculum Authority (QCA) (2005) *Continuing the Learning Journey.* Norwich: QCA.

QCA (2003) *Foundation Stage Profile.* London: QCA Publications.

QCA/DfEE (2000) *Curriculum Guidance for the Foundation Stage.* London: QCA Publications.

Rogers, S. and Evans, J. (2008) *Inside Role-play in Early Childhood Education: Researching Young Children's Perspectives.* London: Routledge.

Rose, J. (2009) *Independent Review of the Primary Curriculum.* London: Department for Children, Families and Schools (DCFS).

Siraj-Blatchford, I., Sylva, K., Muttock, S., Gilden, R. and Bell, D. (2002) *Researching Effective Pedagogy in the Early Years.* HMSO, Research Report 365. London: DfES.

Skelton, C. and Hall, E. (2001) *The Development of Gender Roles in Young Children: A Review of Policy and Literature.* Manchester: Equal Opportunities Commission.

Smilansky, S. and Sheftaya, L. (1990) *Facilitating Play.* Silver Spring, MD: Psychological and Educational Publications.

United Nations (1989) *United Nations Convention on the Rights of the Child.* Available online at: www.everychildmatters.gov.uk.

Vygotsky, L. (1978) *Mind in Society: The Development of Higher Psychological Processes.* Cambridge, MA: Harvard University Press.

Wood, E. (2010) Developing integrated pedagogical approaches to play and learning. In P. Broadhead, J. Howard and E. Wood (eds) *Play and Learning in the Early Years: From Research to Practice.* London: Sage Publications.

Worthington, M. (2007) Multi-modality, play and children's mark-making in maths. In J. Moyles (ed.) *Early Years Foundations: Meeting the Challenge.* Maidenhead: Open University Press.

2 Work or play: how children learn to read the signals about activity type in today's early years provision

Jan Georgeson and Jane Payler

Summary

In this chapter, we explore how children read the signs available in early years settings to help them determine what is expected of them. This chapter:

- suggests theoretical concepts helpful to framing and understanding research into how children learn about what to do, when and where
- explores what is already known about how children perceive different types of activity that could be construed as work or play
- contributes further to this through findings from two research studies
- invites practitioners, many of whom may now be operating in inter-professional integrated early years services undergoing workforce reform, to consider how such knowledge may be used to enhance pedagogy with young children.

Introduction and context

Drawing on research evidence and experience, early years educationalists have fought hard to challenge the automatic association made in past decades between 'work' and 'learning', and to foreground the excellent contribution of play to young children's learning (Moyles 1994; Broadhead 2006; Ranz-Smith 2007). However, during this time, the landscape and context of children's services in England have changed dramatically, particularly for children with special educational needs. The aim of effective multi-agency working has shaped services for young children in England, leading to Children's Trusts and Sure Start Children's Centres (referred to in Anning, Chapter 1). Such initiatives arose following independent inquiries into service failures in England (DoH 2001; DoH and HD 2003), which highlighted ingrained professional demarcations, hindering collaboration and service delivery for children and families. The inquiries led to policies requiring local authorities to create Directorates of Children's Services incorporating education, social services, youth work and partnerships with health services (DfES 2003; DoH and DfES 2004; GB 2004).

In the past, provision for many young children with special educational needs has come within the remit of health services, which has influenced their educational experiences (Grant and Carne 1994; Sebba *et al.* 1995; see also Papatheodorou, Chapter 17). A shift in services has now brought them within the remit of Children's Centres and under the care of early years practitioners or professionals, who come with their own socio-cultural historical contexts. This gives the potential for new collaborations but also new challenges. Research to date suggests that, although the development of Sure Start Children's Centres has begun to show an impact on the lives of young children and families (Melhuish *et al.* 2005; NESS 2006), such collaboration is not without operational difficulties (Edwards *et al.* 2009). Other research has recognised the need for greater focus on the experiences of children and families to inform the future development of integrated services (Tucker *et al.* 1999; Anning 2001; Freeth *et al.* 2002; Anning *et al.* 2006), addressed in part through Broadhead *et al.*'s work (2008).

To aid the culture shift towards integrated practice, the government instigated inter-professional education, particularly in health and social care. However, most children under 5 are educated and cared for by vocationally trained practitioners, many of whom are unlikely to have participated in inter-professional education. Nonetheless, workforce reform for early years is under way; since 2006, the government has committed to training Early Years Professionals (EYPs), achieving Early Years Professional Status (EYPS), to act as graduate leaders for early years care and education. EYPs are to lead the Early Years Foundation Stage (EYFS) with its play-based approach to learning and development, taking account of children's views, interests and needs (DfES 2007). The national standards set for EYPs include two relating directly to integrated practice. One (S6) requires EYPs to know and understand the contribution other professionals make to young children's well-being and development. The other (S36) requires EYPs to contribute to the work of a multi-professional team, often including speech/language therapy and physiotherapy.

What are the challenges faced by EYPs as they try to implement and lead others to implement programmes and interventions? How comfortably does the concept of 'intervention' fit within a play-based curriculum? Because we know that perceptions shape expectations, and that expectations influence participation and outcomes (Donaldson 1978; Gauvin and Rogoff 1986; Thornton 1995; Brooker 1996; Daniels *et al.* 2000; Childs and McKay 2001; David and Goouch 2001; Ranz-Smith 2007), we consider it is worthwhile thinking more about children's *perceptions* of the type of activity they are entering into – is it work or play?

We explore what is known about how children perceive different types of activity and how this affects their participation. We consider findings from two research studies: the first considers how the buildings in which early years provision is offered are perceived by children. The second considers the reality of what children encounter when they enter integrated practice, particularly children with special educational needs for whom the challenges around boundaries between work, play, 'intervention' and learning are magnified by the impetus to deliver therapeutic inputs (see Howard, Chapter 13). Exploring perceptions of and participation in different types of activity for young children will help adults to provide the best available pedagogy for children in their care.

Theoretical underpinning

Our motivation for considering these pieces of research in the context of play in the early years is that, for us, they proved to be *'critical moments'*[1] (Coffey and Atkinson 1996; Byrne-Armstrong *et al.* 2001; Thomson *et al.* 2002) in the sense that they represented important points in our observation of early years activities, which prompted us to stop and reflect on what was really happening. We have found, in the past, that strands of socio-cultural theory have helped us to make sense of what was going on (Georgeson 2009; Payler 2009). Starting from the Vygotskian concept of the social formation of mind, we consider that every social context is the result of the choices people have made about what to do and say, and how to arrange their surroundings. Everything in any social setting is therefore imbued with meaning, and children learn about these meanings in the course of everyday interactions with people, objects and the spaces that contain them. Sometimes children are learning about the perceptual and physical affordances (Gibson 1986; Greeno 1994; Lockman 2000) of the spaces in which they find themselves. This can shape the way they play and the interactions they feel are available to them (Waters 2009). This knowledge builds up over the early years so that, by the time they move into school, children have developed awareness of when it might be appropriate to play and be playful, and when they should be following instructions and adhering to routines (see Fabian and Dunlop, Chapter 15). The everyday practices in the early years of schooling, therefore, introduce children to different pedagogic genres and they become skilled in adopting different ways of talking in different situations, such as circle time and literacy sessions (Christie 2002).

To try to understand how this particular kind of learning happens, we have been considering what signals children might identify as they learn to distinguish between time to play and time to work. We think it is important to take a multi-modal approach to this endeavour; it is not just verbal interactions that signal what might happen next, but sights, sounds, smells, temperature and texture.

Boag-Munroe and Georgeson (2008) have built on this multi-modal approach to develop a framework to help practitioners think about how children and families read the signals from buildings used as early years settings, and how this shapes their understanding about what they can and cannot do in these buildings. The framework encourages practitioners to think about their settings in terms of the experience, the interpersonal relationships, and the cohesion or connectedness of their buildings.

Bernstein (2000: 35) encourages us to recognise that pedagogic discourse will always include both the content of what is to be taught (instructional discourse, encapsulated for most settings in the early learning goals) and the regulative discourse of social order, the often tacit understandings about relationships, who is in charge and who can make choices. Again, there are ways that this is signalled in the physical environment and in specialised ways of talking, and children learn to recognise these signals.

What is known about how children perceive different types of activity and how this impacts upon their participation?

Previous research has shown that, in the course of their early educational experience, children learn to make distinctions between different kinds of activity, and that this contributes to their developing understanding of the difference between work and play, which they will take with them into adult life (Apple and King 2004). While it has been shown that young children clearly associate particular objects (paint, blocks, sand, construction materials, board and computer games) with play rather than work (Wing 1995), other features of the classroom environment (teacher presence, space and absence of constraint) also influence their interpretation (Howard 2002). Wing concluded from discussions with children that a main criterion for interpreting an activity as work or play appears to be whether the activity was perceived as obligatory or not. This can be signalled by the particular words used by adults when discussing the activity, and this was reflected as 'can do' versus 'have to do' in children's comments. However, distinguishing between the modality of an utterance requires a certain level of language comprehension (see Papafragou and Ozturk 2007), which might not be within the receptive language repertoire of some children with special educational needs. Environmental and non-verbal cues to play or work are likely to be more important for these pupils, as well as the recall of or association with feelings of effort and enjoyment, or the perception of these in others (Howard 2002).

Children, especially those with special needs, clearly must learn how to respond physically when confronted with different physical conditions such as slopes, steps, wide expanses or constricted spaces. They must also learn how to use space socially, in conjunction with other people, taking the movements of others into account and interacting with other people as they move through different spaces. But they also need to learn about the cultural constraints and affordances of buildings, the kinds of movements, behaviour and interaction that are expected in particular spaces. As adults, we quickly and unconsciously develop patterns of movement when negotiating familiar spaces; think about how easy it is to carry out tasks in your own kitchen, compared with someone else's. These patterns of movement become so automatic that it can be difficult to explain to someone else how to perform part of your own daily routine, such as finding the way from the car park to the parents room. It is impossible to 'unlearn' how to do this, so it can be difficult to put yourself in the shoes of a child visiting your setting for the first time, but it is important to remember this when we invite children and families to come along to buildings that they have never visited before.

We need to think more about what the buildings and surrounding spaces signal to children and families, and whether they suggest which particular ways of being/doing/saying are acceptable in that particular space. Should they stay put or move around? Be quiet or sing loudly if they want to? Children will already have experience of places where they can move freely and places where there are constraints, so they need to find out what kind of constraints operate in the building. The sense of freedom versus constraint is at the heart of the distinctions that children make between work and play. When considering how the day unfolds, how are time and space punctuated by signs of movement, position, objects and sensory stimuli? Historically, sounds such as bells have been used as punctuation to signal different phases of the day. Signals such as these, by association with particular activities, come to carry meaning and can then be recognised in other situations. They become part of a repertoire of things-we-know-about-places, the multi-modal discourse associated with particular activities. This enables us to read buildings as texts, in just the same way that we draw on our knowledge of letters, sounds and writing genres to understand a piece of writing.

Regan de Bere (2003) points out the value of discourse analysis to unpick how individuals draw on different systems of meaning in order to make sense of their lives in specific situations and times. The type and purpose of activity within settings can be signalled by different discourses; education researchers have noted, for example, the specific and characteristic nature of educational discourse (see, for example, Sinclair and Coulthard 1975; Willes 1983; Mercer 1995), while more recent research has drawn attention to links between pedagogic discourse and young children's learning (Brooker 1996, 2002). Roberts and Sarangi (2005) note that practitioners' knowledge is evident in their practice, but may not be completely evident in what they say. It is important, therefore, to look beyond words to ways in which the actions, words, space and objects together create and communicate dialogue.

This chapter contributes to the body of literature exploring the ways in which early years practice is experienced by people for whom integrated services are designed, particularly young children with special educational needs.

Examples from our own research

Learning to read buildings for early years provision

Children's capacity to read buildings from their external appearance seems to develop from first a recognition of people and objects contained within them, then later responding to what might be described as architectural features. As part of a study into differences in interaction and pedagogy in preschool settings (Georgeson 2006), I invited children (aged 3 and 4) to talk about photographs of familiar and unfamiliar preschool settings. Occasionally children might label objects or parts of buildings that they recognised (such as pictures of toys or cartoon characters, or doors and windows), or they might spot and ask questions about children in the photographs, even if these were children they didn't know. When looking at photographs of the outside or approach to an unfamiliar building, children either said they didn't know what it was, or declared it to be a particular place known to them, often trying to connect it to people they knew – for example, by commenting 'That is my grandma's house' in response to a picture of a tall wooden fence with a gate, which they had never seen before.

As soon as I moved on to photographs of the interiors, they readily labelled or commented, sometimes confirming, sometimes changing their initial interpretation from the photographs of the exterior. And some of the older children were able to use objects or other features, such as doors and windows, as signals to the building's use. This sometimes led to a conjecture that the unfamiliar building belonged to a particular class of buildings: 'It's a pub!' (in response to a photograph of heavy double doors covered in notices): 'It's a playgroup' (in response to a hallway with a teddy border above the dado rail, from a child whose setting used a teddy bear in its logo). This influenced their perceptions of what sort of things happened inside.

The extracts presented below illustrate some of the findings outlined above. The first extract is from a conversation with a 4-year-old girl who had recently moved into the village from a nearby town (still in England) and attended a playgroup in a village hall. She is looking at photos of two unfamiliar nurseries, one (Nursery 1) housed in a Victorian semi in a residential street, and the second (Nursery 2) in a large detached Edwardian house set in its own grounds at the end of a drive, with lots of wood panelling and an impressive staircase inside the inner doors. The second extract is from a conversation with two 4-year-old girls from a playgroup in an inner-city area, also looking at photographs of Nursery 2.

Extract 1

Photograph	**Child's comments** *Researcher's questions*
Nursery 1: Side of house in street	Have you come here before – I haven't seen you – I've just moved into this country *Where do you think this is?* I don't know
Frontage of Nursery 1	England *somewhere in England* It's near David's house
Room in Nursery 1	Look there's the children *What are they doing?* They're playing in the water
Inside same room in Nursery 1	What are they called? *I don't know* Are they at your . . . your place? *No . . .*
Nursery 2: drive with wrought-iron gates	*Where do you think that is?* I don't know *What sort of place do you think it is?*
Frontage of Nursery 2 including car park	I think it's David's house
Front door of Nursery 2 (from outside)	I think it's David's house
Inner double doors, with large brass handles and notices	That's not David's house . . . that's a pub
Hall, stairs and landing, with dark wood panelling	It must be a hotel

Extract 2

Photograph	Child's comments
Nursery 2: drive with wrought-iron gates	It's the park, it's the park – my daddy took me to the park in the car. Yesterday my daddy took me to the park
Front door of Nursery 2 (from outside)	It's a school – look, I see the name. I am going to school . . .
Child with mosaic tiles	What she doing? She do drawing
Messy painting	[excitement] Look, look at them. They do painting

Commentary

Both extracts point to children trying to 'read' the buildings by connecting them to people they know – and when that failed, to me as a possible source of information about the unfamiliar people (in this case children) who used the buildings. Their interpretation of buildings was shaped by the people and places that were important to them, but if they couldn't see a connection to their own experience, they weren't interested.

The children's interpretation of the two nurseries was influenced by the sort of buildings that were common in their own communities. The design of early years spaces sometimes consciously borrows from buildings in the community of the children who attend; this is particularly true of the municipal infant and toddler centres and preschools of Reggio Emilia, where the idea of workshops around a piazza is reflected in the arrangement of rooms in the preschools and echoed in an approach to activities that combines the seriousness of work with the freedom of play (Rinaldi 1998). But not all children will be sufficiently well embedded in mainstream culture to benefit from cultural references like this (Brooker 2002) and not all children have the same expectations of involvement in work and play, as will become apparent in the next section, describing a second example from research.

Examples of different discourses

The research referred to in this section is a re-analysis of data (Payler *et al.* 2008) from a small-scale study into the experiences of 4-year-old children with learning difficulties attending both special and inclusive preschools in England (Nind *et al.* 2007). Payler *et al.* use two examples to show that the children were not only required to 'cope' with moving between the three different environments, but also had to cope with shifts in communicative environment and different discourses *within* settings. The children attended settings that aimed to provide therapeutic input to ameliorate their needs, as well as early years education according to the curriculum of the day (currently EYFS: DfES 2007). Early years practitioners provided 'therapy' during the usual preschool sessions: such inputs were designed, planned and intermittently monitored by professional therapists (such as speech and language therapists), most of whom were not based at the settings. However, the delivery on a daily basis was largely carried out by early years practitioners following the guidance to the best of their ability and reporting back to therapists.

Jamie[2] is a 4-year-old boy attending a special inclusive preschool, and had been allocated a place on the basis of his developmental delay in relation to speech and language and other developmental difficulties. Speech therapy episodes took place in a small separate room and usually lasted for around 8–10 minutes. The content of the sessions had been designed and planned by a visiting speech and language therapist (SLT) and the sessions were delivered one to one by Jamie's key person, Tom, an early years practitioner. The following outlines a session between Tom and Jamie, exemplifying the speech therapy and the transition from therapy to usual discourse.

> Jamie sat at the small table in the speech therapy room. On the table was a row of plastic animals of varying size. Tom sat on the floor facing Jamie and asked Jamie to find the 'little elephant'. Jamie pointed at an object on the table, murmuring 'There'. Tom, using a clear voice, gentle tone and Makaton[3] hand signs, said 'That's the BIG elephant. Where's the little one?' Makaton signs were used to emphasise the words that were the focus of the speech therapy, for example, 'big' and 'little', and to identify the animals. Jamie watched Tom attentively before pointing to another object. Tom praised Jamie, 'That's it. Good boy', and made a note of the response in the records. Jamie waited quietly, his hands folded together in front of his mouth, chewing a finger, gazing at the animals. Tom regained Jamie's attention and asked Jamie to find the big horse, again using hand signs as support. Jamie pointed to one of the animals. Again, Tom praised, 'Good boy!' and recorded the response. This continued for several more minutes, Tom supporting Jamie's understanding through hand signs, praising and recording responses. Jamie was compliant and eager to please. His movements and comments were restricted to the openings provided by Tom within the routine discourse and format of the therapy session.
>
> At the end, Tom asked Jamie to put the animals back into the box. Jamie immediately became more animated, standing up and energetically putting the animals back. Jamie commented on the duck, pointing out that they had not used it and asking Tom if the gorilla, the largest of the animals, also had to go in the box. Jamie pointed to

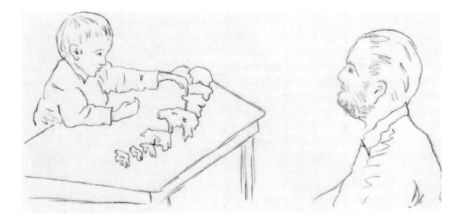

Figure 2.1 Jamie in speech therapy with Tom: 'Find the little elephant'.

the pot of bubble-blowing mixture, stating that he wanted to 'do that', his usual 'reward' for taking part in speech therapy. Tom held the bubble mixture container as Jamie dipped into it, blew the wand and tried to catch the bubbles. He became animated and engaged. The discourse changed, with Tom speaking more naturally to Jamie, 'Ooh, only one! You got it? Caught it? Oh gone! Right, last one, then you can go back into the hall'. As Tom offered to blow bubbles for Jamie to catch, Jamie became even more active, dashing into a space in the room, jumping up and down in anticipation and catching the bubbles with great delight.

It was during these moments alone together at the end of the speech therapy that Jamie had begun to talk more (reported by Tom in interview). It appeared that the time one to one, away from the hustle and bustle of the rest of the preschool, had benefits for Jamie's speech and language beyond the controlled exercises.

The distinctive features of the speech therapy discourse were:

- controlled use of specific words
- use of Makaton signs to supplement words
- rhythm
- adult-controlled, closed interactive space (Payler 2007)
- shared understanding, developed over time, of expectations in relation to discourse and format.

Jamie was clearly interpreting and making sense of quite complex tacit rules in relation to expectations of him during speech therapy. The contrast

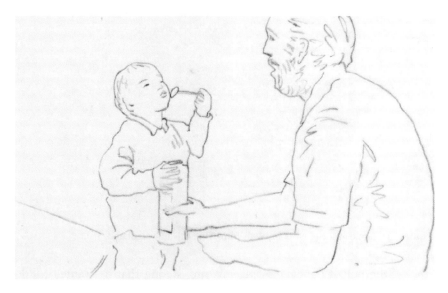

Figure 2.2   Jamie's reward at the end – animated and natural interaction.

between his communication during speech therapy episodes and immediately afterwards, evident from his actions and words, is striking. During the speech therapy session, he communicated within a closed interactive space determined by the opportunities afforded and shaped by the adult interaction and the demands of the exercises. Jamie did not co-construct meanings (Payler 2009) during speech therapy, initiate contributions or show emotional responses beyond his keenness to provide the correct responses. As soon as the episode was declared over, he began to do each of these, communicating within the affordances now available. Jamie appeared to manage the shift in discourse from therapy to playful exchange with Tom successfully.

We turn now to another of the case study children, Mandy, a 4-year-old girl with Angelman's syndrome. Mandy attended a specially resourced Children's Centre where she had speech therapy at least termly, occupational therapy occasionally (primarily focusing on feeding herself) and physiotherapy weekly for 10 minutes. However, Mandy's routine interaction with the early years practitioners also often involved a short session of physical therapy, particularly walking exercises encouraging her to use a frame for support. I will now consider an episode exemplifying Mandy's transition from play into 'therapeutic' discourse, which Mandy appeared to find difficult to negotiate.

> At the beginning of the episode, Mandy lay on the activity rug exploring a favourite toy with her mouth. She crawled across the room to a

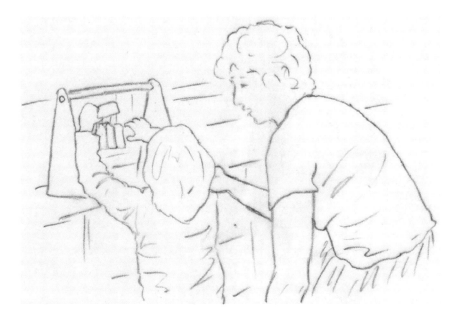

Figure 2.3   From exploring musical toys . . .

worktop to look at and touch the musical toys on display. One of the early years practitioners, Amy, initially supported Mandy in her interest in the musical toys. Amy assisted Mandy to a standing position at the worktop, commenting on Mandy's interest. She used one of the toys as a joint focus of attention, demonstrating how to make a noise with the beater, then placing the beater into Mandy's hand, praising and encouraging. Mandy participated with interest.

Very quickly, however, Amy decided to use this as an opportunity to carry out physical therapy exercises to improve Mandy's walking. Although Mandy showed no indication of having lost interest in the toys, Amy called for Mandy's walking frame and, enlisting the somewhat reluctant help of another child, attempted to encourage Mandy to walk with her walking frame. The discourse used by Amy changed at this point. Shifting from extending and building on Mandy's interest during which she had used words and actions to facilitate Mandy's fuller participation in Mandy's chosen activity, Amy adopted a more directive and restrictive discourse. Although Amy still attempted to use an object which had meaning for Mandy (a favourite soft toy) as a focus for joint attention, Amy directed the other child to hold it out of Mandy's reach as an incentive for Mandy to attempt to walk towards it.

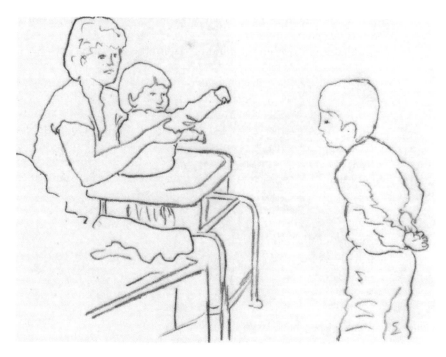

Figure 2.4 . . . to walking therapy; Amy enlisted the help of another child.

Mandy was given no choice; Amy used verbal direction and physical guidance, lifting Mandy to hold on to the walking frame in an attempt to ensure Mandy's compliance. The combination of words used as imperatives, 'Got to move you' and 'Walking, Mandy!', the positioning of Amy's body, standing behind Mandy with her arms around Mandy, and the use of physical repositioning (lifting Mandy under the arms, repositioning her at the frame several times) ensured that this was non-negotiable. Mandy was presented with a closed interactive space, defined by words and actions, in an attempt to ensure her compliance with the specific objective of the therapy. Mandy's lack of interest in the objective to improve her walking, and her consistent desire to move away from the frame back to the worktop, were clearly communicated. Mandy finally succeeded in crawling away and Amy appeared frustrated.

The distinctive features of the physical therapy discourse were:

- tightly focused and exclusive adult-led objective
- strong adult control of child's actions, using body and words

- reduction of Mandy's agency with her lack of involvement clearly communicated
- considerable effort from the adult to sustain the discourse.

For Mandy, the shift from playful exchange to therapy appeared to be unhelpful and poorly received, causing consternation for both Mandy and Amy.

Mandy and Jamie's experiences of and reactions to shifts between activity type during a preschool session were markedly different, though in quite subtle ways. By examining the similarities and differences, we can begin to unpick the features that may help young children to understand expectations of them during activities and to participate more meaningfully. The similarities included:

- 'closed interactive space' during 'therapy', communicated verbally and bodily (Payler 2007)
- a clear objective, tightly controlled by the adult.

The differences included:

- *clear demarcation* in time and space between 'therapy' and 'non-therapy' by the use of a separate room/time for Jamie, but not for Mandy
- *negotiated* beginning and end to therapy sessions for Jamie, but not for Mandy
- *shared understanding* developed over time between Jamie and Tom with valuable use of a 'reward' time, not evident for Mandy.

Effective early years professionals need to be aware of expectations relating to participation for different types of activities, and how these are signalled to children if they are to facilitate children's meaningful participation. Attention needs to be paid to signs determined by the:

- physical and temporal environment – time and space
- social features of the activity – power, control, choice, relationships
- cultural features – the child's prior knowledge of and alertness to 'rules' of games, rules of control and social exchanges
- potential 'collision' of discourses derived from differing principles – for example, early years practice principles linked to 'play', and therapy principles linked to precise, controlled 'work' towards objectives.

Conclusion: what does this mean for practitioners/early years professionals?

Contexts are signalled by the choices people make about how they arrange their surroundings, how they organise time, and about what to say and do. Children need to be able to read the signs of what is expected of them. Practitioners need to be alert to children's cues as to whether or not they understand the signs so that practitioners can facilitate and build from that understanding. The *nature* of children's participation and their willingness/ability to do so depends on this understanding. Such integrated practice on a daily basis is something that professionals in health and social care have evidently struggled with for years (Cooper *et al.* 2001; Reeves *et al.* 2008). The time is ripe for early years staff to grasp the nettle.

Questions to set you thinking

1   How might practitioners seek and act upon children's beliefs about what is expected where and when to enhance children's participation and learning?
2   How might practitioners further influence the design, layout and use of buildings, time and space to define and shape affordances for children and families?
3   How might early years practitioners become more fully involved in negotiating the nature of therapeutic inputs and activity plans with other health and social care professionals to ease children's transitions between discourses and activity types?

Notes

1   Previous authors have used the term 'critical moments' in varying ways to describe pivotal times in the research process or in the lives of 'researched' subjects. We use the term in a similar way to describe our own 'noteworthy' moments during data collection or analysis.
2   All names have been changed and outline tracings of video stills are used to preserve the anonymity of participants.
3   Makaton is a selected purposeful signed vocabulary for use with people with learning difficulties.

References and further reading

Anning, A. (2001) Knowing who I am and what I know: developing new versions of professional knowledge in integrated service settings. Paper presented to the British Educational Research Association Annual Conference, University of Leeds, UK.

Anning, A., Cottrell, D., Frost, N., Green, J. and Robinson, M. (2006) *Developing Multiprofessional Teamwork for Integrated Children's Services.* **Maidenhead: Open University Press.**

Apple, M.W. and King, N. (2004) Economics and control in everyday school life. In M.W. Apple (ed.) *Ideology and Curriculum* (3rd edn). New York: Routledge.

Bernstein, B. (2000) *Pedagogy, Symbolic Control and Identity: Theory, Research, Critique.* Lanham, Rowman and Littlefield.

Boag-Munroe, G. and Georgeson, J. (2008) Architextures of early years settings and the kinds of identity they might construct. Paper presented at First UK and Ireland ISCAR Meeting, University of Bath, July.

Broadhead, P. (2006) Developing an understanding of young children's learning through play: the place of observation, interaction and reflection. *British Educational Research Journal*, 32(2): 191–207.

Broadhead, P., Meleady, C. and Delgado, M.A. (2008) *Children, Families and Communities: Creating and Sustaining Integrated Services.* **Maidenhead: Open University Press.**

Brooker, L. (1996) Why do children go to school? Consulting children in the reception class. *Early Years*, 17(1): 12–16.

Brooker, L. (2002) *Starting School: Young Children Learning Cultures.* Buckingham: Open University Press.

Byrne-Armstrong, H., Higgs, J. and Horsfall, D. (eds) (2001) *Critical Moments in Qualitative Research.* Oxford: Butterworth-Heinemann.

Childs, G. and McKay, M. (2001) Boys starting school disadvantaged: implications from teachers' ratings of behaviour and achievement in the first two years. *British Journal of Educational Psychology*, 71(2): 303–314.

Christie, F. (2002) *Classroom Discourse Analysis: A Functional Perspective.* London: Continuum.

Coffey, A. and Atkinson, P. (1996) Narratives and stories. In A. Coffey and P. Atkinson, *Making Sense of Qualitative Data.* London: Sage.

Cooper, H., Carlisle, C., Gibbs, T. and Watkins, C. (2001) Developing an evidence base for interdisciplinary learning: a systematic review. *Journal of Advanced Nursing*, 35(2): 228–237.

Daniels, S., Shorrocks-Taylor, D. and Redfern, E. (2000) Can starting summer-born children earlier at infant school improve their National Curriculum results? *Oxford Review of Education*, 26(2): 207–220.

David, T. and Goouch, K. (2001) Early literacy teaching: the 'third' way. *Education 3 to 13*, June: 20–24. UK: Primary School Research and Development Group.

Department for Education and Skills (2003) *Every Child Matters* (Green Paper). London: The Stationery Office. Available online at: http://publications.every childmatters.gov.uk/default.aspx?PageFunction=productdetailsandPageMode =publicationsandProductId=CM5860and (accessed 23 December 2009).

Department for Education and Skills (2007) *The Early Years Foundation Stage.* Nottingham: DfES.

Department of Health (2001) *Learning from Bristol: The Report of the Public Inquiry into Children's Heart Surgery at the Bristol Royal Infirmary 1984–95.* London: The Stationery Office.

Department of Health and Department for Education and Skills (2004) *National Service Framework for Children, Young People and Maternity Services.* London: The Stationery Office 3779.

Department of Health and Home Department (2003) *The Victoria Climbié Inquiry: Report of an Inquiry by Lord Laming.* London: The Stationery Office.

Donaldson, M. (1978) *Children's Minds.* London: Fontana Press.

Edwards, A., Daniels, H., Gallagher, T., Leadbetter, J. and Warmington, P. (2009) *Improving Inter-professional Collaborations: Multi-agency Working for Children's Wellbeing.* Abingdon: Routledge.

Freeth, D., Hammick, M., Koppel, I., Reeves, S. and Barr, H. (2002) *A Critical Review of Evaluations of Interprofessional Education, Occasional Paper No. 2.* London: LTSN Centre for Health Sciences and Practice.

Gauvin, M. and Rogoff, B. (1986) Influence of the goal on children's exploration and memory of large scale space. *Developmental Psychology*, 22: 72–77.

Georgeson, J. (2006) Differences in preschool culture: organisation, pedagogy and interaction in four selected settings. School of Education, University of Birmingham. Unpublished EdD thesis.

Georgeson, J. (2009) Co-constructing meaning: differences in interactional microclimate. In T. Papatheodorou and J. Moyles (eds) *Learning Together in the Early Years: Exploring Relational Pedagogy*. London: Routledge.

Gibson, J.J. (1986) *The Ecological Approach to Visual Perception.* Hillsdale, NJ: Erlbaum (originally published 1979).

Grant, M. and Carne, F. (1994) *Managing Special Educational Needs.* Bristol: National Development Centre for Educational Management and Policy.

Great Britain (2004) *The Children Act.* London: The Stationery Office.

Greeno, J.G. (1994) Gibson's affordances. *Psychological Review*, 101(2): 336–342.

Howard, J. (2002) Eliciting young children's perceptions of play, work and learning using the activity apperception story procedure. *Early Child Development and Care*, 172(5): 489–502.

Lockman, J.L. (2000) A perception–action perspective on tool use development. *Child Development*, 71(1): 137–144.

Melhuish, E., Belsky, J. and Leyland, A. (2005) *Early Impact of Sure Start Local Programmes on Children and Families*, SS Report 13. London: DfES.

Mercer, N. (1995) *The Guided Construction of Knowledge – Talk Amongst Teachers and Learners*. Clevedon: Multilingual Matters.

Moyles, J. (ed.) (1994) *The Excellence of Play*. Buckingham: Open University Press.

National Evaluation of Sure Start (NESS) (2006) *Changes in the Characteristics of Sure Start Local Programme Areas between 2001/2 and 2003/4*. Nottingham: DfES.

Nind, M., Flewitt, R. and Payler, J. (2007) The experiences of young children with learning disabilities attending both special and inclusive preschools. Final report for Rix, Thompson, Rothenberg Foundation.

Papafragou, A. and Ozturk, O. (2007) Children's acquisition of epistemic modality. *Proceedings of the 2nd Conference on Generative Approaches to Language Acquisition North America (GALANA)*, ed. Alyona Belikova *et al.*: 320–327. Somerville, MA: Cascadilla Proceedings Project.

Payler, J. (2007) Opening and closing interactive spaces: shaping four-year-old children's participation in two English settings. *Early Years: An International Journal of Research and Development*, 27(3): 237–254.

Payler, J. (2009) Co-construction and scaffolding: guidance strategies and children's meaning-making. In T. Papatheodorou and J. Moyles (eds) *Learning Together in the Early Years: Exploring Relational Pedagogy*. London: Routledge.

Payler, J., Flewitt, R. and Nind, M. (2008) 'Therapy' at pre-school: experiencing the disparate discourses involved in integrated practice. Paper presented at the EECERA 18th Annual Conference, 3–6 September, Norway.

Ranz-Smith, D.J. (2007) Teacher perception of play: in leaving no child behind are teachers leaving childhood behind? *Early Education and Development*, 18(2): 271–303.

Reeves, S., Zwarenstein, M., Goldman, J., Barr, H., Freeth, D., Hammick., M. and Koppel, I. (2008) Interprofessional education: effects on professional practice and health care outcomes. *Cochrane Database of Systematic Reviews*, Issue 1. Art. no. CD002213.

Regan de Bere, S. (2003) Evaluating the implications of complex interprofessional education for improvements in collaborative practice. *British Educational Research Journal*, 29(1): 105–124.

Rinaldi, C. (1998) The space of childhood. In G. Ceppi and M. Zini (eds) *Children, Spaces, Relations; Metaproject for an Environment for Young Children*. Reggio Emilia: Reggio Children.

Roberts, C. and Sarangi, S. (2005) Theme-oriented discourse analysis of medical encounters. *Medical Education*, 39(6): 632–640.

Sebba, J., Byers, R. and Rose, R. (1995) *Redefining the Whole Curriculum for Pupils with Learning Difficulties* (revised edn). London: David Fulton.

Sinclair, J. and Coulthard, M. (1975) *Towards an Analysis of Discourse: The English used by Teachers and Pupils*. Oxford: Oxford University Press.

Thomson, R., Bell, R., Holland, J., Henderson, S., McGrellis, S. and Sharpe, S. (2002)

Critical moments: choice, chance and opportunity in young people's narratives of transition. *Sociology*, 36: 335–354.

Thornton, S. (1995) *Children Solving Problems*. Cambridge, MA: Harvard University Press.

Tucker, S., Strange, C., Cordeaux, C., Moules, T. and Torrance, N. (1999) Developing an interdisciplinary framework for the education and training of those working with children and young people. *Journal of Interprofessional Care*, 13(1): 261–270.

Waters, J. (2009) 'There was a dragon over there'. Child initiated interaction: an analysis of the opportunities for interaction offered by the outdoor environment to 4–7 year old children. Paper presented to BERA Annual Conference, Manchester, September.

Willes, M. (1983) *Children into Pupils*. London: Routledge and Kegan Paul.

Wing, L.A. (1995) Play is not the work of the child: young children's perceptions of work and play. *Early Childhood Research Quarterly*, 10: 223–247.

3 Permission to play

Kathy Goouch

Summary

This chapter draws on research to support ideas for the creation of a pedagogy that is both centred on play and playfulness. Underpinning this chapter will be a core principle that adults can frequently be most useful to children's learning and development if they serve the immediate intentions of children who are playing rather than preset education agendas. It will make clear the importance for all practitioners to increase their knowledge of play and to understand what children do when they play. It will explore the varying and complex roles that are required of adults in support of children at play and specify possibilities for, and advantages to, adults themselves becoming 'players'. Examples will be given from research data demonstrating adults drawing from a repertoire of roles, including, for example, adult as play narrator, in role in play, play resource provider, play negotiator, disseminator and reporter, play guide and support. These examples will serve to both illustrate research findings and exemplify potential for practice. This chapter will typically raise questions of what we understand by play, the purposes of play (particularly in education settings) and, perhaps the most significant question of all, what the role of the adult(s) could most usefully be in play contexts.

Introduction

The central theme of this chapter relates to one of the key findings of the Review of Literature for the Birth to Three Framework (David *et al.* 2003) – that is, that *people* matter to babies and children as they grow, develop and learn. As play can frequently be seen to be central to most children's lives, then adults who play also matter in children's growth, development and learning. This chapter draws on considerable research evidence that emphasises the social nature of learning (Bruner 1986; McLean 1991; Dunn 2004), the importance of attachment to significant adults (David *et al.* 2003; Nutbrown and Page 2008) and the significance of emotional well-being to children's learning potential (Immordino-Yang and Damasio 2007). The work of neuroscience indicates the overwhelming contribution that conversation makes to the growth and shape of children's brain development (Gopnik *et al.* 1999; Greenfield 2000). Observations from everyday family lives are supported by research from across the world, which points to the overwhelming significance of human relationships in children's lives.

Among all of this attention from research, the child at the centre of her world is busy making and shaping human and cultural sense of the mass of information that surrounds her. Rather than being 'an amorphous blob' (Gopnik *et al.* 1999), merely absorbing information, we now know that the brain of the baby/child is constructing its own shape based partly on genetic potential and partly on the surrounding environment, especially including people, at this particularly formative time (Greenfield 2000; see also Parker-Rees, Chapter 4). The brain's plasticity in the early years has long been acknowledged (David *et al.* 2003) and this, coupled with the phenomenal rate at which brain cells proliferate at this stage (Greenfield 2000), reflects the deep significance of this time of life in relation to future development and healthy growth. Research also suggests the importance of relationships during early development, and friendships in particular (Dunn 2004).

It would seem, then, that information from research across disciplines clearly indicates that young developing minds require conversation, inter-action and affective engagements with others in order to grow (see Whitehead, Chapter 5). Given what we know, it seems essential that the education of young children in early years settings demands a complex but relational pedagogy (Papatheodorou and Moyles 2009). Indeed, support for focusing attention on the needs of young learners, rather than the needs of a national primary curriculum policy directed by politicians, has recently been gathering speed (Alexander 2009). In the Final Report of the *Primary Review*, Alexander argues that 'childhood's rich potential should be protected from a system apparently bent on pressing children into a uniform mould at an ever-younger age' (p. 2) and recommends that the early start of formal educational practices in England should be reconsidered.

Reconceptualising children and childhood and the meaning of early edu-cation is important if lessons are to be learned from research, and this requires politicians and policy makers to construct children as other than 'defective adults' (Gopnik 2009: 5) and childhood as a special time 'devoted to learning about our world and imagining all the other ways that world could be' (Gopnik 2009: 11). In such a new conceptualisation, play would be assumed as the site for such learning and imagining. A site is necessary for children's pretence, their hypotheses, possibility thinking, and a place for those possibilities to be tested, mediated and mapped into broader sense-making, world-making patterns, which then serve children in their next steps. Play would seem to offer the physical and conceptual opportunities for children to achieve all of this, and it is 'the signature of childhood' (Gopnik 2009: 14). However, it would be a mistake to think of pretence, hypothesising, creating and playing as a natural, incremental and developmental process for all children. Instead it may be more useful to think of children's early learning as a puzzle or a developing picture, with experiences, images, language, encounters all being drawn together as children develop an inner life as well as the outer manifestation. The part that significant adults play, then, is not one of *selecting* the puzzle pieces but more that of a mediator and guide, helping to ensure the world-making pieces fit together and that the child is, and feels herself to be, the artist and architect of the design and of the developing product – herself in her world.

A complex pedagogy: complex pedagogues

It is hard to find new language to describe what babies and young children do and the activities in which they engage, without employing the term 'play' – however slippery or misinterpreted the term itself has become. Play is the best word we have. It is not a new concept. It is, however, becoming better understood as the result of a range of international and national research (see, for example, Abbott 2001; Jenkinson 2001; Goldschmied and Jackson 2004; Moyles 2005). Children play to explore possibilities and thus to learn about the world. Young children at play have been described variously as *scientists* (Piaget 1959), *statisticians* (Xu and Garcia, cited in Gopnik 2009), *systematic experimenters* (Gopnik 2009); they are clearly *explorers, problem solvers, role takers* and *dramatists, 'wild pretenders'* (Gopnik 2009: 73), *risk takers* and *apprentices* (Rogoff 1990). All of this world-making is undertaken and sometimes accomplished through physical, intellectual and social actions and interactions that can be identified as play. It could also be argued that the same could be accomplished through direction and instruction by adults, parents and teachers. However, the accompanying behaviour by young children in play is also credited with improved well-being, developing autonomy and self-esteem, and learning the worth of independent and interdependent acts as well as the development of agency (Rogoff 1990; Super and Harkness 1998). Such essentials of life and life-enriching development and learning are more difficult, or perhaps impossible, to acquire through structured, instructional activities with adults.

To accompany children in their play is a sophisticated role that can be achieved only by those who know and understand children, who are able to allow the sometimes complex intentions of children at play to take precedence and who will demonstrate respect for such intentionality. For some adults this kind of 'knowing' and 'respecting' is intuitive as they braid together implicit know-how and explicit knowledge (Atkinson and Claxton 2000: 3; see also Georgeson and Payler, Chapter 2). It has been suggested that this kind of behaviour towards children by adults is determined by biology – that is, just as children are:

> intrinsically motivated to learn . . . the parent is intrinsically motiv-
> ated to share his knowledge . . . and has a biologically determined
> capacity to modify the form of conveying knowledge to the infant in
> accordance with the developmental state and momentary course of
> the infant's integrative capacity.
>
> (Papousek and Papousek 1983, cited in Gopnik 2009: 94)

The intuitive behaviour defined above, then, is supported by the idea that it may be biologically determined. Of course, such mutuality in learning contexts presupposes an acknowledgement that learning is a social process (Vygotsky 1978; Rogoff 1990), which, as Bruner claims, appears to be indisputable: 'we now know beyond any reasonable doubt that human intelligence depends upon and is strikingly specialized to assist us in communal and interpersonal enterprises' (Bruner 2004: xi).

In the early years of children's lives as 'the biological heritage of the human species and the cultural inventions of the human species become aspects of each other' (Rogoff 1990: 39), it seems important for the child and adult to form and nurture a special relationship to support this development as both biology and culture entwine to create a sense of identity. Although perhaps a natural occurrence between *parents* and young children, in the early years of education and care, such relationships, while not biologically formed, may still be constructed and nurtured by *teachers* for the purpose of accompanying young children as they make sense of their world. Working with children in this way in nurseries, schools and other settings is sometimes described as organic or intuitive, as above. However, the suggestion of a complex and evolving pedagogy produces something of a dichotomy for teachers as the particular educational climate of the moment, in England, is one of political certainties in relation to education, of robust managerial drives towards prescriptive curricula and tightly controlled levels of accountability. All of this seems to be counter to ideas of intuitive practices and organic pedagogy. The dominant culture, and therefore the dominant discourse, in contemporary educational policy appears to recognise only technicist/rationalist ideologies (see Anning, Chapter 1). Further, it is clear that in some educational fields, for example primary literacy education, where central government has taken new and overarching control, 'teachers may be regarded as blank slates, or "palimpsests", tablets on which successive scripts are written' (Bryan 2004: 143), which results in the development of a scripted pedagogy (Gibson and Patrick 2008) to which many practitioners have now become accustomed. In consequence, and to interpret, enrich, develop or sometimes to subvert governmental scripts, teachers need to be aware not only of the direct needs, intentions and interests of the young children in their care but also of the ways that this information fits into a bigger picture – that is, they find themselves to be considering 'the interests of children, what is in their interest and what is in the public interest' (Peters 1966: 167). Such teachers believe, like Freire (1976), that 'education is not the transference of knowledge but the encounter of subjects in dialogue' (p. 143). They are accomplishing this, however, by occupying *'the plane of the personal'* rather than a *'purely functional position'* (Peters 1966: 94). The 'plane of the personal' in these early years contexts is evident at all levels, in all interactions, spoken and otherwise, but takes a very visible form in storying, story play and play narratives, and is consciously valued and given time, and both physical and conceptual space, by some teachers, in some settings. It is during these moments of often incidental intimacy between the teacher and one child or an infinite number of children, when the children's own discourse takes precedence, their intentions are paramount and their choices apparent, that an attendant aspect of the teachers' role invariably becomes visible.

It is simple to see how children, defining their own space, time and narrative in an organic pedagogy centred on play purposes, will inevitably be affectively involved in their play practice. In addition, by being close to, listening to, playing with and responding to children, it is impossible for teachers to be disengaged from them and often also affectively involved. But 'engagement' may imply merely 'surveillance' in Bernstein's terms (1997: 60), or simply allowing for such events to occur. Affective engagement requires rather more. It demands empathy and emotional connection with children as players; genuine interest in their play; attention to their problems and their solutions; and acute sensitivity. This level of professional activity also requires professional 'knowhow' – that is, knowledge of children and childhood, development and learning, skills and their application, together with pedagogical understandings.

Attention to emotion rather than, or in addition to, technical or rational acts and involvement can sometimes be considered of little or lesser importance in educational practice, particularly as it is not simply measurable for purposes of accountability. However, some research is now providing new information, making closer connections between cognitive development and emotion. An interesting analogy has been made to claim a fundamental role for emotion in education:

> emotions are not just messy toddlers in a china shop, running around breaking and obscuring delicate cognitive glassware. Instead, they

are more like the shelves underlying the glassware; without them cognition lacks support.

(Immordino-Yang and Damasio 2007: 5)

In this recent research from neuroscience, work with brain-damaged adults and children indicates that emotion is essential in cognitive development, decision making, problem solving, social interactions and social functioning. This research with 'damaged' patients illuminates 'the nested relationship' between emotion and cognition. The findings from the study confirm that 'neither learning nor recall happen in a purely rational domain, divorced from emotion' and that if educators attempt to create a purely 'rational domain' then they will be encouraging children to 'develop the sorts of knowledge that inherently do not transfer well to real world situations' and, further, that 'knowledge and reasoning divorced from emotional implications and learning lack meaning and motivation and are of little use in the real world' (Immordino-Yang and Damasio 2007: 9).

The ability to construct such a 'nested relationship' requires layers of sophisticated professional knowledge – knowledge of children, their development, their lived lives, significant relationships, as well as professional knowledge in relation to curriculum and subject knowledge. Influential authors and educators in the field of early education, including Froebel in the nineteenth century and Montessori in the early twentieth century (Bruce 1987; Nutbrown *et al.* 2008), have particularly emphasised the respectful relationship between educator and learner; and, later, the work of Malaguzzi in Reggio Emilia has pursued this idea of a 'pedagogy of relationships' (Rinaldi 2005; see also Parker-Rees, Chapter 4). Although research and some international practice supports a relational pedagogy, there is also concern that teaching has been reduced to curriculum delivery rather than 'an engagement with other minds' (Pring 2004: 68) and it requires deep commitment and also professional courage to challenge prevailing policy and curriculum doctrine. This kind of professional also needs to understand herself, her own biography, her intentions, values and educational aims. In her sensitively reported 'interpretive' enquiry into the practice of early years educators, McLean argues that the 'internal aspects of the person who is the teacher (self concept, beliefs about learning and teaching, awareness of own biography)' connect with the physical environment, and subsequent teacher behaviour will be 'complex, reflexive and multi-directional' (McLean 1991: 7). Reflecting upon and understanding who we are, as teachers and as learners, our influences, mentors and professional values, while being central to the process of understanding the role of teacher in the early years, are rarely afforded time in initial teacher training or indeed in practice.

There are layers of research across discipline boundaries that form the firm underpinning for a complex pedagogy centred on play. In addition, there is the suggestion that, just as babies are predisposed to learn, so too are adults close to them predisposed to teach – in the broadest sense of the term. Understanding the complexity of a relational pedagogy brings with it, however, enormous implications if we believe this to be the case, not least for initial and continuing professional development, in order to help professionals to consider and reflect on their role (Moyles 2010). As a first step it is important to recognise those professionals already engaging in professional encounters with children at this deep relational level, while maintaining professional levels of accountability.

Listening to teachers

In an attempt to understand the practice of those teachers who operate in a relational way, two teachers were provided with an opportunity to take part in a study involving research conversations in order to deconstruct their work with children and to try to establish their intentions. Both had been observed to behave apparently intuitively in their practice and to allow play in their settings to develop in an organic manner. The teachers were asked to consider what they were doing in their professional work and to define the overarching aims of their work with young children, their influences and their intentions in playing with children. To facilitate this study, both teachers were systematically observed, both collected video of their practice, interviews were conducted and three-way conversations undertaken. As a result, some conclusions were drawn about the potential for 'teaching' in the early years of education and some defining elements of practice were constructed. Overall, it became clear why these two teachers appeared to permit themselves to play with the children who are playing in their settings.

One of the key founding elements of the practice of both teachers was that they subscribed to the view, first, that play is the preferred site for children to learn and develop, and, second, that 'children choose to play, they cannot be made to play' (Bruce 2005: 132). In both classrooms the *idea* of play is completely accepted as the context where children will learn. The maximum amount of time possible is given to children for them to play. The nursery classrooms consist entirely of play resources, play areas and ranges of play possibilities. There are consistent, fixed areas and flexible spaces as well as opportunities for change, resources to be added, moved, transported by the children and adapted. There are routines, but these are also flexible.

In both nurseries, everything – space, resources, routines, time, adults and interactions – are all arranged to best fit the perceived day-to-day needs of the children: their physical, social, emotional and cognitive needs. The adults mostly follow the children's lead, their interests and their intentions while at play. One teacher's comment here is significant in understanding her place in children's world of play: 'The more our interactions fit in with the child the more likely that they will be of use to the child in developing and extending, understanding whatever it is they are exploring.' It is this idea, that adults need to be present in order to be of use to children at play, that is of importance and it is also evident in other responses: 'I was waiting to see, to give them time to use me if they wanted to, or ignore me if they wanted to – use me to bounce ideas off, tell me something, help them, explain something, be there as another body . . .'. In these practices, the teachers are of use to children in their conceptual development as well as physically. They both, at different times, emphasise that they *help* children. This may sound simplistic and basic but it is in fact a very significant idea and it appears to form the bedrock of their practice; they are both clear that they are there to service children's play and thus their learning. This is not an idle or a passive role, however, although significantly different from the instructive, management role that many teachers of young children adopt (see Introduction). The evidence of the teachers' own words indicates that it is an informed choice, based on experience, information from a range of sources and their deeply reflexive approach to all aspects of their work.

The teachers explained their stance as follows.

J: Children learn best when they're interested and focused and for such very young children that's when they choose what they do themselves . . . and actually the quality of learning is an awful lot better, visibly – you can visibly see their involvement level and their concentration level and even the outputs are so much higher quality and detailed if you don't over-direct them.

M: I think it's important not to have an agenda sometimes when I go to play with children because otherwise I think I start doing and saying things that I want, that are not necessarily what they want . . . I was waiting to see, to give them time to use me if they wanted to, or ignore me if they wanted to – use me to bounce ideas off, tell me something, help them, explain something, be there as another body . . .

J: If they've got you there playing with them then you're there playing and you need to play.

Both teachers felt very strongly that it is often appropriate to wait for the children to lead them, the teachers, into the play action. They were also observed to employ different 'voices' during play. These were, variously, as described below.

Narrator of the play

This involved the teachers in describing action as it occurred, sometimes together with the children and sometimes as a simple accompaniment. If the play narrative itself serves the purpose of satisfying the urge to 'repeat or represent for consideration what was in actuality a transient happening, giving it shape and pattern and consequently some kind of meaning or significance (Whitehead 1997: 90 and Chapter 5 this volume) then the occupation of the teacher in creating an accompanying narrative to function as a bridge in supporting that meaning making can be helpful. In the example in this study, the teacher made no attempt to direct the play or lead it with her narrative voice, but saw her role as simply to follow the action, describing the event as it flowed, drawing in children as they approached, helping to solve problems without interrupting the flow of the play.

Voices within play

Both teachers in this study were able to participate as actors in the play. In one example the teacher was moving dinosaurs around in the sand tray and speaking as the dinosaur, 'I want my mummy . . .' and 'Help me, I'm lost . . .'. Such examples were frequent and happened either incidentally or through the direction of the children. The teachers were able to tune in to children's play, valuing the children's intentions and the context but also drawing on their professional skills of modelling, observing, interpreting and playing (see Kitson, Chapter 7). One teacher commented that 'You see what the child's intention is – you feed into it.'

The addressee

During one observation it became very clear that the teacher had understood his role to be the opposite of director. During a 20-minute observation of a play period the teacher made only 17 short utterances, which were all very unobtrusive. The contributions to the play were sometimes barely audible and they served to complement rather than narrate the action. This teacher invariably placed the children in the role of expert. He asked questions of the children and avoided instructional talk. He saw his role as helping children to accomplish their task of the moment. His physical presence was close to the children but not inside their play. He was used by the children to fetch and carry resources, was accepted but not deferred to. He left respectful spaces for the children and observed more than played. His physical presence was nevertheless important to the children. As an addressee, he was 'a listener who can also have a creative role to play in a dialogue, even if sometimes only a silent non-verbal one (Carter 2004: 68).

Their personal voice born from their own lived lives

In the study, when asked if they knew where their practice emerged from, one teacher commented that 'My practice comes from a big run of very positive, very committed interactions with people.' She spoke enthusiastically about a range of other professionals that she had worked with at the beginning of her career. However, she also spoke about her father as a key mentor and a strong influence on her behaviour with children, particularly in the way that he treated children as 'worthy':

> I don't think about it consciously but when you try and unpick it, I suppose that's what I do, although at the time I don't think 'Oh I must be respectful', but maybe that's where that comes from, you know if children talk you stop and listen just as when a grown up talks. And if they talk over you, you try very hard to say 'Excuse me one minute: I'll talk to you in a moment', but you do go back and say 'What was that you were telling me; I couldn't listen properly', rather than the kind of seen and not heard thing.

Their professional voice

Both teachers were able to reflect seriously on their work with the children and to demonstrate a professional voice that represented their respect for the culture of the school and that of a public servant with statutory responsibilities. They talked about 'having high expectations of children and wanting them to achieve as much as they possibly can and more than that'; 'I think about what I do a lot and why I do it and I think about the children a lot, what they're doing and why they do it and how I can support them to do it, what they might need to help them get to where they might want to go . . .'; 'When you're meeting the child's needs, you're meeting your own need to have the child's needs met; that's your need as a teacher isn't it, your professional need . . .'.

In the settings of both teachers it was frequently unclear who led the stories during play, who created them, defined the action or who transformed it. The voices that were heard reflected the joint actions of children and adults together – for example, resolving conflict at the sand tray, discussing midnight feasts and sleepovers, or constructing pathways for dinosaurs. Adults and children were multi-voicing (Carter 2004); at one level they were constructing story narratives together, on another they were 'doing the voices' in the story, on another they were directing the play according to the socially constructed narratives of home experiences and frequently instructing other players. In addition, the teachers were controlling the adult pedagogic narrative, retaining the narrative of monitoring and assessment, and sometimes modelling and supplying language. Adults and children in these practices were both inside and outside the play action, inside and outside of reality and fantasy. Voices representing individual consciousness were melded in play and support was often mutual.

Permission to play

Both teachers valued and enjoyed play, and were commonly accepted by the children as players. However, their value as teachers stretched further. Both teachers' metacognitive abilities were very high; they were able to consider, reflect upon and articulate their practice, their learning, their activities and their professionalism with ease and confidence. The questions and challenges they set themselves were always of a high order, and the aims of practice they identified were powerfully expressed:

> Empowerment is the ultimate purpose, I think, so that children believe they can do it, take a risk, have a go, be themselves, be creative, use me, not use me. The outcome I expect is that I want children to feel empowered. What is important is that children find their place, their space or identity in the world outside their family and are comfortable and competent in it; that they get support, encouragement and affirmation of their own developing skills and understandings. It's the research and enquiry and the disposition to be a learner that I am trying to promote . . .

In the teachers' practices, talk and play are both distinctive features. However, the significance of this rests in the teachers' abilities to value, reflect upon and understand the fundamental importance of three key elements in their work with children: intentionality, narrative constructions and voice. Through their demonstrations of absolute respect for children's expressions of intent and for their story narratives in play, the teachers were able to sustain in the children very high levels of motivation, deep concentration and involvement in play. The children in turn trusted the teachers and this trust was clearly manifested in the children's confidence to talk and to collaborate with their teachers and to permit the adults to play with them. The teachers recognised the value of play as a site for developing metacognition as children both enacted worlds but also explored what the actions could mean (see Howard, Chapter 13). This is similar in some respects to the work of educators in Reggio Emilia and the pedagogy of relationships and listening (Rinaldi 2005) that takes place there.

The teachers are both very skilled practitioners, able to intellectualise play, giving it value and status in children's learning. They also employ time and energy in understanding the worlds that children employ in their story narratives so that they can both co-join in the play and account for it in their professional dialogues; thus creating a discourse to legitimise children's intentions and their activities. Their insider knowledge of children and of play produced a pedagogy of consistent questioning, such as: *What are the children doing? What do they know? What are they demonstrating that they know? What then do they need? What am I doing and why? What else could I do? What do I know about this content? How can I help?* In their explorations of their own roles, an activity already embedded in their practice but made explicit in this study, the teachers applied a meta-language to their engagements in play – for example, 'You could see it in his eyes, a connection and an ha ha moment.' Just as children engage in self-making through their reflective play acts, so too did the teachers in their thoughtful engagements and their deconstructions of children's learning.

Conclusion

Rather than engaging with 'a state theory of learning' (Alexander 2009: 307) the teachers in this study demonstrated their commitment to the value of play in children's early learning. The teachers both enthusiastically permitted play but also sought and gained permission to play with the children. Play contexts are risky spaces to inhabit and occupying play spaces with children demands a level of confidence and trust – in children and in the learning potential of play, as well as in children's own ability to cope with uncertainty, which itself demands strong trusting relationships. Both the teachers and the children felt safe in not knowing potential outcomes but in seeking them in each other's company. Through this engagement the children and their teachers were learning a great deal, not least:

> the importance of the imagination; of dialogue and joint activity which both motivate pupils and capitalise on what is now known about how brain, mind and understanding develop during the early and primary years and of generating that sense of empowerment allied to skill through which learning becomes inner-directed and autonomous rather than dependent on pressure from others.
>
> (Alexander 2009: 257)

If, as observed in this study, it is possible to achieve even this one powerfully stated aim through permitting children and their teachers to play, then practice that does not embrace play would be questionable at every level.

References and further reading

Abbott, L. (2001) Perceptions of play – a question of priorities? In L. Abbott and C. Nutbrown (eds) *Experiencing Reggio Emilia: Implications for Pre-school Provision*. Buckingham: Open University Press.

Alexander, R. (2009) *Cambridge Primary Review: Children, their World, their Education. The Final Report.* Available online at: www.cambridgeprimaryreview (accessed 4 January 2010).

Atkinson, T. and Claxton, G. (2000) *The Intuitive Practitioner: On the Value of Not Always Knowing What One is Doing.* Buckingham: Open University Press.

Bernstein, B. (1997) Class and pedagogies: visible and invisible. In A.H. Halsley, H. Lauder, P. Brown and A.S. Wells (eds) *Education, Culture, Economy, Society.* Oxford: Oxford University Press.

Bruce, T. (1987) *Early Childhood Education.* Sevenoaks: Hodder and Stoughton.

Bruce, T. (2005) *Early Childhood Education* (3rd edn). London: Hodder Arnold.

Bruner, J. (1986) *Actual Minds, Possible Worlds.* Cambridge, MA: Harvard University Press.

Bruner, J. (2004) Foreword. In J. Dunn, *Children's Friendships, the Beginnings of Intimacy.* Oxford: Blackwell.

Bryan, H. (2004) Constructs of teacher professionalism within a changing literacy landscape. *Literacy,* 38(3): 141–148.

Carter, R. (2004) *Language and Creativity: The Art of Common Talk.* London: Routledge.

David, T., Goouch K., Powell, S. and Abbott, L. (2003) *Birth to Three Matters: A Review of the Literature.* Nottingham: DfES Publications.

Dunn, J. (2004) *Children's Friendships, the Beginnings of Intimacy,* Oxford: Blackwell.

Freire, P. (1976) *Education: The Practice of Freedom.* London: Writers and Readers Publishing Cooperative.

Gibson, H. and Patrick, H. (2008) Putting words in their mouths: the role of teaching assistants and the spectre of scripted pedagogy. *Journal of Early Childhood Literacy,* 8(1): 25–41.

Goldschmied, E. and Jackson, S. (2004) *People Under Three* (2nd edn). London: Routledge.

Gopnik, A. (2009) *The Philosophical Baby.* London: The Bodley Head.

Gopnik, A., Meltzoff, A. and Kuhl, P. (1999) *How Babies Think.* London: Weidenfeld and Nicolson.

Greenfield, S. (2000) *The Private Life of the Brain.* London: Penguin.

Immordino-Yang, M.H. and Damasio, A. (2007) We feel, therefore we learn: the relevance of affective and social neuroscience to education. *Mind, Brain and Education,* 1(1): 3–10.

Jenkinson, S. (2001) *The Genius of Play: Celebrating the Spirit of Childhood.* Stroud: Hawthorn Press.

McLean, S.V. (1991) *The Human Encounter: Teachers and Children Living Together in Preschool.* London: Falmer Press.

Moyles, J. (ed.) (2005) *The Excellence of Play* (2nd edn). Maidenhead: Open University Press.

Moyles, J. (ed.) (2010) *Thinking About Play: Developing a Reflective Approach.* Maidenhead: Open University Press.

Nutbrown, C. and Page, J. (2008) *Working with Babies and Children from Birth to Three.* London: Sage.

Nutbrown, C., Clough, P. and Selbie, P. (2008) *Early Childhood Education: History, Philosophy and Experience.* London: Sage.

Papatheodorou, T. and Moyles, J. (2009) *Learning Together in the Early Years: Exploring Relational Pedagogy.* London: Routledge.

Peters, R.S. (1966) *Ethics and Education.* London: George Allen and Unwin Ltd.

Piaget, J. (1959) *The Language and Thought of the Child.* London: Routledge and Kegan Paul Ltd.

Pring, R. (2004) *Philosophy of Education.* London: Continuum.

Rinaldi, C. (2005) Documentation and assessment: what is the relationship? In A. Clark, A.T. Kjorholt and P. Moss (eds) *Beyond Listening, Children's Perspectives on Early Childhood Services.* Bristol: The Policy Press.

Rogoff, B. (1990) *Apprenticeship in Thinking, Cognitive Development in Social Context.* Oxford: Oxford University Press.

Super, C.M. and Harkness, S. (1998) The development of affect in infancy and early childhood. In M. Woodhead, D. Faulkner and K. Littlejohn (eds) *Cultural Worlds of Early Childhood.* London: Routledge and the Open University.

Vygotsky, L. (1978, transl.) *Mind in Society, The Development of Higher Psychological Processes.* Cambridge, MA: Harvard University Press.

Whitehead, M. (1997) *Language and Literacy in the Early Years* (2nd edn). London: Sage.

4 Hunting and gathering: how play helps us to let in, as well as to get in, information about our environment

Rod Parker-Rees

Summary

In this chapter I will suggest that our understanding of play may be helped if we recognise a distinction between two different kinds of learning which can both be supported by play. One kind of learning can be characterised as 'getting in' information; this is learning that results from the purposeful, active engagement with our environment when we 'work out' how things can be expected to behave. If this learning is thought of as a form of hunting for understanding, tracking it down and 'taking it out' or abstracting it, the other kind of learning can be thought of as a form of gathering, of 'picking things up' as we go along and without necessarily knowing in advance what we might come across. This 'letting in' of information is perhaps even less intentional than the word 'gathering' might suggest – an intuitive process that enables us to 'get to know' extraordinarily complex webs of relationships between objects, events and people in our environment without needing to trouble our conscious awareness. Perhaps we should think of gathering more as a social process, because relaxed, social gatherings are particularly conducive to this letting in of knowledge about other people, customs and cultural values.

Introduction

The distinction between hunting and gathering echoes differences in the ways in which the left and right hemispheres of the brain divide up the task of managing our interactions with our environment (see Anning, Chapter 1). A lot of nonsense has been written about 'left brain' and 'right brain' activities, styles of behaviour and even types of people, but there are significant physiological differences between the hemispheres, brilliantly represented in Guy Claxton's analogy of a penlight and a candle (1994: 45). The predominance of grey matter in the left hemisphere means that tightly focused, close connections can be picked out for detailed attention while the higher proportion of white matter in the right hemisphere allows more wide-ranging, dispersed connections to be simultaneously illuminated. As Claxton points out, having both a candle and a torch enables us to find our way around a dark cave much better than if we had two candles or two torches. Baron Cohen (2003) has suggested that each of us occupies a position along a spectrum from the extreme 'male brain' associated with autism to the extreme 'female brain' associated with Williams syndrome but, like Claxton, Baron Cohen stresses that this variation is beneficial to any social group, since different people will contribute different sets of skills and interests. Play that focuses on 'hunting' or 'getting in' information may be more associated with left-hemisphere activity and typically male interests, while 'gathering' or 'letting in' forms of play are more associated with right-hemisphere activity and typically female interests, but I will argue that children (and adults) should be allowed and encouraged to develop their ability to combine and integrate both forms of play.

We are all familiar with models of development and education that focus attention on the pursuit of knowledge. This form of learning may seem well matched to a curriculum that specifies what individual learners need to acquire but, by creating an artificial separation between the 'work' of the hunt for knowledge and the 'play' of social gatherings, this approach distorts our understanding of how we come to know about our environment. In this chapter, I hope to make a case for greater recognition of the role of easy, enjoyable, social processes in gathering or letting in the contextual information that gives body and vitality to what we know.

Cameo 4.1

Six-month-old Rosie is sitting at the kitchen table with her mother. On the table is a pack of fat felt-tip pens and some paper. Rosie holds a pen lightly in her left hand as she picks another up in her right hand and begins to 'draw' on the paper – she clearly knows what pens are for – but the pen still has its lid on. Her mum reaches out, 'Shall we take the lid off?' Rosie murmurs assent but when mum has to take a firmer hold, with two hands, to get the lid off, she makes eye contact and shrieks with frustration – 'Wait, wait, wait, wait – Oh it's hard. There you go, go on, you do it then – on there – Oh', Rosie now pants with excitement, waving the freed pen but also making an exaggerated expression with wide open mouth – 'Oh – funny face'.[1] Rosie tries to put the pen back in its box, mum holds out the lid 'There's the lid' and Rosie immediately tries to fit the pen into the lid as mum carefully adjusts its position, 'Push it back in, clever girl'. As soon as the pen and the lid are connected Rosie yanks the pen, with its lid, out of mum's hand and waves it about triumphantly. Mum gasps to share her delight and Rosie immediately puts the lid end back in mum's hand to be gripped so that Rosie can pull the pen free – 'Take it off – oh!' and then try to put it back in, 'Put it back in'. This takes several attempts, with mum moving the lid to meet the pen as Rosie concentrates fixedly on controlling its movement, making little gasps of effort with each stab. After six near misses, mum uses her other hand to guide the pen into the lid, 'Ooooooh come on, do it!' – she is clearly giving the least possible support, so that Rosie remains in control. Rosie again flashes eye contact and then murmurs 'aaaah' (echoing mum's 'oooooh') as the pen and lid finally make contact, 'Yeeaah!' but she immediately pulls the pen out again, 'Oop!'. Rosie says 'Eh, eh, Geh! Geh!' as she manoeuvres the pen and mum echoes, 'Try again? – eh – there!' – 'Aah oooh oh, deh! There!' as the pen and lid are again fitted together. Again, Rosie immediately snatches the pen back out of the lid but with her eyes still fixed on the opening of the lid she quickly brings the pen back, saying 'Deh – adeh – oh-oh-oh' as she again joins the dance of fitting pen to lid. Both Rosie and her mum are accompanying the effort with extended sounds, which rise in intensity until both reach a simultaneous peak as Rosie again manages to pull the pen, with its lid, out of mum's hand. Rosie gazes for a few seconds at the point where pen and lid meet – 'Done!' – before she puts the lid back into mum's hand again, 'Deh – Take it off? – off' and then again concentrates on fitting them together again, with mum's help – but the lid slips from mum's hand and falls to the floor just as the pen makes contact with the paper. Rosie switches her attention to making a mark – 'Oooh – Deh!, Dere'. She flashes a glance at the camera and then sings, echoed by her mum, as she draws.

Rosie is clearly engaging actively with her world, making sense of the made sense that surrounds her, with a particular, earnest focus on exploring the way in which the pen and its lid can be put together and taken apart.

This process of getting in information about our environment by actively experimenting with it and noting how our actions affect what we perceive is central to our understanding of how play supports learning. The repetition and variation that characterise playful activity allow us (at any age) to jiggle and adjust, to finesse the fit between our personal idiosyncrasies and the public possibilities our environment offers us. Whether fitting a pen into its lid, wiggling a piece from an inset puzzle until it slips into its place or exploring how we can fit our principled practice into a prescribed policy framework, play enables us to adjust the way we fit in to our environment (see also Bruce, Chapter 18).

While Rosie is playing with the pen and its lid, and getting in information about the way they fit together, her absorbed engagement is kept afloat by a sea of cultural support. Everything about her environment is unnatural, everything has been made to afford possibilities for certain kinds of action: the kitchen provides a safe, comfortable place for focused interactions; the table and highchair ensure that everything is conveniently kept where she can reach it (until the lid falls to the floor); the pen and lid have been designed to be held by small hands and to snap together in a satisfying (if rather challenging) way; her mother provides sensitive, responsive assistance to scaffold her efforts at manipulation, and uses her voice both to provide a running commentary and to echo Rosie's shifting moods. While Rosie does not seem to be consciously aware of the circles of support that surround her as she plays – focusing more on 'in and out', 'tightness' and fine motor control – she is, nevertheless, letting in a mass of information about her place in a cultural world of made things and in a relationship with her mother.

This relationship of active, intersubjective engagement between adult and child seems to be uniquely human (Parker-Rees 2007). Where other animals may have opportunities to learn by imitation of adults, human infants are constantly exposed to a pedagogical social environment – a world in which adults are willing to give up time to enter into the intricate, sophisticated sort of partnership seen in Rosie's mum's sensitive support for her engagement with cultural tools, practices and values. Human children are not left to blossom untended in a natural environment; they are projects, nurtured, shaped and made by the social and cultural environment that surrounds them, and that is also influenced by them – not only in terms of the sheer volume of 'stuff' that parents accumulate but also the new behaviours that children train their parents to adopt. Tronick (2005: 311) insists that we should see this negotiation of roles as co-creation rather than co-construction, because co-construction 'implies a pre-existing plan', whereas co-creation 'emphasizes that the meaning made is a process in which each individual's meaning is changed and created into a new meaning'.

Our first experiences are always dyadic. While we are still in our mother's womb we are gathering information about her as well as about our own processes, so our first environment is intensely mutual and social. Trevarthen has shown how this mutuality develops into 'primary intersubjectivity' as both babies and parents delight in the reciprocity of 'liking', of co-creating a match in the timing, rhythm and dynamics of their movements, sounds and gestures (Parker-Rees 2007). The pleasure of being liked fuels sustained bouts of gooey wallowing in each other's attention, providing an emotional pattern for the later enjoyment of social play and conversation with friends.

Trevarthen noted that this short period of primary intersubjectivity gives way, after about 4 months, to a period when developing motor skills and active exploration of objects fuel an explosion of 'hunting' or exploratory play. But even when babies are most absorbed in their 'little scientist' engagement with their physical environment they depend on the 'intentionally supportive teaching behaviours that more experienced partners offer' (Trevarthen 2005: 84). Rosie may not be aware of her mother's role in getting the lid where it needs to be, or of the way her vocalisations and dynamics are matched, but everything about her mother's support will be gathered up with her experience, informing her expectations about how the world will meet her.

As infants become more adept and experienced in their handling of objects they need to devote less of their attention to the physical processes of manipulation and exploration, allowing them to 'look up' and notice how other people respond to things and events. This ability to read through another person's activity and gather information about their attitude to aspects of their experience is described by Trevarthen as 'secondary intersubjectivity' and by Hobson (2002: 102) as a 'relatedness triangle', and it illustrates how hard-won direct knowledge can provide a foundation that makes us more able to let in more intuitive perceptions about other people. We have to know an object ourselves before we can really draw inferences from another person's way of using it. The 'to and fro' between preoccupation with relationships and fascination with things in the first year illustrates the intricate ways in which active theory finding and more receptive 'tuning in' to underlying complexities can support and enable each other. As infants are helped to co-create hypotheses, event representations, scripts and theories about how the world can be expected to behave, they free up more of their attention for gathering more subtle, less tidily organisable 'local colour', which in turn allows them to refocus their interests – the dim light from the candle provides useful information about where to direct the beam of the torch so that shadowy forms can be lit up for examination.

Getting to know people

The close, familiar and intensely supportive environment of home provides a manageable, contained frame within which infants can be helped to develop their ability to engage with the complexities of cultural life. Among family a child is richly and deeply familiar to people who are also richly and deeply familiar to her. Of course the degree of familiarity will vary but, relatively speaking, a child can count on being known and understood better by family than by strangers. Meeting strangers and finding one's place in new and unfamiliar groups is, therefore, a special challenge and early experiences of encounters with children from other families can be both daunting and fascinating.

Among family a child is known for who she is, but among strangers she may be reduced to a shell, and all she can know about unfamiliar people is what their shells reveal to her. As adults, especially as urban adults, we must learn how to interact with people we do not know and who do not know us, but for young children this can be particularly daunting. However, it can also be exciting to have opportunities to play with peers 'on a level' – an experience that is refreshingly different from playing with familiar adults or siblings. What children gather from being in new, unfamiliar situations is likely to colour the way they respond to unexpected, novel and strange situations later in life. As they begin to engage with unfamiliar people they need plenty of time and space to circle around each other, check each other out, notice when they have been noticed, play alongside each other, and venture into imitation and shared play (see Broadhead, Chapter 14 on friendships).

Although every unfamiliar person may be no more than a shell to begin with, each comes trailing clouds of home, bearing exotically different ideas about what is fun, what is naughty, what is interesting and what is special. Without resorting to profiles or checklists, children begin to size each other up – especially if they are given time and space to play freely around each other but, even in the most rigidly managed classrooms, they will still find ways to gather intelligence about their peers.

Hobson (2002), Rochat (2004), and Carpendale and Lewis (2006) argue that our awareness of a self, which lifts us out of the undifferentiated melee of infant egocentrism, results from our gradual discovery of differences between the selves of others. As we let in information about the 'person patterns' or regularities in other people's behaviour, we notice ways in which they are like or unlike each other and, as a result, we can then begin to notice ways in which they are like or unlike us. Of course, we will have been told what we are like for a considerable time before this, especially if we have older brothers or sisters, but it is only when other people's ways of talking about us meet up with our own dawning awareness of our differentiated selves that we can really be said to bob to the surface of the social flow and into our own conscious awareness.

This co-creation of a self requires awareness of patterns in what usually happens and what people can be expected to do, an awareness that is actively co-created by the pursuit of knowledge, but it also requires less purposeful 'boundary work' to let in the much more intricate social awareness of individual identities:

> the self is in continual negotiation with the other and the situation in which it finds itself with the other, working to define itself as a diverse unity. It is both an individual and part of a whole structure that is more than the sum of its parts – a borderline phenomenon, which takes its identity from the selves with which it shares boundaries as much as from some individual teleological principle within itself. The subject-in-process is defined as much by this border or boundary-work – the history and process of its relations with its margins and interfaces – as by an idea of internal structure or core.
>
> (Kennedy 2006: 120)

An important part of the self we construct for ourselves will be determined by our own style of meeting other people. Some are particularly adept at tuning in to other people's interests and concerns; others find meeting people more of a challenge and may need prolonged exposure before they get the hang of a new acquaintance's personal ways and patterns. For these latter in particular, social playfulness may be a particularly important way of softening personal boundaries. Adults may need the support of specific social contexts, and even alcohol, to help them to relax into the unstructured, meandering forms of interaction that allow us to get to know each other. Children, just beginning to tune in to the nuances of social interaction, need extensive opportunities for relaxed, unhurried and undirected play, but there is considerable variation in the extent to which early years settings are able to meet these needs (see Georgeson and Payler, Chapter 2).

Hedegaard (2009: 72) points out that the forms of practice afforded by settings both shape and restrict children's activities and 'become conditions for their development'. In some countries, such as Norway, Sweden and Denmark, preschool provision reflects what the *OECD* (2006) has described as a 'social pedagogy' tradition, where 'greater emphasis is placed on learning to live together and supporting children in their current developmental tasks and interests' (*OECD* 2006: 60) but in other countries, including the UK, the USA, France and the Netherlands, the 'schoolification' (2006: 61) of preschool practice reflects a 'pre-primary' approach to early education with a greater emphasis in curriculum documentation on identifying *what* children should learn. How children play in different settings both reflects these cultural differences and contributes to different perceptions of the nature of play (see Anning, Chapter 1). Where, for example, children's play is separated out from the work of learning into designated playtimes and playgrounds, this is bound to affect the ways children play. The release of children into the playground for a short playtime, like opening a fizzy drink, can result in a rather frantic, wild form of play, which scares civilised adults into further efforts to limit and manage it.

Early years practitioners who have themselves experienced the UK education system, for example, will have experienced many years of being released into playgrounds for short doses of playtime and, even if this is not the way they manage play in their settings, they may see this sort of 'binge playing' as the 'true' essence of play, so that calmer, quieter play may feel rather flat by comparison. Where children are given greater opportunities to manage their own activity, however, binge playing may be relatively rare (see Knight, Chapter 12). In the celebrated preschools of Reggio Emilia, for example, children show that, given the chance, they enjoy exploring ideas and developing their skills and knowledge. In Steiner kindergartens, where children are allowed plenty of time and space to play with older and younger peers, they are able to exercise and develop their abilities through casual interactions, observations and opportunities to 'let in' knowledge about their social world within a reassuring framework of consistent routines, rhythms and structures (Drummond and Jenkinson 2009).

The following observation took place in a Steiner kindergarten. Thirteen children were present for this session, eight boys and five girls, aged between 3:8 and 5:4 years.

Cameo 4.2

Carol is crawling into Warren's sanctuary – a secluded spot behind a large wooden crate of logs – he calls out 'Stop that you naughty rascal!' – clearly enjoying the game – but Carol says 'I'm your dog' and starts spitting at him. Warren says 'Those dogs are such a idiot' to Damien, who is sitting with him in their corner, watching Mark and Tim, older boys who are throwing balls into a basket on the roof of the house they have built out of clothes horses, planks and pieces of cloth. Tim comes to get a big piece of hollow log from the crate – Warren shouts 'Stop taking our hockey balls!' – Tim smiles and says, 'Now I've got a new game – watch' and he shows Warren how he can use the hollow log as a new target.

Five minutes later, Warren and Damien are still sitting in their cosy corner chatting and planning their play. They have snuggled under a piece of cloth to 'go to sleep'. Patrick, another older boy, plays at 'attacking' Warren and Damien – 'Can I be a snow-lion or a snow-tiger? They're both really strong'. Warren responds with 'Who do you think you are looking at, tomato-head?' Carol has joined in and is poking at Warren with a walking stick. Patrick attacks again, 'I'm a Tyrannosaurus rex!' but Warren is safe behind his wooden crate – 'Can't hurt me anyway!'

Tim has picked up on Patrick's reference to T-rex and has found a pair of wooden clogs. He puts them on and stamps around – 'Tyrannosaurus rex had noisy feet and big feet'. Now lots of children are involved in roaring.

Xavier and Patrick are again 'attacking' Warren and Damien – the mood turns when the bigger boys take Warren's bucket of 'hockey balls', which upsets him. He asks for his wooden crate back so he can retreat behind it into his corner.

Warren, Otto and Damien are negotiating with Mabel over the balls. Warren says, 'He [Otto] is the middle one, so he's big AND little'. He then persuades Otto and Damien to join him in another cosy spot, tucked under a big shelf in an alcove, 'Come down here and I'll tell you something'. He has to work at this as their attention is taken up by watching other children, but he persists and finally manages to tell them, 'We're like numbers, you [Damien] are three, you [Otto] are four and I'm five'. It was clearly important to him that he should share this observation with them.

Leo is playing at the table where Barbara was cutting vegetables – he declaims in a very stagey voice, 'I am not dead. One bite shall not kill ME! I am not an ordinary Panda'. Banging on the table seems to remind him of a judge's gavel – 'Silence in court! Silence and die!' In the same voice he asks Patrick, 'How many people have you shot since you have been a marshal?' Patrick replies, 'A thousand he has shot'.

Warren, Otto and Damien are still tucked under their shelf, but are now 'armed' with various sticks and logs, which they brandish at anyone who approaches. Tim peers into their hideaway. Leo and Patrick are talking light sabres and superheroes – 'I jumped and it was such a force!' When Otto tells his friends that Patrick is a baddy, Patrick replies – 'I don't care, I've got a light sabre – just chop my leg'. Otto 'chops' at his leg with his penknife (a short piece of log) and Patrick says 'You chopped your own penknife!' Patrick then steals one of the hockey balls and Warren shouts, 'He's absolutely foggy!' and laughs.

Warren is doing more gathering or 'letting in' than hunting or 'getting in' here. He clearly enjoys watching what the older boys are doing and being cosy with the younger boys – protecting them and explaining things to them. The older boys seem to recognise his need to tuck himself away but they also include him in their play by occasionally pretending to 'attack' – Warren certainly seems to enjoy their attention. He is allowed to find his own ways of managing his need for security and he is given time to make his own decisions about when and how far he will emerge.

In this Steiner kindergarten the protective environment of structure, routines and 'a place for everything', the adults' consistent reminders about a shared understanding of 'how we do things' and the mix of children of different ages all combine to enable everyone to get to know each other in particularly satisfying ways.

Meaning for us, for them, for you and for me

As they gather awareness of the subtle differences between other people's unique ways of performing common roles, children co-create a web of relationships between the kinds of meanings that tangle around objects, ideas and events. Everything acquires multiple meanings: 'meaning for us' – the lingua franca that emerges out of shared frameworks, contexts, experiences and stories; 'meaning for them'. This allows us to refine our understanding of how others – 'babies', 'old people' or 'teachers', for example – may have different patterns of responses; individual versions of 'meaning for you'. These can be noticed in terms of different people's ways of engaging with a shared culture, which build into awareness of differences in personality, character and temperament, and 'meaning for me'. This is particularly intense, rich and deeply rooted in personal experience but rises to the surface of awareness as we notice differences between our own meanings and those of other people.

Curriculum models have to focus on common, shared ideas rather than the messy tangle of relationships that complicate and colour the meanings in any particular setting (see Anning, Chapter 1). But the bare, snow-capped peaks of abstract 'meanings for *all* of us' cannot hover, unsupported, in mid-air. They have to be grounded in the warmer, richer lowlands and valleys that teem with an irreducible ecosystem of lived relationships. The webs of personal associations that weave knowledge into understanding are much too complex and individual to be mapped on to a sequence of learning activities. Early years provision must allow children to gather the rich variety of social and cultural meanings that swarm around them as well as encourage them to look up towards the clearer, simpler ideas that can be seen by all.

Effective early years environments appear to be characterised by a blurring of divisions between 'work' and 'play' so that people are allowed space to find their own ways of fitting in and of contributing to the co-creation of shared understandings (see Georgeson and Payler, Chapter 2). Sawyer (1997) argued that the unplanned flow seen both in children's pretend play and in playful conversation between adults should be understood in terms of improvisation. Both forms of interaction allow participants to get to know each other by combining emergent frames of common elements and rules with opportunities to notice individual differences in how these are creatively performed. In many 'work'-focused environments, however, playfulness is discouraged because it tends to slow things down and may make it harder to keep to a planned agenda or curriculum. The challenge, then, is to manage social environments so that focused, coordinated 'hunting' activities are securely grounded in looser, more playful activities that allow people to gather intricate, intuitive knowledge about how things may have different meanings for different people. Such environments are 'convivial, playful, cooperative and non-judgemental, as well as being purposeful and professional' (Claxton 2000: 48; see examples in Goouch, Chapter 3). They feel more enjoyable and exhilarating, but they also provide the conditions in which old ideas can be reinvigorated with new interpretations that allow them to adapt to changing cultural circumstances.

Conclusion

The greatest challenge to maintaining a balance between the purposeful pursuit of knowledge and the more relaxed getting of wisdom seems to be a lack of trust in intuitive processes. When practitioners know that they will be held accountable for what they understand about children's progress, they are likely to pursue recordable, 'hard' facts rather than trust to the more relaxed processes that they can rely on when getting to know friends and colleagues. When practitioners are unsure about their status in the eyes of parents they are more likely to adopt cooler, more 'professional' relationships, which are more about getting information than about the co-creation of a supportive community. Yet practitioners also know that they can learn more about children from joining them in chat, sharing mealtimes with them or going out with them on a social outing than from hunting down the 'facts' required to complete a formal assessment. They know that relationships built on friendly chat with parents make it much more likely that conversations about children will contribute to the emergence of shared understanding. They also know that tightly structured businesslike staff meetings run more smoothly when colleagues also have opportunities to get to know each other through more relaxed, informal gatherings.

Ten years ago, I argued (Parker-Rees 2000) that we needed to relax a little in order to allow for more playful interaction at all levels of education. The *Early Years Foundation Stage* (DCSF 2008) now clearly recognises the importance of play in early learning, but it is still not easy for early years practitioners to feel comfortable about relaxing their control and allowing space for children to enjoy each other's company as they play. As long as play continues to be seen as a challenge to getting work done, rather than as a necessary component of any form of social interaction, playfulness, in adults as well as in children, will continue to be discouraged (see Moyles 2010). 'Hunting' play may be acceptable, where practitioners can show that the hunt is likely to be successful and result in the capture of valuable knowledge, but the forms of play that allow children to gather less immediately impressive, albeit essential, ingredients may still have to be squeezed in around the margins, concealed from public view and given little encouragement or support. We can continue to hope that playful early years practitioners and playful children will continue to change the landscape until convivial, enjoyable, relaxed playfulness can be recognised as a necessary part of all forms of social interaction.

Questions to set you thinking

1 Think about one particular child you care for (not a member of your family) and one adult friend. How well do you know each of them? How well do they know you? How did you get to know them? What might help you to get to know them better?

2 In your experience, what are the main differences between how you feel about work meetings and how you feel about more playful gatherings? In what ways might work meetings benefit from being a bit more playful?

3 What is the balance between 'hunting' play and 'gathering' play in different children's activities in different parts of your setting and at different times?

Note

1   The meaning of Rosie's wide-mouthed expression becomes clear later when mum has left and, noticing the open end of a lid, Rosie again opens her mouth wide before looking at the student filming her then looking away and quickly putting the pen in her mouth. She appears to be imitating the lid with her mouth, or perhaps making a connection between the sight of the pen fitting into the lid and earlier experiences of putting things into her mouth. She also seems to be aware that this action may provoke disapproval.

References and further reading

Baron Cohen, S. (2003) *The Essential Difference: Men, Women and the Extreme Male Brain*. London: Allen Lane.

Carpendale, J. and Lewis, C. (2006) *How Children Develop Social Understanding*. Oxford: Blackwell.

Claxton, G. (1994) *Noises from the Dark Room: The Science and Mystery of the Mind*. London: HarperCollins.

Claxton, G. (2000) The anatomy of intuition. In G. Claxton and T. Atkinson (eds) *The Intuitive Practitioner: On the Value of Not Always Knowing What One is Doing*. Buckingham: Open University Press.

Department for Children, Schools and Families (DCSF) (2008) *Practice Guidance for the Early Years Foundation Stage*. Nottingham: DCSF Publications.

Drummond, M.J. and Jenkinson, S. (2009) *Meeting the Child: Approaches to Observation and Assessment in Steiner Kindergartens*. Plymouth: University of Plymouth.

Hedegaard, M. (2009) Children's development from a cultural-historical approach: children's activity in everyday local settings as foundation for their development. *Mind, Culture, and Activity*, 16(1): 64–82.

Hobson, P. (2002) *The Cradle of Thought: Exploring the Origins of Thinking*. London: Macmillan.

Kennedy, D. (2006) *The Well of Being – Childhood, Subjectivity and Education*. Albany, New York: State University of New York.

Moyles, J. (2010) Practitioner reflection on play and playful pedagogies. In J. Moyles (ed.) *Thinking about Play: Developing a Reflective Approach*. Maidenhead: Open University Press.

OECD (2006) *Starting Strong II: Early Childhood Education and Care*. Paris: OECD Publications.

Parker-Rees, R. (2000) Time to relax a little: making time for the interplay of minds in education. *Education 3–13*, 38(1): 29–35.

Parker-Rees, R. (2007) Liking to be liked: imitation, familiarity and pedagogy in the first years of life. *Early Years*, 27(1): 3–17.

Rochat, P. (2004) Emerging co-awareness. In G. Bremner and A. Slater (eds) *Theories of Infant Development*. Oxford: Blackwell.

Sawyer, K. (1997) *Pretend Play as Improvisation: Conversation in the Preschool Classroom*. New York: Lawrence Erlbaum Associates.

Trevarthen, C. (2005) Action and emotion in development of cultural intelligence: why infants have feelings like ours. In J. Nadel and D. Muir (eds) *Emotional Development*. Oxford: Oxford University Press.

Tronick, E.Z. (2005) Why is connection with others so critical? The formation of dyadic states of consciousness: coherence governed selection and the co-creation of meaning out of messy meaning making. In J. Nadel and D. Muir (eds) *Emotional Development*. Oxford: Oxford University Press.

PART 2
Play, language and literacy

5 Playing or having fun? Dilemmas in early literacy

Marian Whitehead

Summary
This chapter starts from the current requirements in England that early years practitioners must facilitate play-based learning for children and also introduce the systematic teaching of phonics in a fun way to very young children. The following discussion has several aims: • to raise awareness of the possible dilemmas in these requirements • to look again at the nature and complexity of play • to review the relationship between play, literature and literacy • to consider the role of fun in teaching and learning • to provoke serious thought about child-initiated learning.

Introduction

In a fascinating article on dilemmas in early childhood teacher education in the United States, Katz (2008) defines a dilemma as a choice between alternative courses of action that are equally problematic. Where there is a choice to be made between alternative courses of action, we always have to ask what might be lost if we choose 'A' rather than 'B'. Here we have the core concern of this chapter, but I take comfort from the conclusion reached by Katz that professional practitioners must go for the 'least worst' errors (2008: 21). As we nurture young children's literacy development, we have to think about the nature and complexity of play, what is involved in tackling phonics in a fun way and accept that these approaches may not be entirely compatible. In other words, before we can choose the least worst errors we have to understand the competing alternatives.

Cameo 5.1

In the early days of the National Curriculum in England, I was observing a class of 5 and 6 year olds who were having a science lesson about the parts of a tree. This involved a focus on the naming of the parts and, as the teacher confirmed and repeated the correct name for the main stem of a tree, a child near me muttered 'elephants have trunks'. When the teacher went on to identify the outer layer of the trunk as 'bark', another child at the back of the group made quiet 'woof-woof' noises.

Deep play and being subversive

This observation has stayed with me and influenced my thinking about what is play and what is not. It was also a sharp reminder that children do have their own ways of responding to curriculum initiatives and are not passive recipients of the latest care and education package. The children's whispered interventions demonstrated considerable skill in subverting a formal lesson that was not engaging them in any way and was also underestimating their existing knowledge and understanding. This kind of subversion of authority and power is risky – hence the whispers at the back of the group – but it was apparently worth the risk as it clawed back an element of power and control in a teacher-dominated session. It also provided some momentary excitement for these young captives on the carpet and allowed them to display their broad linguistic skills. Such extraordinary high-risk play has come to be categorised as 'deep play', and twentieth-century anthropologists identified it in many cultures around the world (Geertz 1976). It is certainly not restricted to children and the likely originator of the term, eighteenth-century political philosopher Jeremy Bentham, viewed it as dangerously irrational behaviour when it occurred in adult social and political life. Deep play is not just about subverting external authority, it often involves personal risk taking of the kind that drives explorers, climbers, gamblers, athletes, artists, scientists and thinkers to 'get in over their heads', or push themselves to the limits of endurance and sensible behaviour. So why do it?

Many forms of artistic activity and creative thinking display features of deep play. These activities often frighten and offend other people, but they also push out the boundaries of what is known and safe, and formulate new ways of solving old problems and exploring human experience. They seem to be part of a drive to make life meaningful, and can range from the child's explorations and imitations of adult behaviours, to the novelist's investigations of the human condition and the scientist's inquiry into the origins of life. Deep play distances the player from the practical demands of the here and now and creates a special situation, a special place, where it is possible to go overboard, take a leap into the unknown and push a 'what if' question to the limits. Deep play does this by effecting a kind of disconnection from the demands of everyday reality, and creates a virtual reality or 'third area' (Winnicott 1971) where we are more able to be ourselves. It is not unreasonable to link these speculations with Vygotsky's description (1986) of a zone of proximal development in which a child in partnership with an older or wiser mentor can reach higher levels of thinking. Goswami (2008) has revisited Vygotsky's ideas about the role of language in children's thinking, and she suggests that language and imaginative pretend play enable children to:

- reflect upon and regulate their own cognitive behaviour
- develop a deeper understanding of the beliefs and emotions of other people (Goswami 2008: 412–413).

If we return to the cameo of the children on the carpet, we can see that their secretive, witty contributions were not just challenging a lesson, they were a form of sophisticated language play. This risky deep play with the unpromising content of a formal lesson created a fleeting zone of proximal development that raised the level of the thinking going on, at least at the back of the group. The children subverting the lesson were supporting each other in exploiting the rich metaphors and multiple meanings of two words in the English language. So they understood and demonstrated that there are several kinds of 'trunk' and more than one meaning of 'bark'! This shows considerable linguistic skill and knowledge and, I must admit, a great sense of fun. The sound play with 'woof-woof' is a reminder that onomatopoeic, rhyming and alliterative nonsense words are frequently used by children to ridicule excessive adult talk or 'nagging'. The currently popular form in the UK is 'blah-de-blah', while in the USA it comes out as 'ya-dah, ya-dah'. So useful is this method of pinpointing and being dismissive about boring empty talk, that adults are adopting it too and using it in their language play. Have you heard adults summing up a whole lot of talk and explanation as 'blah-de-blah', or have you said it yourself recently?

Play, literature and literacy

Although not all play is deep and subversive, there is a thread of risk taking and boundary pushing that runs through play, literature and literacy. One way of defining play emphasises the 'Who's in charge?' question, because control of the nature and direction of genuine play must stay with the player(s). The significance of this for taking risks is obvious: we cannot tell children to be exploratory and think outside the box if we dictate all aspects of their play activities. If we want play to be free flowing (Bruce 2009 and Chapter 18), and to contribute to children's thinking and meaning making, we have to follow the children's lead and learn to be co-explorers and thinkers with them in their play. This is a challenge for practitioners, but help is at hand if we share a wide range of stories and literature with children, because literature can often be subversive, challenging and deeply playful. In stories and books the power and direction of the narrative is up for negotiation between the teller and the listener because the tale becomes a kind of plaything that can be reshaped and reused in many different ways. Clearly young children are taking control of stories and thinking with them when they try out a wild rumpus dance in the garden, or repel a fierce wolf who is attempting to climb down the playhouse chimney! These life-and-death scenarios, played out every day in early years settings, are a reminder of the challenges that stories and literature offer all of us.

Literature is a high point of deep play with language but it is also the foundation of literacy. It provides a powerful motivation for children (and adults) to become readers and writers so that they can access the power of written words for themselves. Literature also offers examples of language at work. The patterns of syntax, new words, letter combinations, features of punctuation, page layout and conventions of illustration, and so on, become teachers of literacy. If children have ample opportunities to explore for them-selves the nature of written marks, drawings, signs and letters, and use all the ways they can to communicate important messages, they will start to discover the power of literacy. However, written language is a cultural invention and children are in the roles of young apprentices who need older and wiser lit-eracy partners to tutor them and share in their explorations. In such truly educative partnerships, young children can interrogate written texts and come up with reasonable hypotheses about 'what that says' and 'how you write that'.

It is all too easy for practitioners, especially in England, to become so focused on the alphabetic and phonological systems of English that they think only of the rules and tricks that children must learn if they are to break the code. The danger of falling into this trap is increased by the official view that learning the 'phonic rules' of English is easy and reading is 'simple'. In fact, fluent reading depends on doing lots of it, and taking risks and making intelli-gent predictions, or guesses, based on many pleasurable and meaningful engagements with stories, books and print of many kinds. Children who are scared of making mistakes become too cautious and sound out every letter and familiar digraph, to the point at which they render the text in front of them meaningless. There must be a trade-off between accuracy and speed, and enjoyment if young children are to become readers and writers who make literacy their own tool and plaything.

Two dilemmas

1　If deep play is a personal risk-taking activity and all genuine play must belong to the player(s), what happens when it is taken over by practitioners and structured towards meeting externally imposed goals? Is it still play? Perhaps not, but used judiciously, it might be a form of good pedagogical practice that humanises curriculum demands by relating them to the interests of the children.

2　Literacy is a system that represents the sounds and words of a language using written signs. To this extent it is a tight formal system that functions in a particular language community and culture, and must be passed on to children. However, this passing-on process is not totally dependent on schools and explicit instruction: far more meaningful and enjoyable learning about the system occurs when it draws on familiar community literacy (Makin and Whitehead 2004; Serpell *et al.* 2005), and appeals to children's delight in playing with marks, signs and letters.

Don't you dare . . .

Play, books and stories can be free flowing, chaotic and unpredictable teachers of literacy, as I found out when I bought an unconventional picture book to share with Mattias, my 9-year-old grandson. Mattias is high-functioning autistic and has struggled to make sense of formal reading instruction, although he loves books, and has a strong sense of narrative and drama. The book, which has fascinated all the family, is *Don't Read This Book* by Jill Lewis and Deborah Allwright (2009). The plot centres on a vain and hot-tempered king and the panic that is caused when the king's official story writer loses a new story he has promised to produce. The picture book starts with furious attempts by the king to stop readers reading the book, hence the title, because 'There is no story here'! However, these attempts to get rid of the reader are accompanied by many sly references to the reader who is already turning the pages: 'Yes, I do mean you.' As the frantic search for the lost story progresses, more and more familiar characters from traditional tales pop up to offer advice and add to the king's fury! So we encounter three blind mice, a beanstalk and a giant, Red Riding Hood's Grandmama (plus the wolf) and a gingerbread man. We only discover what the missing story is about on the last double spread of the book when characters, plot and title are found and hastily put together. Part of the fascination and challenge of this text arises from the fact that it is a story about the nature of stories. But the deeper appeal of the book for a child is probably the narrative focus on the spiralling monumental rage of the king. This anger is openly directed at the reader on pages that feature huge coloured letters and dire threats of imprisonment if the reading does not stop immediately. The final page is Mattias's favourite as it repeats the king's constant threat: 'Go away. And don't you dare read this book again!'

Of course Mattias does just the opposite and enjoys innumerable re-readings of the book, always preceded by his own cheeky response to the book's title: 'I'm gonna!' He knows the text word for word, and the phrase 'Don't you dare read . . .' has become part of family talk and is applied to the appearance of any print, from postcards and magazines, to road signs and Mattias's birthday cards.

Most children will draw comfort and reassurance from the theme of unmanageable rage that is controlled and contained within the safe shared reading situation and held within the pages of a picture book. This is particularly significant for Mattias, who is sometimes overwhelmed by his own frustrations and confusions and reacts with angry outbursts.

A struggling reader is likely to be intrigued and encouraged by a book that is trying to stop them reading! Mattias has shown a new confidence in his encounters with literacy since becoming fascinated by this book, and seems to realise that he can exercise choice and control over all his reading. So much so, that he was recently observed in his school classroom politely but firmly refusing to read a controlled phonic text with his teacher. He argued very convincingly that he should be allowed to read his own *Star Wars* reading book that he had brought from home: 'It is mine because my mum has put my name on it'! He is passionately interested in *Star Wars* Lego but had some trouble with the school text as it was called 'I am water' and he, like many autistic people, can be very literal and was anxious to assert that, 'I am Mattias'! These indications that Mattias was learning about control and power in literacy, and willing to take risks and play for high stakes are reminders that deep play can emerge suddenly in homes and classrooms, if practitioners and families are brave enough to let it.

What about fun?

Cameo 5.2

The children in a reception class are creating amusing pictures and thinking up words that rhyme and words that start with the same sounds. Their own unique take on this conventional phonics play is focused on some recent work about the polar regions and the animals who inhabit them. Delightful pictures and verses about penguins that 'live in a hole in the south pole' are part of a colourful wall display. In another part of this large reception unit, a display of paintings beautifully embellished with glitter and fabrics seems to consist of self-portraits of the children. But the human figures are sprouting elaborate branches, leaves and blossoms, and it is only when we read the captions written by the children that the nature of this particular game with imagination and language becomes clear. The children have thought about creating pictures of themselves as trees and chosen the kind of imaginary tree they would like to be and, of course, the names of the trees are the same as the names of their creators.

The children in the cameo are clearly having fun as they learn about letters, sounds, phonemes, blends and words as concepts. The practitioners who work with them understand the importance of alphabetic and phonological awareness in early literacy, and are able to interpret the official advice set out in government documents (DfES 2007) in the context of the meaningful interests and passions of the children in their class. If children are to enjoy their early encounters with the amazingly varied and irregular system of English phonology they need meaningful contexts, plenty of fun and a wide range of approaches. They also need confident practitioners who follow the children's interests and enthusiasms and know that these can provide the best possible ways into literacy, no matter how narrow and simplistic the official curriculum (see Anning, Chapter 1).

There are lots of traditional materials available for children and practitioners who need fun, inspiration and linguistic riches, but they are to be found in collections of nursery rhymes, poems and the half-remembered action and finger rhymes of infancy, not in curriculum guidelines. This ancient material has been carefully analysed and explained for a new generation of practitioners and families who may not know that English-speaking cultures have a rich resource of language play and experimentation just waiting to be used (Bruce and Spratt 2008). These distinguished experts locate the essentials of literacy in baby songs, finger and action rhymes, nursery rhymes and poetry.

A similar approach, using much of the same traditional material, and displaying an equal delight in the fun that can be had with language and literacy, was published in 2006 (Featherstone 2006). The timing of this was crucial as the pressure of the formal teaching of synthetic phonics was beginning to be felt in early years settings. There is plenty of fun and phonics in this exhilarating collection of helpful guidance from a team of respected early years experts who put child development and understanding at the heart of the literacy curriculum. So we find that we can explore initial sounds and digraphs by 'sorting the laundry', develop fine auditory discrimination as we play with puppets, and explore alliteration in made-up nonsense rhymes and phrases. The advice at the end of this book, to 'keep it active, keep it fun' (2006: 177), brings us back to a consideration of the role of fun in early literacy.

It would seem that fun has some positive advantages:

- fun lightens the context and the imposed nature of the activities
- fun starts to introduce the possibility of subverting a tight structure
- fun legitimates exploration of the sound system of the language
- fun supports investigation of multiple meanings in the language.

Cameo 5.3

I am talking to a 12-year-old boy in a school in the USA and he tells me that he is doing an enrichment class in English for gifted students. They are studying old English riddles and he is keen to try one or two out on me, and he also wants me to find some more for him. It has been many years since I thought about this very old tradition of language play with meanings, rhymes and rhythms, but it was exciting to share it again with a youthful speaker of a distinctive branch of the English language. Whoever first thought of an egg as a palace could not have dreamed that it would one day delight children living in a totally different culture on the far side of a vast ocean. And we still create similar riddling questions, as this twentieth-century favourite shows:

> *What is black and white and red all over?*
> A newspaper!

Another dilemma

There are dangers in the endless pursuit of fun because it is essentially light-hearted and superficial. Too much emphasis on such amusing approaches can become trivial and undermine young children's serious and thoughtful engagements with language and print. An example of so-called 'fun ways with phonics' in the classroom was observed by an American researcher (Meyer 2002). Each child had been given the individual letter cards 'm', 'n', 'c', 'd', printed in black, and 'a' printed in red. The children were told to make words and sound them out to the group. This activity went fairly smoothly until one boy said he could make 'candy' if he had a 'y'. The teacher replied, 'That is harder than we're supposed to make' and seemed clearly distressed by the rigid lesson imposed on her (2002: 20). It is worth noting that systematic intense phonic instruction took off in the USA several years before it was introduced to the UK and has been big business for US educational publishers. The publishers of these phonic schemes, games and cards clearly consider them to be fun and some children may be helped by such support, but they also need a full range of letters and permission to be adventurous!

Questions for practitioners

Do both play and fun have roles in the early years curriculum and early literacy?

Clearly they do, but we have to be more aware of their nature and the differences between them. The implications of both for children's well-being and learning must be understood. For example, fun is usually a light-hearted and superficial response or activity, but it can certainly make dull routines, repetition and drudgery manageable. In contrast, play can be 'deep' and challenging for children and adults as it pushes at boundaries and flows in unpredictable directions (see also Howard, Chapter 13). Play of this kind raises issues of power, direction and control for practitioners and for families (see also Georgeson and Payler, Chapter 2). Nowhere is the issue of power in the learning and teaching situation more challenging than in attempts to encourage child-initiated learning.

What is the place of child-initiated learning in the curriculum?

For many experienced and deeply thoughtful practitioners, child-initiated learning must be at the heart of the curriculum. This philosophy is grounded in the belief that what matters to children is their first-hand experiences (Rich *et al.* 2005) as they learn about their world, their significant people and relationships, and themselves. This approach understands that children are learners, learning is what they do (see Goouch, Chapter 3). The kind of learning that matters to children 'is driven by their urgent desire to make sense of the world' (Rich *et al.* 2008: 2) and can be described as having four interrelated domains: being, acting, exploring, thinking (2008: 2). Similarly, other studies of child-initiated learning (Featherstone and Featherstone 2008) focus on the powerful and self-motivated ways in which young learners set about gathering the experiences they need to make sense of the world and, in the process, creating the essential neural connections for thinking in their brains.

This may seem very challenging, if not risky, for practitioners, and certainly takes us all out of our comfort zones. It means that we have to start learning to trust children as thinkers and begin to learn alongside them. In the process, we will find out what interests and motivates them, and what happens in their deeper engagements with learning. In terms of special needs, we will also learn about the different strategies that different kinds of brain connections prioritise, as we see in Cameo 5.4.

Cameo 5.4

Mattias has picked up some information about extreme weather features in a school science lesson and waits behind to ask the teacher a question that is concerning him: 'What colour is a tornado?' Mattias categorises the world and thinks about it in very literal ways, so he needs information about features he can point to and identify. He certainly hasn't experienced a tornado and may well feel anxious about so powerful and incomprehensible a phenomenon. Yet this could be the start of some exciting explorations of wind power and movement, spirals and whirlpools, stories and dance.

Do we understand the nature of language and literacy learning?

This question produces a whole cluster of related questions for practitioners. But studying the development of language and literacy with many questions in our minds is the best possible way to tackle this huge topic (Whitehead 2010). As we formulate our questions, we are already halfway to answering them. So, what are the functions of marking, drawing and writing, and what part do they play in young children's drive to communicate? Are they essential aspects of literacy? What is the nature of stories and literature (see also Whitebread and Jameson, Chapter 6)? Must children grasp how oral and written stories work if they are to become book lovers and readers? If literacy is more than learning sounds and decoding a system, do children have opportunities to play with meanings – as well as sounds? What are the advantages of being bilingual, or on the way to becoming bilingual? How do the children we work with move between two, or more, phonological systems, inside and outside early years settings? What about all the other related systems of meanings, writing, culture and feelings? What about all the babies and toddlers in early years settings? Do we realise how important it is to play one-to-one games that involve communicating, making eye contact, babbling, squealing and gurgling, for example?

How do we plan for the developmental stages and special needs of children?

Do we prioritise gesturing and signing in our settings? Are we aware of how very significant this is in supporting the language development of babies and toddlers, young bilinguals and children with degrees of hearing loss?

Are we providing visual cues (picture cards); little play scenarios (pretending to eat a sandwich); and intense one-to-one interactions, for hearing impaired children, children with language delay and children on the autism spectrum?

Do we plan for sensory enrichment of the curriculum for children who are visually impaired or on the autistic spectrum? There are so many other ways of learning that can involve all the senses and, if we observe our children closely, they will help us to understand their needs. This approach is not only inclusive in the schooling and administrative sense of the term, it is also truly inclusive in that it leads to appropriate high-quality care and education for all children.

Cameo 5.5

All this summer Mattias has been fascinated by the noise of the cicadas in the trees around the house. Today he asked me to go outside as he wanted to show me something. He stood under his favourite tree and made an almost perfect imitation of the sound of a cicada with his tongue and teeth. (He does understand that the cicada produces this sound with its abdomen.) He then said to me, 'Go on the computer, Granny, and find me a film about cicadas.'

Conclusion

This chapter is full of questions and it may seem a bit thin on answers, but at least that is a refreshing change from all the official strategies that claim to be foolproof and are not up for debate! At a time when national literacy initiatives in England are dominated by simple reading and simple phonic instruction, it is hard to convince anyone of the complexities of language and literacy, and the astounding creativity of the developing human brain. It is even harder to put forward the notion that early literacy teaching may be a matter of making choices and going for the least worst errors in terms of play versus fun approaches. But what if the main dilemma I have identified, that of depth versus surface, is not a stark choice after all? Perhaps one way to get off the horns of this particular dilemma is to admit that both approaches have a role to play in early literacy learning and teaching. So the least worst error means, for the practitioner, being open to wherever deep play takes the children and also ready to use plenty of fun tactics as appropriate. However, this requires considerable practitioner knowledge about child development and language, as well as professional skill and sensitive insights. In contrast, the greatest error would be not to know the difference between play and fun.

Questions to set you thinking

These are included throughout this chapter.

References and further reading

Bruce, T. (ed.) (2009) *Early Childhood. A Guide for Students* (2nd edn). London: Sage Publications.

Bruce, T. and Spratt, J. (2008) *Essentials of Literacy from 0–7*. London: Sage Publications.

DfES (Department for Education and Skills) (2007) *Letters and Sounds: Principles and Practice of High Quality Phonics*. London: DfES.

Featherstone, S. (ed.) (2006) *'L' is for Sheep: Getting Ready for Phonics*. Lutterworth: Featherstone Education.

Featherstone, S. and Featherstone, P. (eds) (2008) *Like Bees, Not Butterflies. Child-initiated Learning in the Early Years*. London: A&C Black Publishers.

Geertz, C. (1976) Deep play: a description of the Balinese cockfight. In J.S. Bruner, A. Jolly and K. Sylva (eds) *Play: Its Role in Development and Evolution*. Harmondsworth: Penguin Books.

Goswami, U. (2008) *Cognitive Development: The Learning Brain*. Hove: Psychology Press.

Katz, L. (2008) Dilemmas in early childhood teacher education: an American perspective. *Early Childhood Practice: The Journal for Multi-professional Partnerships*, 10(1): 6–22.

Lewis, J. and Allwright, D. (2009) *Don't Read This Book!* London: Egmont UK Ltd.

Makin, L. and Whitehead, M. (2004) *How to Develop Children's Early Literacy: A Guide for Carers and Educators*. London: Sage Publications.

Meyer, R.J. (2002) *Phonics Exposed: Understanding and Resisting Systematic, Direct, Intense, Phonics Instruction*. New Jersey and London: Lawrence Erlbaum Associates, Inc.

Rich, D., Casanova, D., Dixon, A., Drummond, M.J., Durrant, A. and Myer, C. (2005) *First Hand Experience. What Matters to Children*. Woodbridge: Rich Learning Opportunities.

Rich, D., Drummond, M.J. and Myer, C. (2008) *Learning: What Matters to Children*. Woodbridge: Rich Learning Opportunities.

Serpell, R., Baker, L. and Sonnenschein, S. (2005) *Becoming Literate in the City: The Baltimore Early Childhood Project*. Cambridge: Cambridge University Press.

Vygotsky, L.S. (1986) *Thought and Language*. Revised and edited by A. Kozulin. Cambridge MA: MIT Press.

Whitehead, M. (2010) *Language and Literacy in the Early Years* (4th edn) London: Sage Publications.

Winnicott, D.W. (1971) *Playing and Reality*. Harmondsworth: Penguin Books.

6 Play beyond the Foundation Stage: storytelling, creative writing and self-regulation in able 6–7 year olds

David Whitebread and Helen Jameson

Summary

This chapter argues for the power of playful approaches and activities in stimulating children's storytelling, creative writing and self-regulation. Despite the recent support for playful approaches in the Foundation Stage, other current developments in primary education have increased the downward pressure to use exclusively formal teaching methods, particularly in the area of literacy, to ever younger children. By contrast, evidence is presented of the potential benefits of playful approaches being extended to older and more able children. The example is discussed of work using Storysacks and other props to stimulate imaginative oral storytelling and high-quality creative writing with highly able Year 2 children.

Introduction

Recent research related to learning within developmental psychology has established the overwhelming significance of the development of children's cognitive and emotional self-regulation. This has implications for their thinking, problem solving and creativity. Major influences have been Bruner's (1972) evolutionary/ethological approach to notions about flexibility of thought, and Vygotsky's (1978) suggestion that in play children create their own zone of proximal development and establish a bridge between the real world of objects and events and the symbolic world of thoughts and ideas. Neo-Vygotskian research (Karpov 2005) has explored the development of cognitive self-regulation and control within play contexts.

The research reported in this chapter is consistent with the view that play impacts upon self-regulation and metacognitive processes and, as a consequence, its effects emerge most clearly in tasks and aspects of development that involve problem solving and creativity.

Age, ability and learning through play

Without doubt, the introduction of *Curriculum Guidance for the Foundation Stage* gave 'official' recognition and status to something that early years practitioners have recognised for many years, namely 'Well planned play is the key way in which children learn with enjoyment and challenge during the foundation stage' (DfEE/QCA 2000: 25).

The importance of play in the Foundation Stage now seems to be accepted and positively encouraged for children up to the age of 5 years through the replacement *Early Years Foundation Stage* (DfES 2007). In contrast, however, play is being squeezed out of the curriculum from the beginning of Year 1 onwards. The emphasis on formal learning in KS1 denies the fact that these children are still in the early years of their development; indeed, the term 'early years' seems to have been hijacked in schools to mean 'under-5s' and has become synonymous with the Foundation Stage, rather than 'under-8s' as was previously assumed. The change in language following the introduction of the National Curriculum regarding the group of children in school aged between 5 and 7 years from 'infants' (with its connotations of babyhood) to 'Key Stage 1' (a much more formal title) again emphasises the move away from regarding these children as still relatively young and in need of a less formal, play-based curriculum (see Anning, Chapter 1).

The only areas where slightly older children are still encouraged to play are those where there is evidence of special educational need or early deprivation. In 2001 the government announced it would be giving £6 million to set up and run 150 toy libraries in deprived areas. This followed research (commissioned by the Department for Education) by London University's Institute of Education, tracking 2800 children between the ages of 3 and 7, which concluded that children who have high-quality play equipment at home outperform those who don't, and that these educational advantages stay with children at least through primary school. The then Education and Employment Minister, Margaret Hodge, was quoted as saying:

> Every parent knows that toys and play equipment can be expensive. As a result many young children from deprived areas are going without essential early play that is crucial to child development.
>
> (*Daily Mail*, 20 February 2001)

Anyone visiting a special school, be it for severe learning difficulties (SLD) or emotional and behavioural difficulties (EBD), cannot fail to notice all the extra play equipment available to the children, and the extra time devoted to and emphasis placed upon play. This is despite the fact that many of the children in these schools are still required to follow (or at least pay lip service to) the National Curriculum. The assumption seems to be that able children from Year 1 onwards, who are doing well in school, do not 'need' to play as much as their less able or educationally less 'successful' peers.

This appears to be a dominant view even among many in the teaching profession (see Moyles, Introduction). As Eyles (1993) reported, when considering the importance of play, it is clear that most of the teachers she interviewed believed that:

> . . . time spent on play activities should decrease with the increased age of the children . . . and many children in Year Two classes did not seem to be involved in any identified play experiences in the classroom . . . By Year Two the overwhelming opinion (of the children) was that they did not play! Where 'play' did take place with the older age-group it was always referred to as 'not work' and therefore learning was not taking place during the activity.'
>
> (p. 45)

Within the teaching profession, the idea of 'readiness' for certain skills and concepts is often assumed; young children who have not reached the position of being 'ready' for a new skill/concept are often encouraged to play in order to develop the necessary pre-skills/concepts and so on. As Moyles has emphasised: 'Immature children are prime candidates for carefully conceived play activities, through which basic conceptual understandings can be achieved' (Moyles 1989).

In contrast, able and successful children are often encouraged to go straight to formal learning and it may be deemed 'unnecessary' to give them the same amount of play opportunities. This is even more apparent as children get slightly older. By the time they are in Year 1 or 2, if they have no learning difficulties, developmental delays or such like, the emphasis on formal, sitting-down, pen-and-paper learning increases to the point of complete exclusion of play, particularly for able, high-achieving children.

Given the opportunity, all children, regardless of age, often choose to play and indeed even adults still like to play (as can be demonstrated in our culture by the phenomenal sales of adult computer games, board games and puzzles, along with the large number of adults taking part in sports, historical re-enactments and activities such as paintballing and tenpin bowling). Despite this, the assumption remains, following Piaget (see Sutton-Smith 1966), that play is indicative of immature functioning, a developmental 'stage' that children go through, and, if successfully transcended, they will then be ready for formal schooling, with little need for any more play in order to learn (a notion stringently challenged in several chapters of this book).

A number of related pressures are currently reinforcing this trend towards squeezing playfulness out of the school curriculum beyond the Foundation Stage and making it difficult for teachers of children of 5 years and older to justify the inclusion of playful opportunities and approaches in their classrooms. The requirements of the National Curriculum, with national tests for 7 year olds, backed up by the publication of school league tables, have clearly increased the downward pressure to use exclusively formal teaching methods with children in KS1. Furthermore, there is a general perception that parents prefer more formal approaches. This is backed up, for example, by research commissioned by the American Toy Institute in the USA (2000), which found that 72 per cent of parents thought it very important for their children to start (academic) learning early, while 54 per cent believed there was already enough playtime in schools. The emphasis on 'delivering' the curriculum in teacher training in recent years has also tended to powerfully reinforce the view among student teachers that children are only learning when they, the students, are teaching (Moyles 1989). In the present climate, the concern is that our young teachers are not being given the opportunity to test out the validity of this view.

This is all exacerbated in the UK, of course, by the extraordinarily young age at which children start formal schooling. Our formal approach in Year 1 is in stark contrast to that of most other industrialised countries around the world, where children are commonly 6 or even 7 years old before they start formal school (Woodhead 1989).

There is still a paucity of research to give us firm evidence as to whether this debate over formal versus playful education and/or the appropriate age for formal schooling to start really matters in the long term. However, one important longitudinal study by Schweinhart and Weikart (1998) followed a group of disadvantaged children who were randomly allocated to attend one of three preschool programmes. The programmes in question were High/Scope (where children are encouraged to follow a pattern of plan–do–review), Direct Instruction (teacher-led, with academic lessons) and Nursery School (teachers used themes and children had free choice of activity for much of the time). Initially, all three groups showed an increase in IQ, followed by a decline to age 10. However, the most startling difference was in the long term. At age 23, both the Nursery and High/Scope groups were doing better on a range of 'real life' measures (e.g. rates of arrest, emotional problems and suspension from work). Schweinhart and Weikart (1998) hypothesised that an emphasis on child-initiated and playful activities in these two preschool programmes developed the children's sense of social responsibility and their interpersonal skills, and that this had a positive impact in later life.

Play and creativity

With this apparent paradox between the emphasis on play-based learning for the Foundation Stage and for educationally disadvantaged children, combined with the sudden introduction of a more formal approach for Year 1 onwards, we have been keen to investigate whether, in fact, for older (Year 1 and above) and more able children, playful approaches to learning may be beneficial. This possibility has seemed to be worth investigating given the powerful range of evidence and theory from psychological research supporting the developmental significance of play, particularly in relation to problem solving and creativity (see Howard, Chapter 13).

Psychologists have been researching and developing theories about the nature and purposes of children's play since the middle of the nineteenth century. It has been suggested as a mechanism for letting off steam, for providing relaxation, for relieving boredom, for practising for adult life, for living out our fantasies, and many more (Moyles 2005). That it is important in children's development, however, has never been in doubt. As Moyles (1989) demonstrated, for every aspect of human development and functioning, there is a form of play.

It is only in the past 20 to 30 years, however, that its significance for thinking, problem solving and creativity has been fully recognised. Bruner (1972), in a famous article entitled 'The nature and uses of immaturity', is generally credited with first pointing out to psychologists and educationalists the relationship across different animal species between the capacity for learning and the length of immaturity, or dependence upon adults. He argued that, as the period of immaturity lengthens, so does the extent to which the young are playful and that play is one of the key experiences through which young animals learn, the means by which their intellectual abilities themselves are developed. The human being, of course, has a much greater length of immaturity than any other animal, plays more and for longer, and is supreme, of course, in flexibility of thought. The more recent neuroscientific evidence has very much supported Bruner's position (see Moyles, Introduction).

Play, in Bruner's view, is all about developing flexibility of thought. It provides opportunities to try out possibilities, to put different elements of a situation together in various ways, to examine problems from different viewpoints. This is very close to Craft's (2000) more recent definition of creativity as 'possibility thinking'. Bruner demonstrated this in a series of experiments (e.g. see Sylva *et al.* 1976) where children were asked to solve practical problems. Typically in these experiments, one group of children was given the opportunity to play with the objects involved, while the other group was 'taught' how to use the objects in ways that would help solve the problem.

Consistently, the two groups subsequently performed at a similar level, in terms of numbers of children completing the task with total success, when they were individually asked to tackle the problem. However, in the 'taught' group there tended to be an 'all or nothing' pattern of responses, with the children either succeeding immediately by accurately recalling and following their instructions, or giving up following an initial failure. By contrast, the children who had the experience of playing with the materials were more inventive in devising strategies to solve the problem and persevered longer if their initial attempts did not work. The same proportion of children as in the 'taught' group solved the problem almost immediately, but many of those who didn't, solved the problem at a second or third attempt, or came close to solving the problem, by trying out different possibilities.

Observation of children at play gives some indication of why it might be such a powerful learning medium. During play children are usually totally engrossed in what they are doing. It is quite often repetitive and contains a strong element of practice. Two further elements that have been highlighted by psychological research and theory also contribute to an understanding of its vital significance in learning and creativity. These relate to its role in children's developing sense of control and self-regulation of their own learning and to their developing powers of symbolic representation. Both emerge from the influential theoretical writing of the Russian psychologist, Lev Vygotsky (1978). According to Vygotsky's position, during play children create what he has famously referred to as their own 'zone of proximal development' – that is, they set their own level of challenge and so what they are doing is always developmentally appropriate (to a degree that tasks set by adults will never be). This also involves the notion that play is spontaneous and initiated by the children themselves; in other words, during play children are in control of their own learning.

Guha (1987) has argued that this element of control or 'self-regulation' is particularly significant. There are many examples in psychological research of tasks where being in control has turned out to be crucial for effective learning. Guha cites, for example, experiments concerned with visual learning in which subjects are required to wear 'goggles' that make everything look upside down. They are then required to sit in a wheelchair and learn to move safely through an environment. The results of such experiments show that subjects moving themselves around the environment (and having a lot of initial 'crashes') learn to do this much more quickly than those who are wheeled safely about by an adult helper.

The parallels here with Bruner's 'play' and 'taught' groups are striking. There are also clear implications for how we can most effectively help young children to learn. Whenever a new material, task or process is introduced, it is clear that children's learning will be enhanced if they are first allowed to play with them in a relatively unstructured manner. When new information is being introduced, children need to be offered opportunities to incorporate this into their play also.

The other important implication of Vygotsky's notion of the 'zone of proximal development' for teachers, however, is that there is an important role for the teacher in participating and intervening in children's play. Smith (1990), in an extensive review, examines the evidence relating to the issue of structured and unstructured play. He concludes that there is a role in learning for both kinds of play; sensitive adult intervention can usefully enhance the intellectual challenge, mainly by opening up new possibilities and opportunities (see Goouch, Chapter 3).

In relation to its role in the development of creativity, the other element in Vygotsky's analysis of the cognitive processes in children's play relates to its pivotal contribution to the development of symbolic representation. Human thought, culture and communication, Vygotsky (1978) argues, are all founded on the unique human aptitude for using various forms of symbolic representation, which would include drawing and other forms of visual art, visual imagination, language in all its various forms, mathematical symbol systems, musical notation, dance and drama, and so on. Play, crucially, is recognised in this analysis, as the first medium through which children explore the use of symbol systems, most obviously through pretence. Play becomes, in this view, a 'transition' from the purely situational constraints of early childhood to the adult capability for abstract thought (Vygotsky 1978). So, as an adult, when you have had an interesting experience upon which you wish to reflect, or a problem to solve, or a story to write, you have the intellectual tools to do this in your mind. Lacking these tools, the argument follows, children require the support of real situations and objects with which the ideas are worked out through play.

The precise ways in which play, thinking, learning, development and creativity influence one another have been the subject of extensive research (for useful reviews see Craft 2000; Whitebread 2000; Lillard 2002). Lieberman (1977), for example, revealed a general relationship between playfulness traits and various measures of divergent thinking over 20 years ago. Of particular relevance to our own research, which we report in the final part of this chapter, are two empirical studies related to children's storytelling, both carried out as long ago as the 1980s. Pellegrini (1985) showed that the verbal narratives of preschoolers who especially enjoyed pretending were more elaborate and cohesive than those of age mates who preferred other forms of play. Dyachenko (1980, cited in Karpov 2005) showed that 5–6 year olds' ability to retell a story was significantly enhanced by the use of representational objects such as sticks, paper cut-outs etc., and that their ability to retell a story without the use of these objects was subsequently enhanced.

A very plausible mechanism through which this kind of play may facilitate problem solving and creativity is that referred to by Vygotsky as 'private speech'. In Vygotskian theory young children's tendency to talk to themselves, or self-commentate, while they are undertaking a task, is of great significance, as he argues that such speech is an important step in the processes by which children learn to represent ideas to themselves in language and learn to use language to self-regulate their activities. Berk *et al.* (2006) reported a series of observational studies of 2–6-year-old children in which they recorded the incidence of 'private speech'. They found particularly high levels of private speech and verbal self-regulation among 2–6-year-old children during open ended, make-believe or pretend play.

One of the chief areas of contention, however, in the research literature has been the direction of causality. Is more sophisticated play responsible for stimulating, or just the product of, particular aspects of cognitive development? This is clearly a crucial issue pedagogically. The study reported in the following section attempted to unravel this kind of issue.

A study of pretend play and imaginative storytelling

We have previously replicated, in a variety of content areas, the study by Sylva *et al.* (1984) in which the impact of play on practical problem solving in young children was investigated. As in the original study, on each occasion, children given the opportunity to engage with the material to be learned in playful contexts, performed as well as 'taught' groups in situation-specific aspects of the task, but also demonstrated more creative approaches and more positive dispositions, which seemed likely to have long-term benefits in relation to their development as learners.

Construction, both by its nature and within the framework of a primary school curriculum, is a practical activity, easily developed through play. Given the more formal prominence placed upon developing reading and writing skills, we were interested, however, to see if the same kind of pattern observed between play and taught conditions would emerge in relation to the rather different area of children's oral and written storytelling. The sample chosen for this research (Whitebread and Jameson 2003) consisted of Year 1 and Year 2 children (aged 5–7 years) in an independent school. We were particularly interested to be able to study a very specific sample group of children who were all (with the exception of two 'intellectually average' children) of at least 'above average' intellectual ability (as measured by Raven's Progressive Standard Matrices IQ Test). In fact, the average IQ of the group was 131, which is within the top 2 per cent of the population as a whole. Every child in the group had a reading age at least 6 months above his/her chronological age. Given that this was an independent, fee-paying school all the children come from reasonably affluent backgrounds. All of the children in the sample were of a white British ethnic origin with English as their first language. All of the children had had experience of nursery/preschool education and many opportunities to play during school time up until the end of their Foundation year. However, none of them had had experience of playing with Storysacks or story props prior to the start of the research. All the children had a great deal of experience of stories being read to them at school and also of being asked to write stories of their own.

This sample would normally be expected, according to the generally held views discussed earlier, to have the least 'need' for play: consequently we were intrigued to have the opportunity to discover if play would actually have any beneficial effect upon their storytelling and writing.

Following the general structure of the original study by Sylva *et al.* (1976), 35 of this group of able 5–7 year olds in an English independent school were asked to produce oral and written stories after they had been read a story and had experience of story props under 'play', 'taught' and 'control' conditions.

In order to engage in the 'play' condition 'Storysacks' were used. In English schools, there has been an increasing use in recent years of Storysacks as originally devised by Griffiths (1997). These consist of sets of toys and artefacts relating to items and characters in a story. In a letter from Neil Griffiths to the second author of this chapter (2004) he made the following observations:

> Storysacks are a tried and tested practical approach for strengthening literacy, involving parents and families in their children's learning. They are highly flexible and versatile in their use and by their nature offer a tactile, participatory approach to learning. Above all, they are a resource that motivates, raises confidence, extends concentration and listening skills and helps to gain a greater insight and understanding of a storyline for children and adults alike. A Storysack allows a child to enter the three-dimensional world of a story.

Within our study, sets of Storysack materials were used for three stories appropriate to the age range. The children were read each of the stories and then had follow-up activities that varied according to a 'play', 'taught' or 'control' condition. The order of stories and conditions was varied for different sub-groups within the sample in order to control for the differential effects of the three stories, and for ordering effects between the three conditions.

The children were read the stories in groups of 10–15, using a picture book version. In the 'play' condition, the group was then allowed 10 minutes to play with the story props in groups of five without any intervention from the teacher. In the 'taught' condition, the teacher then worked with the group for 10 minutes discussing and modelling with the story props other possible stories, but did not allow the children to handle the props. In the 'control' condition, the children were shown photocopied sheets of the story characters with their names, but no further help or guidance was offered. All the groups were then asked to write their own stories containing one or more of the characters in the story they had just heard. It was emphasised that this should be different from the original story.

These written stories were analysed according to the time taken to write them, the number of words they contained, their 'National Curriculum level', using national government guidelines (QCA 2001), and the number of points of information, beginnings, conflicts and resolutions that were the same as or different from those in the original story.

Later in the day, after each condition, the children were also given the opportunity to record an oral story using the same story characters. They were assessed for the time taken to tell them, the number of 'prompts' needed and the confidence with which they were told. The children were also assigned a General Confidence score (outside of the experimental conditions) by one teacher who had taught all of the children.

The results of the analysis of the children's written stories arising from the three conditions showed that in the 'taught' condition, although the children included more conflicts and resolutions in their written stories than the control group, they spent less time writing their stories than in the other two conditions, and they included more 'same' points in relation to the original story than the 'play' condition and fewer 'different' points than either of the other two conditions. They also included more 'same' resolutions than either of the other two conditions.

In the 'play' condition the children also included more conflicts and resolutions than the control group. However, more of these conflicts and resolutions were different from those in the original story than in either of the other two conditions, and their stories were of higher quality (as measured by NC levels) than in the 'taught' condition.

The analysis of the children's oral storytelling showed that in the 'play' condition the children showed more confidence than in either of the other two conditions. This difference appears to have been mostly attributable to a greater number of children lacking confidence after the 'taught' condition. After the 'play condition' the children also showed more confidence in this oral storytelling than in their regular classroom activities.

It was extremely interesting to observe that, despite investigating a completely different area of learning to Sylva *et al.* (1976), our findings, like theirs, clearly showed the value and importance of play in enabling children to be confident and creative. Similarly, children who have 'observed the principal' (taught group) show heightened anxiety when faced with a task and responded with an 'all or nothing' approach, as defined by Sylva *et al.* (1976).

The results of our analysis of various aspects of the stories showed a high level of congruence with each other and supported the theory that children who were not given an opportunity to play but had only the experience of watching the teacher (control and taught groups) felt that they had to model the teacher as closely as possible in order to be able to complete the task. This inhibited these children's creativity and, for many of them, also appeared to increase their anxiety and fear of failure.

Considering that the only difference between the independent variables was an isolated 10-minute opportunity to play or be taught, it was impressive just how significant these results were. In a curriculum that is increasingly pressed for time to fit everything in, it is reassuring to note that just 10 minutes spent playing has such a significant effect on both confidence and creativity (among other things). That these results were obtained with a deliberately able group of children suggests that the idea that such children in the 5–7 age range do not 'need' to play to learn may be seriously misguided.

Conclusion

Our research confirms that play is indeed vital in enabling young children to be confident, persevering and creative learners in more than one area of the curriculum. It is also crucial to note that, far from detracting from children's learning, the standard of writing actually rose after play. Given that the sample were all slightly older and very able children (who are often assumed not to need or benefit from play in the same way as younger and/or less able children) this is especially important. This should enable us to feel less 'that children are only learning if they are being taught' and more secure about making play the basis for learning in the early years and beyond.

However, the fact that children in the 'taught' group did appear to have higher confidence scores than the control group, as well as a higher total number of conflicts and/or resolutions present, would also seem to be important, and is of some little consolation to teachers that teaching does appear to have at least some positive benefits. Our education system currently relies upon children being able to learn, remember and regurgitate facts, details and information at increasingly higher levels as they progress through it. The National Literacy Strategy requires children to be able to read and write well at a young age (certainly much earlier than in many other countries, as already discussed). It would appear that a combination of play (to encourage confidence and creativity) alongside teaching/modelling (to introduce and develop new concepts and skills) might provide the best possible pedagogical environment to foster young children's learning.

Thus we have seen the benefits of pretend or fantasy play upon storytelling and writing for children, including very able children, up to at least Year 2. Observations on such a wide range of ages and backgrounds, showing that all children benefit from having opportunities for this kind of structured imaginative play, should encourage practitioners to incorporate more of this kind of opportunity into their curriculum planning. It seems likely that this will enhance their children's confidence and creativity as learners.

More generally, this work supports the increasing body of evidence concerning the role of play, particularly pretend or symbolic play, which might involve objects or other children, in providing a context in which children can develop their skills and dispositions as self-regulated learners. The first author of this chapter and others have written elsewhere concerning the now considerable body of evidence relating the development of self-regulation to children's success as problem solvers, creative thinkers and learners, and the implications for the classroom environment, for learning activities and for teacher–child interactions (Bronson 2000; Featherstone and Bayley 2001; Perry *et al.* 2002; Whitebread 2007; Whitebread and Coltman 2007). Particularly at this time, with the pressures on early years education that we have discussed, it is critical that the procedures and practices that these authors have promoted, and most importantly that support children's imaginative play, are well understood by early years practitioners, and form the foundation for their practice.

References and further reading

American Toy Institute (2000) *The Power of Play*. Factsheet. New York: ATI.

Berk, L.E., Mann, T.D. and Ogan, A.T. (2006) Make-believe play: wellspring for development of self-regulation. In D.G. Singer, R.M. Golinkoff and K. Hirsh-Pasek (eds) *Play = Learning: How Play Motivates and Enhances Children's Cognitive and Social-emotional Growth*. Oxford: Oxford University Press.

Bronson, M.B. (2000) *Self-regulation in Early Childhood*. New York: The Guilford Press.

Bruner, J. (1972) *The Relevance of Education*. Sydney, Australia: Allen and Unwin.

Craft, A. (2000) *Creativity across the Primary Curriculum*. London: Routledge.

DfEE/QCA (2000) *Curriculum Guidance for the Foundation Stage*. London: DfEE/QCA Publications.

Department for Education and Skills (DfES) (2007) *Early Years Foundation Stage*. London: DfES.

Eyles, J. (1993) Play – a trivial pursuit or meaningful experience. *Early Years*, 13(2): 45–49.

Featherstone, S. and Bayley, R. (2001) *Foundations of Independence*. Market Bosworth: Featherstone Education.

Griffiths, N. (1997) *Storysacks: A Starter Information Pack*. Bury: Storysacks Ltd.

Guha, M. (1987) Play in school. In G.M. Blenkin and A.V. Kelly (eds) *Early Childhood Education: A Developmental Curriculum*. London: Paul Chapman.

Karpov, Y.V. (2005) Three- to six-year-olds: sociodramatic play as the leading activity during the period of early childhood. In Y.V. Karpov, *The Neo-Vygotskian Approach to Child Development*. Cambridge: Cambridge University Press.

Lieberman, J.N. (1977) *Playfulness: Its Relation to Imagination and Creativity*. New York: Academic Press.

Lillard, A. (2002) Pretend play and cognitive development. In U. Goswami (ed.) *Blackwell Handbook of Childhood Cognitive Development*. Oxford: Blackwell.

Moyles, J. (1989) *Just Playing? The Role and Status of Play in Early Childhood Education*. Buckingham: Open University Press.

Moyles, J. (ed.) (2005) *The Excellence of Play* (3rd edn). Buckingham: Open University Press.

Pellegrini, A.D. (1985) The narrative organisation of children's fantasy play. *Educational Psychology*, 5: 17–25.

Perry, N.E., VandeKamp, K.J.O., Mercer, L.K. and Nordby, C.J. (2002) Investigating teacher–student interactions that foster self-regulated learning. *Educational Psychologist*, 37(1): 5–15.

Qualifications and Curriculum Authority (QCA) (2001) *English Tasks Teacher's Handbook*. London: QCA/DfES.

Schweinhart, L.J. and Weikart, D.P. (1998) Why curriculum matters in early childhood education. *Educational Leadership*, 55(6): 57–60.

Smith, P.K. (1990) The role of play in the nursery and primary school curriculum. In C. Rogers and P. Kutnick (eds) *The Social Psychology of the Primary School*. London: Routledge.

Sutton-Smith, B. (1966) Piaget on play: a critique. *Psychological Review*, 73(1): 104–110.

Sylva, K., Bruner, J. and Genova, P. (1976) The role of play in the problem-solving of children aged 3–5 years. In J. Bruner, A. Jolly and K. Sylva (eds) *Play: Its Role in Development and Evolution*. Glasgow: Penguin.

Vygotsky, L. (1978) The role of play in development. In L. Vygotsky, *Mind in Society*. Cambridge, MS: Harvard University Press.

Whitebread, D. (2000) Teaching children to think, reason, solve problems and be creative. In D. Whitebread (ed.) *The Psychology of Teaching and Learning in the Primary School*. London: RoutledgeFalmer.

Whitebread, D. (2007) Developing independence in learning. In J. Moyles (ed.) *Early Years Foundations: Meeting the Challenge*. Maidenhead: Open University Press.

Whitebread, D. and Coltman, P. (2007) Developing young children as self-regulated learners. In J. Moyles (ed.) *Beginning Teaching Beginning Learning* (3rd edn). Maidenhead: Open University Press.

Whitebread, D. and Jameson, H. (2003) The impact of play on the oral and written storytelling of able 5–7 year olds. Paper presented at the 33rd Annual Meeting of the Jean Piaget Society, Chicago: USA.

Woodhead, M. (1989) School starts at five . . . or four years old? The rationale for changing admission policies in England and Wales. *Journal of Education Policy*, 4(1): 1–21.

7 Children's fantasy role play – why adults should join in

Neil Kitson

Summary

This chapter highlights the importance of fantasy role play and socio-dramatic play in the cognitive, social and emotional development of young children. Socio-dramatic play offers great learning potential for those working with young children. Structuring the play enables practitioners to extend and enhance children's learning through creating situations and generating motivation to encourage the children to behave and function at a cognitive level beyond their norm. This is most effective when done through sympathetic and interactive interventions. Educators using socio-dramatic play can stimulate, motivate and facilitate the play, encouraging the children to work at a deeper level than they would if left to their own devices. Not only does the adult in role provide the children with a model of behaviour but the role can be altered to bring a galaxy of 'people', problems and challenges into the play. Only when educators acknowledge and recognise the importance of their role in children's fantasy play will they feel able to intervene and begin to develop its true potential.

Introduction

Cameo 7.1

In the corner of the nursery is a 'shop'. This has been made from screens and the adults have been successful in getting real objects for the children to play with. Indeed they are proud of their success and consider this to be a rich and valuable environment for the children to develop role play in. Kisha, Ashok and Michael have been in the 'shop' for some time now. Kisha is singing on the phone while Ashok and Michael are repeatedly putting money in and taking money out of the till. The children are all busy and, yes, they are engaged but these superficial activities have little of the promise of dynamic role play. Enter the adult in role as a confused older person; can't remember what they came in for, can't remember what they needed for tea and needs help getting home. At once the 'play' takes on a perceptively different quality. No longer are the boys playing tag with the money but as shopkeepers working out what I need. They patiently explain that I must pay for my shopping when I try to just walk out. Kisha uses the phone to call 'my house' to confirm the orders, to arrange a lift home, to tell my family off for sending me to the shops on my own. They use language in sophisticated ways, have a developed understanding of morality and display an ability to solve complex problems that would never had occurred if they had been left to themselves, to the phone and the till.

I don't know if you have ever watched young children like Kisha, Ashok and Michael when they are involved in role-play games; I mean really *watched* and not just seen them while they're playing. What they are able to do is quite amazing. One of the most fascinating things for me is the way that they are able to negotiate the rules of the game and what is going on without ever seeming to formally agree on them. The game just rolls and turns, and they all seem to instinctively understand. Now, clearly there is more to it than that and, as we go through this chapter, we'll look in a bit more detail at what these things might be. But seeing as the children appear to be able to do this so effortlessly wouldn't it be great if we as educators could use this ability to help *us* teach *them*?

There are a number of ways in which this could be done. We could just let children get on with it by themselves, as Kisha, Ashok and Michael were doing, but, from all that I have seen, they can get even more out of the experience if we, as adults, join them (see Goouch, Chapter 3). We can shape the game as in the example above, help give it structure, reinforce areas of learning as we go along, challenging them without ever having to be heavy handed and teaching 'formally'. What I'm saying is if this form of play is so valuable that we encourage children to do it, why don't we get involved as well? It's a bit like saying 'You know that reading thing that I'm trying to get you to do? Well if it's OK with you, *I'll* just watch'! In my experience the reason that this wonderful opportunity is not made more of in early years settings has nothing to do with the children but has much more to do with the adults who seem to find it *so* hard to join in.

My task, then, over the next few pages is to offer a few reasons why we should sit on the floor and pretend that the bus is late, or hide in the corner pretending that the Gruffalo is coming to get us. For me this is analogous to encouraging children to read and enjoy books. What we do is share books with children, we read with them, we talk about what has happened and what might be going to happen, we model good practice by allowing them to see us reading (see Whitehead, Chapter 5). We would think it very strange if people tried to develop reading solely by giving the children lots of books to look at. Sharing and participation is good practice and yet, when it comes to fantasy play, at worst (and I know this is a bit of a cliché but I have seen it), we tell the children to go into the corner and make up a story.

There has been growing interest in the way that young children use fantasy play within their basic strategies for learning (Smilansky and Sheftaya 1990; Broadhead 2004; Edgington 2004; Wood 2004). It is seen as a powerful and dynamic tool to engage children in the learning process (Kitson and Spiby 1997). Children seem to develop the ability to engage in fantasy play by themselves independent of educational environments. While it is accepted that these activities are a 'good thing' and situations are provided to allow children the opportunity to involve themselves in such play, what is less widespread is the study of the adults involved becoming part of that learning process.

There is the belief among some adults working with children that we should view children's play as sacred, as being for children only, and feel that fantasy play, even more than other forms of play, allows children to operate without adults almost as a form of therapy (see Georgeson and Payler, Chapter 2, and Howard, Chapter 13). Clearly, engaging in such activities allows children a sense of intellectual freedom – it is their story played out to their evolving rules. My concern is that from all of the work that I have observed (Kitson and Spiby 1997), children will frequently repeat very similar if not identical forms of play, engage in very similar role-play activity, model the same if not identical behaviours, and resolve similar problems time after time. If playing the same fantasy game over and over, children will have only a limited cognitive area in which to develop and grow their thinking, their skills and their imagination (Hendy and Toon 2001).

Effective intervention can channel children's learning, helping them to construct new problems and challenges, encouraging and supporting individuals, and extending and motivating language performance and ability (see Manning-Morton and Thorp 2003; Duffy, Chapter 8). Perhaps we should learn to see this as *engaging in learning* rather than *intervening*. By engaging with children's learning we are also structuring the learning, not by telling children what to do but rather offering them a scaffold, around which they can intellectually explore (Parker-Rees 2004; Dolya 2009). This then is the crux, as it were, of my argument – this is the case for adult intervention.

So what do we mean by fantasy play?

Children engage in a wide variety of play activities – this can be seen throughout the chapters of this book. Fantasy will occur at differing levels within individual children's play and games and at different levels of maturity. Socio-dramatic play is, for the most part, concerned with the nature of role and of social interaction, while other types of play involve bodily activity or the use and exploration of objects (see Part 3 of this book for examples). At its simplest, it can be argued that there are four main types of play – functional play, constructive play, rule-governed play and socio-dramatic play – and the one that we are most concerned with here is socio-dramatic play.

In socio-dramatic play children demonstrate a growing awareness of their social surroundings, consciously acting out social interactions and experiencing human relationships actively by means of symbolic representation. The key difference between socio-dramatic play and dramatic play is that in the latter children can pretend on their own. They can act out a situation to the exclusion of others, while the more mature socio-dramatic play, as Smilansky and Shefatya (1990) define it, requires interaction, communication and cooperation. Dramatic play is imitative, it draws upon first- or second-hand experiences, and uses real or imaginary objects (Hendy and Toon 2001; Rogers and Evans 2008). This play becomes socio-dramatic play if the theme is elaborated in cooperation with at least one other person and the participants interact with each other in both *action* and *speech.*

Smilansky and Sheftaya (1990: 22) suggest six elements necessary for fantasy play, as follows.

1   *Imitative role play:* the child undertakes a make-believe role and expresses it in imitative action and/or verbalisation.
2   *Make-believe with regard to toys:* movements or verbal declarations and/or materials or toys that are not replicas of the object itself are substituted for real objects.
3   *Verbal make-believe with regard to actions and situations:* verbal descriptions or declarations are substituted for actions or situations.
4   *Persistence in role play:* the child continues within a role or play theme for a period of at least 10 minutes.
5   *Interaction:* at least two players interact within the context of the play episode.
6   *Verbal communication:* there is some verbal interaction related to the play episode.

The first four of these apply to dramatic play but the last two define only *socio-dramatic* play. This difference can be illustrated with a couple of examples.

Three-year-old Joseph puts a cape on his shoulders and runs around the nursery saying, 'I'm Batman. I'm flying and I'm getting the baddies.' This behaviour has elements of 1 and 3 present, so it can be defined as dramatic play. In another example, two girls are playing 'hospital' in the doctor's surgery. They are wearing white coats and are giving each other instructions such as, 'I'll go and use the phone.' Questions like, 'Can I have the listening thing now?' and statements such as, 'I've got the medicine spoon' suggest elements of imitative role play are present; they are acting but not *interacting* – merely informing each other what is going on. They are engaging at the very basic level of socio-dramatic play.

Contrast this with two children pretending to build a house together for a pigeon, using make-believe tools, talking and acting as if they are doing the job, sharing their ideas and developing the story together; this would be an example of higher-level socio-dramatic play as elements 2, 3, 4, 5 *and* 6 are present. This is a richer, more involving form of play offering the children who are playing more opportunities to learn by testing things out. Bolton (1979) would argue that all socio-dramatic play and drama is a metaphor for the children's lives, and that it is the function of the teacher to help the children to reflect on the significance of their play in order to learn from it. And what better place to reflect from than from within the drama as a part of the story?

Why is socio-dramatic play important?

Key to the value of socio-dramatic play is the psychological benefits drawn from the theories of Freud, Piaget and Bruner. Although it is a crude distinction, one can look at the research in terms of psychoanalytic theory, as exemplified by Freud (1961), and of cognitive processing theory, as suggested by Piaget, to which can be added the more functionalist views put forward by Bruner (see Howard, Chapter 13). Irrespective of their differing views on the contribution to child development, all three stress the importance of fantasy play and argue for its inclusion in the ongoing education of individuals (Edgington 2004).

Freud saw fantasy as a way to gain access to the psyche. Emphasising the function of the child's instincts in fantasy play, he suggested that through play children will show their 'inner selves'. Play becomes like a mirror to the child's subconscious.

Piaget examined fantasy play in terms of assimilation and accommodation. He set up the theoretical notion of 'schema' (a collection of associated ideas) to which new ideas and new relationships of existing ideas are conjoined through experiences. This process he calls assimilation. In fantasy play the fantasy elements within the play can be assimilated into a particular schema. If children make up a story about going on a journey, they draw upon existing knowledge of journeys (their existing schema) and add to it any new information obtained through the play. As a result, new interconnections will be made. Fantasy play can help children test out ideas and concepts, and help them make sense mainly through assimilation (Bruce 2001).

Through their fantasy play, children create new pretend situations. These can contain within them a wide range of seemingly unconnected elements all drawn from the child's previous experiences. Fantasy acts as a way of unifying experiences, knowledge and understanding, helping the child to discover and control the links between the individual components. Young children engaged in a fantasy about a space journey will selectively combine a wide range of components about 'space' and 'journeys'. They will consider what it is like to go on a journey, how to get ready, how time does not stand still during absence, how good it feels to arrive; and they will consider aspects of space, such as darkness, distance, and the need for oxygen and special clothes.

The manifestation of the fantasy element (the play) develops as the child grows older. According to Piaget, children progress through stages of functional play, through dramatic play and on to socio-dramatic play (Cole-Hamilton and Gill 2002). Throughout, children bring to the fantasy play existing knowledge, skills and understanding of the world, which they then assimilate within existing schema or create new and novel interconnections (Wood 2004).

Bruner *et al.* (1976) see fantasy play as a precursor for social rules. What we learn through fantasy play forms the basis of rule-governed behaviour. They illustrate this through simple peek-a-boo games played by young children, showing how these lead to the development of structured interactions with turn taking. I have noticed that the fantasy element in play, which develops up until about the age of 7, slowly becomes submerged if it is not sustained and actively encouraged. These observations are supported by Singer and Singer (1990), who suggest that fantasy play goes underground at around 7 years of age, to manifest itself later either as daydreaming or outward expressions of internal thought such as poetry, art or theatre.

What is needed in the early years is the development and extension of fantasy play, the legitimising of it, so that children themselves can come to understand the value of it. Through this play considerable learning about people's lives, human interactions, the workings of society and the individual's role within it can take place. Children can begin to learn to cope with life, and with a range of complex social issues such as failure, loneliness and disappointment. Bolton (1979) argues that all socio-dramatic play and drama is a metaphor for the children's lives, and that it is the function of the teacher to enable the children to reflect on the significance of their play in order to learn from it. Singer and Singer (1990: 152) suggest, 'Imaginative play is fun, but in the midst of the joys of making believe, children may also be preparing for the reality of more effective lives.'

We can see that there is a value in fantasy play, and that it has therapeutic, diagnostic and cognitive developmental functions. This is something of a paradox for educators: while cognitive growth is enhanced by fantasy/socio-dramatic play, the very fact of this cognitive development will mean that children have less need of the fantasy in order to explore simple behaviour patterns and motives through observation of those immediately around them. Peters and Sherratt (2002) shed some light on why fantasy play should begin to

disappear around the age of 7. They support the idea that the increasing influence the child actually has on the world, coupled with the decreased need
to test out and explore family roles and the development of reading, enable
children to open up and explore new horizons without the need for fantasy
play. Educators need to move children beyond these immediate horizons
so that they can begin to look at the deeper level of 'role' and the greater
complexity of life. For this to happen, children need to be challenged.

Socio-dramatic play in action

There is a sound argument in both psychodynamic and cognitive developmental theories for the specific benefits of encouraging children to engage
in fantasy play. The advantages of assimilation and role learning are clear, but
how might these be developed in an early years context? The potential benefits to be gained from fantasy play are difficult to quantify but we can discuss
them in general terms. Singer and Singer (1990) identify three areas where the
benefits of fantasy play can be seen:

1   actual spontaneous verbal output (around 50 per cent) in socio-
    dramatic play
2   a corresponding increase in social interaction
3   a significant improvement across a range of cognitive skills after
    'training' in imaginative play.

Singer and Singer (1990: 151) go on to provide clear evidence that the benefits
to children's learning, self-awareness, language complexity and adaptability
go well beyond this.

Smilansky (1968) proposes a range of generalisations relating to the value
of socio-dramatic play that show how socio-dramatic play can influence the
creativity, intellectual growth and social skills of the child. Among Smilansky's
generalised notions of the benefits of socio-dramatic play are the following:

1   Creating new combinations out of experiences.
2   Selectivity and intellectual discipline.
3   Discrimination of the central features of a role sequence.
4   Heightened concentration.
5   Enhanced self-awareness and self-control.
6   Self-discipline within the role context (e.g. a child who is
    playing a special role within a game might inhibit crying
    because the character in the game would not cry).
7   The acquisition of flexibility and empathy towards others.
8   The development of an intrinsic set of standards.

9   Acquisition of a sense of creativity and capacity to control personal responses

10   Development of cooperative skills since make-believe games in groups require effective give and take.

11   Awareness of the potential use of the environment for planning and other play situations.

12   Increased sensitivity to alternative role possibilities so that the notion of father need not be one's own father but may include many kinds of behaviour associated with the broader concept of fathering.

13   Increased capacity for the development of abstract thought by learning first to substitute the image for the overt action and then later a verbal coding for both the action and the image.

14   Heightened capacity for generalization.

15   A step towards vicarious learning and a greater use of modelling.

(Smilansky in Singer 1973: 224)

It appears that there is evidence that fantasy play provides an opportunity for the child to gain ready access to these opportunities.

Having spent a lot of time with young children, watching them and being part of their fantasy play, it is important to highlight the role that fantasy play has in the development of morality (Peters 1981; Winston 2000). Children test out their ideas and attitudes in a number of different situations and practice what will happen in real life but within the safety of the enactment. Social contact is important to young children and, as Blank-Grief (1976) indicates, role play serves to imitate and facilitate the contact: children develop the social skills they will need later in life.

Why should adults join in children's socio-dramatic and fantasy play?

So far we have talked in general terms about how young children engage in fantasy play, but one of the most valuable contributions that adults can make to such fantasy play is their own involvement. By becoming part of the socio-dramatic play, the adult can capitalise upon the great learning potential outlined above. Skilful interaction can stimulate and act as a catalyst (Moyles 1989), help focus the children's attention and set up challenges (Heathcote 1984), all of which enhance and deepen the child's experiences through intervention in fantasy. It is worth considering here what the writer Vygotsky refers to as the theory the 'zone of proximal development'. An excellent exploration of these theories has been set out by Doyla (2009). What is argued here is that selective interventions on the part of the adults can make the zone of proximal development and the corresponding learning more precise. Children need to be encouraged to struggle with ideas, concepts and morality. In such activities failure doesn't exist since both adults and children are working with fantasy: nothing of the real world has been altered; nothing has changed.

Do we mean interfere or intervene?

As with most forms of play, socio-dramatic play has a structure and rules but, as Garvey (1976) points out, these are often subsumed as part of the action. At first glance this structure is not apparent, but it is there nonetheless. Social play needs rules that we all understand in order for the interaction to take place. Interventions do not mean taking over: they allow for the development of structure within the children's socio-dramatic play. The adult becoming part of the play can facilitate the implementation of the rules as well as act as a behavioural model for the children to copy. Garvey (1976) further points out that in order to play we must understand what is *not* play. It is useful to identify clearly for the children when socio-dramatic play is taking place. This can be done very effectively by the adult working with the children saying, 'We are going to make up a story', or 'We are going to make up a play.' In this way the children are clear about the expectations of the activity and also have a much clearer idea of when they are, and are not, involved in the fantasy. As Rogers and Evans (2008) illustrate, it is equally important for the adult to make it really clear when the socio-dramatic play is over. This is merely the formalisation of what children do for themselves. Their play will begin with, 'Let's pretend . . .' and will terminate when either the rules are broken or the children move away from the activity with, 'I'm not playing any more!' (Garvey 1976: 176).

Any episode of socio-dramatic play entails the exercises of shared imagination and the shared development of the theme of that particular episode. By selective interventions, able adults can monitor the negotiation of the children's ideas and act as facilitators. They can help the children remain consistent within their role and so aid the development of the story. One of the great strengths of this way of working is that, through the fiction, a great many learning areas can be explored. Problems can be set up that children can resolve within the story. The adult working within the fiction is able to set the problems and then keep the children on task, so making them confront the challenges. For example, in a children's story in which they have to get past the queen who guards the gate and into the castle, by persuading the queen to let them into the castle the children are employing and extending social skills.

Their preferred solution may well have been to employ magic but such a solution would have merely avoided the social learning potential generated.

Intervention in socio-dramatic play enables the participating adult to keep the activity going by motivating the children to persist. While some children engage in such play readily, others need to be guided and encouraged to play a full part. The adult can help to refocus the story in order to bring the group together and generate excitement by introducing *tension* into the story. These are both difficult for young children to attain for themselves. Working in a nursery school with a group of 18 children, I was asked to make up a drama on the theme of 'building'. The children wanted to make up a story about building a house for the people in a book that had been read to them. After sorting out what had to be done, the work started. It was not long before the children began to lose concentration in the 'building' as there was little to hold their interest. In dramatic terms there was little or no *tension*. It was at this point that intervention was needed. I pretended to receive a phone call from 'the boss', who was going to come round and check up on our work. We would have to make sure that the house had been put together properly. Immediately the children were drawn back into the fantasy play and found a renewed vigour and purpose, created by the injection of tension and the pressure of evaluation.

Equally effective could have been completing a given task in a set time (for example, 'We've got to build the hut before night comes'), meeting a challenge ('Do you think you could help me put out this fire?'), solving a problem ('What food should we give the animals now the snow's here?') or posing a dilemma for the children to work out ('But if we take the curing crystal how will the people who own it feel?'). These inputs into socio-dramatic play become the subtle tools of the adult working and playing with children. Within the play, the adult is able to enrich and deepen the play, and open up new learning areas for the children.

It is important to remember that, although the adult can guide and, to some extent, shape the socio-dramatic play, essentially the play and action must belong to the children. Their ideas must be used: words spoken must be their words expressing their thoughts. It may perhaps be that the adult simply joins in an existing 'game' with the children without the intention of simply being in the group but rather of moving the children's learning on, placing obstacles in the way of their story so that, by overcoming these obstacles, learning opportunities are created.

Another way of doing this is to construct the story with the children: 'What shall we make up a story about today?' Feeding from the children's ideas, both children and adult construct the fantasy. The adult's role is again that of facilitator, stretching and extending the children while maintaining interest and excitement. This adult participation legitimises the play and encourages the children to see what they are doing as something valuable.

Such adult participation or intervention also allows for the structuring of learning areas for the children through the selection of themes or stimulus areas (Moyles 1989). By setting up stories about post offices, the children are involved with maths, language, social skills, manipulative skills, and so on. If such pretend areas become a garage or a desert island, then a new set of learning potential is created. By selecting appropriate themes for the children's needs, the adults can then give access to appropriate areas of learning.

Is fantasy role play for all children?

Fantasy play and socio-dramatic play transcend normal barriers of learning as perceived in traditional learning settings. The ability to participate in the activity is not governed by other abilities (Peters and Sherratt 2002); rather it is governed by a willingness to participate. Although this idea has been widely explored (Sayeed and Guerin 2000; Peters and Sherratt 2002; Rogers and Evans 2008; and others), it took me a long time working with skilled practitioners to really understand it. Being part of a group who were working with a number of children with severe learning difficulties showed me that these children still got a great deal out of being part of the role play even if their participation was restricted (see Georgeson and Payler, Chapter 2). With children in mainstream education who find accessing aspects of the curriculum difficult, fantasy role play is often very liberating. Coming from a position of not succeeding, role play can enable them to achieve. Practitioners have often commented on the way that children with perceived blocks to their learning have engaged in activities associated with role play (Van Hoorn *et al.* 2003), pointing out that the children exhibit very few of the frustrations and tensions shown when they engage with other subjects. Fantasy role play offers a different way of learning, focusing on different sets of skills that allow young children to develop a different kind of world around them.

Conclusion

In this chapter, I have argued that adults should participate some of the time in children's fantasy role play as a tool to develop learning. We looked first at the development of fantasy play, at the evidence supporting the need for adult intervention in such activities and opportunities for cognitive development. Links were made to learning development and accessibility for all children. It was emphasised that adult interaction has to be sympathetic to the needs of the children and operate within their fantasy. The adult's role is to provide a structure within which the children can interact – this was referred to as a scaffold – to challenge and set up problems to be solved, to encourage children to test out ideas and, perhaps more importantly, to open up personal learning strategies to the children. Practitioners may also find that they thoroughly enjoy, and learn from, role playing themselves!

Some questions to set you thinking

1 If you don't do so already, what stops you from engaging with the children in fantasy and socio-dramatic play? If you do engage in fantasy play with the children what do you feel are the benefits?

2 Do you have particular children in your setting who might be able to 'shine' through involvement in role-play contexts?

3 What is the potential within your setting for developing socio-dramatic/fantasy play areas? What might these be? What are the possibilities for learning?

4 Which of Smilansky and Sheftaya's six elements of socio-dramatic play do children in your setting engage in?

References and further reading

Blank-Grief, E. (1976) Sex role playing in preschool children. In J.S. Bruner, A. Jolly and K. Sylva (eds) *Play and its Role in Evolution and Development*. Harmondsworth: Penguin.

Bolton, G. (1979) *Towards a Theory of Drama in Education*. London: Longman.

Broadhead, P. (2004) *Early Years Play and Learning: Developing Social Skills and Cooperation*. London: RoutledgeFalmer.

Bruce, T. (2001) *Helping Young Children to Learn through Play*. London: Hodder and Stoughton.

Bruner, J.S. (1976) *On Knowing: Essays for the Left Hand* (2nd edn). New York: Atheneum.

Cole-Hamilton, I. and Gill, T. (2002) *Making the Case for Play – Building Policies and Strategies for School-aged Children*. London: National Children's Bureau.

Dolya, G. (2009) *Vygotsky in Action in the Early Years: The Key to the Learning Curriculum*. London: Routledge.

Edgington, M. (2004) *The Foundation Stage Teacher in Action – Teaching 3-, 4- and 5-year-olds*. London: Paul Chapman.

Freud, S. (1961) *Beyond the Pleasure Principle*. London: Hogarth Press and the Institute of Psycho-analysis.

Garvey, C. (1976) Some properties of social play. In J.S. Bruner, A. Jolly and K. Sylva (eds) *Play: Its Role in Evolution and Development*. Harmondsworth: Penguin.

Heathcote, D. (1984) *Collected Writings*. London: Hutchinson.

Hendy, L. and Toon, L. (2001) *Supporting Drama and Imaginative Play in the Early Years*. Buckingham: Open University Press.

Kitson, N. and Spiby, I. (1997) *Drama 7–11*. London: Routledge.

Manning-Morton, J. and Thorp, M. (2003) *Key Times for Play*. Maidenhead: Open University Press.

Moyles, J. (1989) *Just Playing? The Role and Status of Play in Early Childhood Education*. Buckingham: Open University Press.

Parker-Rees, R. (2004) Moving, playing and learning: children's active exploration of their world. In J. Willan, R. Parker-Rees and J. Savage (eds) *Early Childhood Studies*. Exeter: Learning Matters.

Peters, M. and Sherratt, D. (2002) *Developing Play and Drama in Children with Autistic Spectrum Disorders*. London: David Fulton.

Peters, R.S. (1981) *Moral Development and Moral Education*. London: Allen and Unwin.

Rogers, S. and Evans, J. (2008) *Inside Role-play in Early Childhood Education*. London: Routledge.

Sayeed, Z. and Guerin, E. (2000) *Early Years Play. A Happy Medium for Assessment and Intervention*. London: David Fulton.

Singer, D. and Singer, J. (1990) *The House of Make Believe*. Cambridge, MA: Harvard University Press.

Singer, J. (1973) *The Child's World of Make-believe: Experimental Studies of Imaginative Play*. London: Academic Press.

Smilansky, S. (1968) *The Effects of Socio-dramatic Play on Disadvantaged Preschool Children*. New York: Wiley.

Smilansky, S. and Sheftaya, L. (1990) *Facilitating Play: A Medium for Promoting Cognitive, Sociocultural and Academic Development in Young Children*. Gaithersburg, MD: Psychosocial and Educational Publications.

Van Hoorn, J., Monighan-Nouret, P., Scales, B. and Rodriquez-Alward, K. (2003) *Play at the Center of the Curriculum*. New Jersey, NJ: Merrill, Prentice-Hall.

Winston, J. (2000) *Drama, Literacy and Moral Education*. London: David Fulton.

Wood, E. (2004) Developing a pedagogy of play. In A. Anning, J. Cullen and M. Fleer (eds) *Early Childhood Education*. London: Sage Publications.

PART 3
Play and curriculum

8 Art in the early years

Bernadette Duffy

Summary

In this chapter I will explore what creativity is, and why it is important to the child and the wider society. I will also be looking at the development of creativity from birth and how it is expressed in the *Early Years Foundation Stage* framework. This will be followed by a discussion of the links between creativity and the arts, and how they connect areas of learning. The ways in which adults can foster creativity through their interactions with children and the environment they create and systems for planning, recording and documenting experiences will be discussed. The crucial issues of including the child's voice and working with parents and carers are covered. The chapter will emphasise that practitioners are the most important resource children have: in our hands lies the power to hinder and curtail children's creativity, or to nourish it and watch it grow.

Introduction

This chapter emphasises the importance of creativity and the role of the arts in promoting this, drawing on our experiences at the Thomas Coram Centre. The Centre is a partnership between Camden local authority and the charity Coram, and is situated in south Camden. We serve a culturally, religiously, linguistically and economically diverse community, and 20 per cent of the children are referred as children in need.

This site has been a special place for young children for over 300 years, and a place where the arts have always been seen as important in the lives of young children. The practitioners currently working on the campus are continuing this tradition. We are committed to creativity and promoting an approach which ensures that children are encouraged to develop their own personal creative responses.

What is creativity and why is it important?

In recent years the importance of creativity has frequently been stressed: 'Creativity is good for the economy, good for the individual, good for the society and good for education' (NACCCE 1999: Preface). This view is reflected in the *Early Years Foundation Stage* (EYFS) framework (DCFS 2008), which highlights the importance of creativity in the early years of education. One of the four principles that underpin the framework emphasises the importance of creativity and critical thinking in all aspects of children's experience, and creative development is an area of learning in its own right. The recent *Independent Review of the National Curriculum* (Rose 2009) explored the transition from EYFS to KS1, and highlighted the importance of increased flexibility for young children to consolidate their learning and ensure that learning through play continues to be stressed. It is not just England that seeks to promote creativity in education: the European Union declared the European Year of Creativity and Innovation 2009 in recognition of the fundamental importance of creativity and innovation for Europe's future: 'Education should foster more innovation and creative mindsets, focusing on dealing with all-pervasive complexity, encouraging learning by doing, opportunity creation and problem solving rather than knowledge transmission' (European Union 2009).

Creativity is seen as important because it enables us to respond to a rapidly changing world and to deal with the unexpected by extending our current knowledge to new situations and using information in new ways. It encourages us to take risks, think flexibly, be innovative, play with ideas and respond imaginatively.

However, defining creativity is not easy and there is much debate about how it is characterised and identified (Gardner 1993; Fisher 2003). Part of the difficulty is that the term is applied to individuals, to a process and to products. For some, creativity is reserved for a few very gifted individuals; for others it is a human characteristic that we all possess.

Craft distinguishes between 'big C' and 'little c' creativity (Craft 2001). 'Big C creativity' involves invention and a break with past understanding – for example, the creative process engaged in by Einstein. 'Little c creativity' enables individuals to find routes and paths to travel. It is a process of conscious invention and describes the resourcefulness of ordinary people rather than extraordinary contributors. Such creativity involves originality, seeing things in fresh ways and learning from past experiences. It involves thinking along unorthodox lines, breaking barriers, using non-traditional approaches to problems and creating something, whether an idea or object. Creativity means connecting the previously unconnected in ways that are new and meaningful to the individual concerned, to make real something that you have imagined (Duffy 2006).

There has been a lot of discussion about the nature of creativity in young children. Children's creativity is best defined as creativity with a 'little c'. Children are being creative when they use materials in new ways or combine new materials; they are creative when they make discoveries that are new to them. When children are being creative they go further than the information given to create something new and original for them. For young children, the process of creativity – which includes curiosity, exploration, play and creativity – is as important as any product they may create (see Photograph 8.1).

Photograph 8.1 Is creativity a human characteristic that we all possess?

The development of creativity from birth

Children are born with a strong desire to explore the world around them and from this innate curiosity creativity develops. Just watching a young baby shows us that we are curious from birth: we want to find out about the world we are in, the people in it and how it all works. But while we are predisposed to be curious, the start of the creative process, whether this disposition develops or not, is largely the result of the environment and interactions we experience. While creativity is a human characteristic, there are also skills involved, and these need opportunities to be practised and developed. We have all seen young children who come to settings and schools full of curiosity and creativity; sadly, we have also all seen how quickly this can be suppressed when the children encounter an environment that does not value this (see Fabian and Dunlop, Chapter 15).

In recent years we have learned more and more about the brain and how it works. Gopnik *et al.* (2001) show how brain research has revolutionised our ideas about childhood, the human mind and the brain. Babies' brains are designed to enable them to make sense of the world around them. As they use their senses to explore the world, they create mental images and this helps them to make sense of new experiences by comparing them to the images they already have. As more of these images are created, connections form between them and these enable the child to make increasing sense of their environment. Creativity involves connecting the previously unconnected in ways that are new and meaningful to the individual concerned. Recent research has established that more connections, synapses, are made in the first years of life than at any other time of life.

As children grow, their ability to make connections increases as they have more information to combine and more skills to employ. As these abilities evolve, young children are able to explore an ever-widening world. They do not leave behind the interests and understandings of earlier stages but add on to these to develop an increasingly complex view of the world and their relationship to it.

Creativity and the EYFS

As previously mentioned, creativity is a key element in the EYFS and creative development is an area of learning in its own right. The EYFS states that:

> Children's creativity must be extended by the provision of support for their curiosity, exploration and play. They must be provided with opportunities to explore and share their thoughts, ideas and feelings, for example, through a variety of art, music, movement, dance, imaginative and role-play activities, mathematics, and design and technology.
>
> (DCSF 2008: 15)

The aspects of learning included under this heading are those that are often described as 'the arts':

- being creative – responding to experiences, expressing and communicating ideas
- exploring media and materials
- creating music and dance
- developing imagination and imaginative play.

The role of the arts in promoting creativity

Frequently creativity and the arts are seen as the same thing. However, involvement in the visual and performing arts does not necessarily mean involvement in creativity. Many art experiences offered to young children are dull, repetitive and far from creative; rather a way of occupying children and covering the walls; creating something does not necessarily indicate creativity. The arts do have a particular contribution to make, and when they are introduced to children in appropriate ways can enrich and stimulate. ARTS alive!, the QCA curriculum development project, identified ways in which the contribution of the arts to pupils' education can be maximised. The key message to emerge from this research is that investing in the arts can transform schools, raise standards, change attitudes, improve behaviour, and increase the quality of teaching and learning. The 2002 Arts Council of England national study of the arts in the early years also found a strong belief in the value of the arts in early years settings (Clark *et al.* 2002). By using the arts we are supporting the development of positive dispositions and providing meaningful links across the curriculum.

For example, music gives practitioners a vehicle for getting to know children as unique individuals and for bringing them together as a group, which reinforces a sense of community (see Pound, Chapter 9; Young and Glover 1998). At Thomas Coram we have been fortunate in receiving support from the National Foundation for Youth Music to develop a music programme aimed at encouraging the innate musicality of adults and children. 'Finding our Voices' is an example of one such project.

Cameo 8.1: Finding our voices

The starting point for this programme is the belief that musicality is an innate human characteristic and that involvement in music making not only gives children a chance to develop musical concepts and skills but also encourages self-esteem and well-being. As a staff team we were aware that music making was an area in which many of us lacked confidence and we needed an experienced music maker to support our own musical development alongside that of the children. We wanted music to be embedded into the life of the Centre, not to be something a music teacher does once a week with the children. Children, parents and staff attend regular music sessions with the music maker and, as staff confidence develops, they take over the sessions with the support of the music maker. The sessions are linked to the ongoing work of the Centre and the songs and music from the sessions become part of the day-to-day life of the Centre. The children also have the opportunity to listen to and work with visiting musicians from a range of musical traditions, and to share their music making with their parents and the wider community.

Creativity through the arts enables children to communicate their feelings in non-verbal and pre-verbal ways, and to express their thoughts. Translating ideas, concepts and experiences into representations involves many thinking skills. Through the arts children can:

- comprehend, respond to and represent their perceptions
- develop their understanding of the world, experience beauty and express their cultural heritage
- gain self-esteem and create a view of the world that is uniquely their own (see Photograph 8.2).

Creativity across all aspects and areas of learning

Creativity is important in its own right and also because it fosters the development of the whole child by promoting learning across the curriculum. While the EYFS has an area of learning labelled 'creative development', which might suggest that creativity is only to do with the arts, the underlying message is that creativity is part of every area of the curriculum, and all areas of learning have the potential to be creative experiences.

The creative process is as applicable to personal, social and emotional development; communication, language and literacy; problem solving, reasoning and numeracy; knowledge and understanding of the world; and physical development as it is to art, music, dance and imaginative play, as the following examples demonstrate.

- 'Personal, social and emotional development' includes dispositions and attitudes, encouraging self-confidence and social and emotional development. Creativity builds from children's curiosity and encourages a positive approach to new experiences. Children display high

Photograph 8.2   Through the arts children can comprehend, respond and represent their perceptions.

levels of involvement, and are able to select and use resources independently. Through the creative process children can develop concentration, problem solving, planning and persistence. Working together encourages a sense of self-respect and valuing of others.

- 'Communication, language and literacy' includes language for communicating and listening, and the arts offer plenty of opportunities to speak and listen – for example, when sharing resources or creating a shared dance. Reading and writing development draws on the understanding that marks can represent meaning and through this process children can understand the symbolic nature of written language (see Whitehead, Chapter 5). The fine motor skills needed for writing are best developed through meaningful, enjoyable experiences which the arts provide, for instance by manipulating materials and equipment. The narratives children develop through their imaginative play provide the basis for writing stories.

- 'Problem solving, reasoning and numeracy' are supported as concepts of shape, size, line and area are used to classify and sort objects in the visual arts. Dance provides many opportunities to explore spatial concepts, and sequencing events and objects – for example, creating a pattern on a piece of clay helps children to understand patterns.

- 'Knowledge and understanding of the world' is developed through the investigations that occur when children are presented with unfamiliar materials and resources, and exposed to a variety of materials and their properties.
- 'Physical development' is encouraged by the many opportunities to develop and practise fine motor skills – for example, through sculpting, play equipment and materials. Gross motor skills are also encouraged as children involve themselves in movement and dance, and develop body control, balance, coordination and poise.

The voice of the child

The arts have an important role in ensuring that the child's voice is heard (Lancaster 2003). For instance, drawing offers us an insight into children's thinking. Drawing is about looking and the particular things children choose to look at and to draw are likely to be those that have special relevance for them. The content of children's imaginative play also gives us an insight into their preoccupations – for example, the superhero play in which many young boys often engage (Holland 2003; see also Kitson, Chapter 7). But we need to be aware that our attitudes may stop us listening to the voice of the child. Anning and Ring (2004) found that boys' use of drawing for meaning making was unacknowledged by practitioners until they were at the stage of visual realism. Holland (2003) also found practitioners reluctant or unable to accept the child's voice in superhero play. Children with disabilities and special needs can also remain unheard (see Georgeson and Payler, Chapter 2). In some cases, access to the arts is limited because programmes for the children focus on what they cannot do and practitioners concentrate on plugging the gaps. In other cases, lack of imagination on the part of the adults leads to children not having access because the additional support they may need is not forthcoming. Hearing children's voices can occur in many different contexts, such as the following example (Cameo 8.2).

Cameo 8.2: Camden Dance Festival

During the regular music and movement session we had found that, for many children, the medium of dance enabled them to express themselves in a way that words cannot do. Children from Thomas Coram were invited to take part in Camden's Dance Festival. This involved working with dancers to create a dance and then performing this at a local theatre alongside children and young people from Camden's primary and secondary schools. Initially, we had concerns about such young children taking part in a public performance, as we did not want the children to feel pressurised to live up to adult expectations. However, since taking part in the Festival we have revised our ideas. For the children, the experience of being performers in a proper theatre with a real audience has been a magical one. There has been the excitement of going backstage and finding out what happens behind the curtain. Then there has been the pleasure of appearing before an appreciative audience, sharing their work with the wider community and knowing that their voices have been heard. The increase in confidence and self-esteem has been marked.

The role of the adult

The socio-cultural context children experience has a strong influence on their development. Children receive messages from the society they are growing up in related to their cultural identity or gender, and it is clear that young children are interested in these and explore the role models they see around them. While it is essential that children develop a positive self-image, part of which involves their identification with others of the same gender or culture, we need to make sure that this does not limit their access to creative experiences. The challenge is to confront stereotypes that limit access, and offer experiences that extend children's horizons.

The way in which the adults frame an experience is crucial to how the children perceive it and how it motivates them to join in or to avoid the activity. Learning is a communal activity and children's dispositions are very influenced by the adults around them (Anning and Ring 2004).

In order for creativity to flourish it is necessary for the child to be actively involved in the process of learning (Prentice 2000). Creative teaching is an art; it involves practitioners in using their imagination to make learning more interesting, exciting and effective. Creative teaching involves taking risks, leaving the security of structured lessons behind and learning from the children (NACCCE 1999), such as in the dolls' house project (Cameo 8.3).

Cameo 8.3: Dolls' house project

Tom, a teacher at the Centre, was discussing presents with his key group of 3 and 4 year olds. The children decided that they would like to make a dolls' house as a present to themselves and the other children at the Centre. While this was not what

Tom had planned to do with the children, he felt that he should capitalise on the children's enthusiasm for the project. With Tom's help the children spent time researching how to make a house. What did they need to include in their design? How did the different pieces fit together? What were the best materials to use? They used the woodwork skills they had previously acquired to construct the frame and, during the process, had plenty of opportunity to understand why accurate measuring is important. Once the structure was complete they used their knowledge of paint to create wallpaper for each room, and designed and made furniture. Tom documented the process as they worked, especially the children's comments. He used this to plan retrospectively, to look at what the children had learned and relate this to the different areas of learning, demonstrating the cross-curricular nature of creativity. The children had meaningful opportunities to develop mathematical concepts and real reasons to communicate clearly. Working together was essential and the particular skills of different children were used. Boys and girls worked collaboratively on the project and once the house was complete it was interesting to see how much the boys in particular enjoyed playing with it, developing and acting out their own stories.

The Effective Provision of Preschool Education project (Sylva *et al.* 2003) stresses the importance of adult–child interactions. A child's freely chosen play offers many opportunities to promote learning when practitioners recognise its importance and interact with children while they play. We can support learning through modelling possible ways to explore the materials and demonstrating to the children how they might use the new materials and equipment. Open-ended questioning is also very important as are pondering comments or thinking out loud – for example, the adult pondering 'I wonder why that happened?' or 'I wonder what would happen if I add more water?' These comments draw the children's attention to possibilities but do not put them under pressure to find a right answer.

However, when it comes to interacting with children about their art representations many practitioners are not confident (OfSTED 2002). There seems to be a reluctance to intervene based on a fear that this may adversely affect or curtail natural creativity. But when adults intervene with sensitivity and understanding this can deepen children's understanding (see also Kitson, Chapter 7). To intervene effectively we need to have an understanding of creative and artistic concepts, developments and processes, and the vocabulary to discuss them with children. It is also crucial that we tune in to children's preoccupation and understand what they are trying to do. Are they interested in the properties of the materials or resources and their possibilities? Are they exploring concepts such as shape, colour or pattern, pitch or texture? Is their interest in the capturing of a feeling, movement or image from the world around them? It is also important to know when to be silent, pause before speaking and give children the opportunity to speak first. We may help by focusing their attention on a particular part of their representation, recalling experiences to encourage them to make associations and introducing them to the work of others. Hypothesising or making suggestions can also be helpful, especially when the child seems to be experiencing frustration and needs support towards the next step. It is important to give children time to reflect on their work by not taking away work too soon and remembering that it is never too early to discuss with children how their images work (Matthews 2003).

The creative environment

The EYFS framework has enabling environments as one of its four principles, and practitioners are encouraged to create an environment that stimulates children's creativity, originality and expressiveness inside and outside. Each setting will offer its own possibilities and we need to see how we can maximise this potential. Creativity is about making meaningful connections, using ideas and materials in new ways, and the organisation of space and resources will largely determine whether children can do this.

It is important that there is sufficient space to work and easily accessible material and tools. Without access to resources it is hard for children to demonstrate their creativity, especially when trying to create two- and three-dimensional representations. The range of resources we provide will determine what and how the children can create, and how creative they can be. Access to a range of resources enables children to choose the best medium for a particular representation.

The creative process also takes time. Children need sufficient time to explore, to develop ideas and to finish working at these ideas. This means that we need to think about the organisation of the available time to ensure that the children have as much of it as possible to engage in creative experiences. Lack of time is often cited as a reason for curtailing children's creativity, especially in Year R when the perceived demands of the numeracy and literacy strategies seem to eat into the time available. This is an opportunity for practitioners to engage their own creativity! A cross-curricular approach allows us to draw on the appeal and potential of the arts to encourage learning and development in all areas of the curriculum. Such an approach enables children to deepen understanding and make creative connections, and helps practitioners to 'join up' the curriculum. Through the arts, children acquire a range of skills and understandings that are transferable to areas such as literacy or numeracy.

The setting alone cannot provide all that children need and it is important to recognise the role of the wider community in developing children's

Photograph 8.3 Practitioners need to think about time, to ensure that children have as much of it as possible to engage in creative experiences.

creativity. Children are part of the wider creative community, and benefit from the opportunity to work alongside artists, musicians and crafts people, as in the following example (Cameo 8.4).

Cameo 8.4: Case study – the sculpture project

The children at Thomas Coram have had the opportunity to work with artists from our local gallery, the October Gallery. The starting point for this particular project was a practical one – creating seats for the courtyard entrance to the nursery. Artists from the October Gallery worked with the children to create designs for the seats based on animal forms. The practical aspects (how to make the seats stand up) and the aesthetic aspects (how to create pleasing shapes) were both explored. Drawing up prototypes to try out ideas was a new experience for the children, as was the process of selecting the best designs from a range. Working with the artists gave the children a chance to develop new skills, such as drawing up designs, and to work with new materials, such as concrete and tiles. The opportunity to work with a group of artists for over a year meant that children, staff and artists developed an understanding of each other and real relationships were formed. While the process was important, the end results are also very important to the children. The animals they have created to sit on are very precious to them and have become part of the nursery – a number of children greet each animal in the morning and say farewell at the end of the day.

Planning for creativity

There is no single system of planning that suits all settings and all children all the time – it is not a case of 'one size fits all'. But there are principles that should underpin the systems we choose to use. Too often young children are given access to a narrow, limited and superficial range of creative experiences. For example, opportunities to paint can be restricted to using a small number of ready-mixed paints, with no choice of brush or paper texture, size or shape. Freely chosen play activities often provided the best opportunities for adults to extend children's thinking (Sylva *et al.* 2003). Planning for creativity should include time for extending child-initiated play as well as time for adult-initiated experiences (Featherstone and Featherstone 2009).

Practitioners need to differentiate the experiences they present and to match the learning experiences to the needs of the individual children. As there is no prescribed end product, individual children are able to use the materials and ideas in a way that matches their own learning needs. The adult's expertise is in enabling children to develop mastery and the freedom to explore by introducing them to the skills and concepts they need at the time they need them.

Planning should be based on observations of individual children's needs and interests, relate to their previous experiences and actively involve the children. The experiences need to be introduced to the children in ways that excite their curiosity and allow plenty of time for exploration and play. When reviewing the experiences offered, practitioners should reflect on how the children have responded to them, why they have used materials or ideas in a particular way, and how to extend the experiences offered.

Recording and documenting

It is as important to record and document children's artistic development as with any other area of the curriculum (see Papatheodorou, Chapter 17). It is especially important to record the processes as well as any end products.

Portfolios for individual children enable progress to be tracked over time and offer the children an insight into their own learning. Documenting the ways in which groups of children work together on common projects is also important. Digital photography can be used to record individual children's progress with accompanying notes, and to create displays complete with children's comments on their learning. It is also useful to record episodes of play to reflect on with others – the children, in team meetings and with parents. Video offers the opportunity to stand back and view the bigger picture.

Working with parents and carers

The importance of working in partnership with parents is a key theme in the EYFS and this is especially true when it comes to encouraging creativity. Some practitioners express concern and, on occasion, annoyance at certain parents' unwillingness to allow their children freely to explore materials such as paint or clay. In turn, some parents are confused by the practitioner's view that making a mess is important, especially when it involves doing things that are often actively discouraged at home! It is important that practitioners develop a dialogue with parents that enables them to discuss children's creative development, and work together to support and encourage it (see Fabian and Dunlop, Chapter 15). Hands-on joint workshops for parents and children are a good way of introducing parents to painting and drawing, and enabling them to experience at first hand the pleasure and learning children acquire from these materials. Inviting parents to come and make music with their children not only gives parents an insight into the benefits for their child but also strengthens the adult–child bond.

Conclusion

Children are not empty vessels but are creative in their own right, and indeed have much to teach us about being creative. Children are freer from inhibitions about what ought to be and so are more open to possibilities. They have their own ideas and thoughts, their own desire to create. Our responsibility is to ensure that we build on children's current skills and understandings, and expand this by providing new opportunities that develop their attitudes skills and knowledge across a broad range of experiences. Our challenge is to nurture, develop and support each child.

Questions to set you thinking

1 Think over the last week – how have you supported and developed your own and the children's creativity?

2 Think of three things you can do during the next week to develop:

- your creativity as a teacher
- the children's creativity.

3 What kind of creative arts projects might children in your setting engage in over the next year?

References and further reading

Anning, A. and Ring, K. (2004) *Making Sense of Children's Drawings*. Maidenhead: Open University Press.

Clark, A., Heptinstall, E., Simon, A. and Moss, P. (2002) *The Arts in the Early Years: A National Study of Policy and Practice*. London: Arts Council in England.

Craft, A. (2001) Little c creativity. In A. Craft, B. Jeffrey and M. Leibling (eds) *Creativity in Education*. London: Continuum.

Department of Children, Schools and Families (DCSF) (2008) *The Early Years Foundation Stage Framework (EYFS)*. London: HMSO.

Duffy, B. (2006) *Creativity and Imagination in the Early Years*. Maidenhead: Open University Press.

European Union (2009) Manifesto for creativity and innovation in Europe. Brussels, Belgium: European Commission. Available online at: http://www.create2009.europa.eu (accessed 14 November 2009).

Featherstone, S. and Featherstone, P. (eds) (2009) *Like Bees Not Butterflies: Child-initiated Learning in the Early Years*. Market Bosworth: Featherstone Education.

Fisher, R. (2003) Understanding creativity: a challenging concept. *Primary Leadership Paper*, 10 September. London: NAHT.

Gardner, H. (1993) *Creating Minds*. New York: Basic Books.

Gopnik, A., Metfzoff, A. and Kuhl, P. (2001) *How Babies Think*. London: Phoenix.

Holland, P. (2003) *We Don't Play with Guns Here: War, Weapons and Superhero Play in the Early Years*. Milton Keynes: Open University Press.

Lancaster, P. (2003) *Listening to Children*. Milton Keynes: Open University Press.

Matthews, J. (2003) *Drawing and Painting: Children and Visual Representation*. London: Hodder & Stoughton.

National Advisory Committee on Creativity and Cultural Education (NACCCE) (1999) *All Our Futures – Creativity, Culture and Education*. London: DfEE.

Office for Standards in Education (OfSTED) (2002) *The Curriculum in Successful Primary Schools*. London: HMSO.

Prentice, R. (2000) Creativity: a reaffirmation of its place in early childhood education. *The Curriculum Research Journal*, 11(2): 145–158.

Qualification and Curriculum Authority (QCA) (undated) *Art's Alive*. London: QCA.

Rose, J. (2009) *Independent Review of the Primary Curriculum*. London: Department for Children, Families and Schools (DCFS).

Sylva, K., Melhuish, E.C., Sammons, P., Siraj-Blatchford, I. and Taggart, B. (2003) *Findings from the Pre-school Period: Summary of Findings*. London: Institute of Education, University of London/DfES.

Young, S. and Glover, J. (1998) *Music in the Early Years*. Milton Keynes: Open University Press.

9 Playing music

Linda Pound

Summary

In this chapter the term 'playing music' is considered and compared with the language used to describe other playful and creative experiences. The biological functions of play and music are discussed, and their role in learning and development explored. These include a sense of group cohesiveness, supporting memory and the reflection or representation of mood. The importance of including playful music in the curriculum is emphasised, including physicality, which is an integral part of music making in young children. I discuss the ways in which music can be made more playful by giving more opportunities for improvisation, rather than simply playing the music dictated by others; song writing, an activity that most young children engage in spontaneously, but that disappears since practitioners largely ignore it; and physical action, now recognised as essential to all learning.

Introduction

In an effort to convince parents and policy makers that play is of value in school, there was a period during the later part of the twentieth century in early childhood education where everything that happened in the nursery or other early years setting was described as work. Children were asked whether they wished to work in the sand, work in the home corner or work with the blocks. It was hoped that this strategy would give essentially playful activities status, and enable them to be seen as serious and productive. It did nothing, however, actually to present play itself as either serious or productive. The lessons of neuroscience and developmental psychology are supporting educators in seeing not only that 'play is fun with serious consequences' (Greenfield

1996: 75) but that play, along with music and interaction, appears to be part of every child's learning repertoire from their earliest days (Trevarthen 1998). In essence, play (and, as this chapter will demonstrate, music) is not just fun, it is also of fundamental importance.

The way in which we describe musical activity in everyday life gives some interesting clues to its relationship with play. Our choice of the term 'playing music' contrasts with the language we use in relation to other subject areas or areas of the curriculum. We would not talk of working with musical instruments nor would we suggest playing painting. Although we use the expression 'playing music' in everyday life for a vast range of activities ranging from concert pianists to a rap CD, we do not generally describe many of the music-making activities that go on in the classroom as playing music. While we talk of children playing instruments, we generally describe other activities simply as singing, dancing or listening to music. We do not generally ask if they would like to play with songs or play dancing.

In other areas of the arts, while we may talk to children about playing (or working) with clay, we are more likely to describe their artistic endeavours as painting, drawing or dancing. Artists do not generally talk about playing painting, playing sculpture or playing dance, although we know that engagement in these creative acts involves a great deal of playful activity. Picasso and Mozart, for example, are frequently characterised as essentially childlike in their passionate and creative behaviour.

Perhaps less surprisingly, people rarely talk about playing mathematics or playing physics. Yet it is said that Richard Feynman's Nobel prize-winning work in physics sprang from playing in the canteen with paper plates. Seymour Papert, inventor of Logo – software that enabled children to create their own programs – describes his childhood passion for playing with gears and other rotating objects. He goes on to describe his excitement and to generalise this to all learning – the exploration and passion being seen as vital components (1980). Shakuntala Devi, acclaimed by the *Guinness Book of Records* as the world's fastest human computer, states that, at the age of 3, she 'fell in love with numbers'. She continues: 'Numbers were toys with which I could play' (Devi 1990: 9).

Small (1998) suggests that the word music should be used as a verb – musicking – to remind us that being engaged in music (either playing it or listening to it) is an active process that involves others. The term 'playing music' does of course denote action but is not in everyday language applied to all areas of musical activity in the comprehensive way that Small envisages. Although, as indicated above, we *play* recorded music, we do not play live music – we merely listen to it! Small would describe all such activities as musicking. Since music appears to have a particular place in our vocabulary we can speculate that music may also have a particular place in our living and playing.

What is music for?

Since musicking is a universal feature of human endeavour we can speculate that it has a biological purpose. In all societies, music plays a number of important functions or roles in human living and learning (Pound and Harrison 2003).

Music supports social interaction and group identity

The development of group cohesion through music can be seen in places of worship and at football matches, in armies and in the performance of school songs. It is evident in the way in which educators use song in particular to hold the interest of a group of children coming, for example, to sit on the carpet for story time.

Cameo 9.1

Three-year-old Joshua found it difficult to leave an activity. Staff found that, having given forewarning of story time, sitting quietly on the carpet and singing familiar songs helped Joshua to join the group. He no longer needed constant reminders but joined in happily, feeling like a member of the group.

Bowman (2004: 44) describes music as essentially a matter of identity 'as much a matter of who [children] become as what they do'. This is also evident throughout life – both in the fiercely defined types of pop music and in the clientele attending the opera house. Music is culturally specific, and even very young children recognise and enjoy music that has cultural significance. Siegel (1999) suggests that cultural awareness is among our earliest memories.

More recent research (Cross and Morley 2009) suggests that the combination of play and music is particularly effective in developing the level of interaction and bonding required to foster the engagement of babies and children in a community. Their research indicates that play and music have a number of features in common. In addition to learning through action and exploration, and creating 'self-stimulating fun' (Cross and Morley 2009: 73), both help to develop negotiation and cooperation.

Music helps to create and express or reflect particular atmospheres or moods

This is evident in everyday life – at funerals and parties, in hotel lobbies or supermarkets, the choice of music helps to put even the apparently passive listener into a particular frame of mind. As adults we are often highly discerning about whether a particular piece of music will suit our mood – either in reflecting it or in helping us to overcome it. We may choose music to relax, revive or rally us. This function is also evident in the universal use of lullabies and soothing songs with young children. Not even babies and toddlers are exempt from the energising influence of music – even before they can move independently, a piece of lively music will have them bouncing and waving excitedly.

Hargreaves (2004) has described music as 'a sound track to life', suggesting, perhaps conservatively, that around 40 per cent of our time is accompanied by music – listening, singing, whistling, and so on. This inevitably means that our responses are being shaped by the choice of music being heard.

Cameo 9.2

When 10-month-old Layla joined the nursery, to help her get to sleep she needed a recording of the familiar lullaby her mother sang to her. As she settled she began to associate the singing of 'Happy birthday' with a celebration and was eager to join in.

Music supports memory

Certain pieces of music can conjure up memorable situations – just hear the opening notes of a particular song or piece of music and you are transported to a particular time or place. Advertisers exploit this. The rhythm and cadences of their jingles (whether or not they are set to music) remain lodged in the brain, often to our annoyance when we no longer wish to think about toothpaste or chocolate. But educators are also aware of music's potential – rhymes work because learning a string of apparently unrelated words (one, two, three, or Monday, Tuesday, Wednesday) or letters (A, B, C) and being able to recite them in a helpful order is made easier if they are set to music. MacGregor's (1998) songs set to familiar tunes exploit this link, in describing circles, triangles and squares in memorable ways. Mention triangles and a group of children familiar with the song will be away – singing the song to the tune of 'Three blind mice'.

Control and discipline

Music can help children to move from one space or one activity to another in an orderly fashion. Many settings use a particular tune or song to signal clearing-up time, for example. Similarly, songs can be used to help children to learn social values and behaviours, which might include taking turns or saying 'good morning' to the group (based on Hildebrandt 1998).

This emphasis on group management and conformity was openly acknowledged by Robert Owen who, when setting up his innovative and philanthropic venture at New Lanark in the early part of the nineteenth century, gave music a focal place in the curriculum, for children from 2 years of age. He viewed music and dance as a means of 'reforming vicious habits . . . by promoting cheerfulness and contentment . . . thus diverting attention from things that are vile and degrading' (Donnachie 2000: 170). More recently, Hildebrandt (1998) reminds us that, all too often, despite the rich potential offered by music the main use made of it is in getting children to conform – all doing the same thing at the same time. That same thing might be focused on the music – all singing the same words or doing the same actions – but it might equally be to do with discipline; all lining up nicely to go out to play or march into assembly. Hildebrandt suggests that this contrasts with other areas of the curriculum, where exploration and experimentation are more effectively encouraged. With painting and drawing we are more likely to welcome idiosyncratic responses, valuing the importance of the imagination, which underpins children's work. With music, however, we are anxious about keeping in time, about getting the tune, words and actions 'right'.

Communication and music

Music eases communication in situations where it would otherwise be difficult (Papousek 1994).

- Distance may make communication difficult but music can make words or sounds more easily heard and understood. Yodelling, whistling and drumming are familiar examples of this. However, the technique is put into practice in day-to-day situations where the distances are less great but still a barrier to communication. When wanting, for example, to call children from the far side of the playground, adults commonly adopt a rhythmic chant or exaggerate the intonation so that it has a music-like quality.
- Music has a unique role in aiding communication where the feelings expressed would be difficult to put into words (Mithen 2005). Music can enable us to vent anger, and to describe love, joy or sorrow, or in short allow us to express 'that which cannot be said and on which it is impossible to be silent' (Hugo, cited in Exley 1991). As Bowman (2004: 32) aptly writes, 'Music sounds like feelings feel.'
- Music plays a part in supporting the vital but potentially difficult

job of drawing babies, who have not yet learned language, into the culture by 'reducing the distance and highlighting the emotions'; capturing the baby's attention; developing shared meaning; and communicating feelings (Pound and Harrison 2003: 13). Hearing, the first of the senses to develop (Bowman 2004) and the last to leave us (Pound 2002, citing Storr), is first stimulated by the 'intra-uterine symphony' (Bowman 2004: 37) that surrounds the unborn child.

The role of musicality in supporting development and learning continues throughout infancy. Adults and even very young children raise the pitch of their voices and use a sing-song melody in their talk with babies. Babies' hearing allows them to differentiate languages and voices – their preferences being their mother's voice and her first language. They also prefer complex sounds, including music and 'highly intonated speech' (Eliot 1999: 228). The intonations chosen by adults are now known to convey a range of emotions, which show an apparently universal pattern. Thus the tunes and pitch used to communicate, for example, approval, disapproval or comfort show significant similarities whether the language used is English, French or even a tonal language such as Mandarin (Fernald 1992; Powers and Trevarthen 2009).

From 3 or 4 months of age, babies and adults engage in playful musical interactions, which involve songs, rhymes and chants that may be traditional but increasingly may also be versions of popular music adapted to display the features common to these games (Trevarthen 1998). The common features (Pound and Harrison 2003) include the fact that the musical form of what Trevarthen (1987: 189) has called 'baby songs' and 'baby dances' appears to be essentially the same across different languages and different cultures. They provoke interest through repetition with variations in tempo and pitch. They have a story-like structure and invite an emotional response, often associated with a delayed climax.

- Music is often well used to support communication with those for whom it would otherwise be difficult, namely children with special educational needs. Even children with severe expressive speech difficulties can sometimes join in songs on cue, carried as they are by the rhythm of the music. This has been described by Bowman (2004: 38) in the following words: 'Sound seldom reflects the periphery of the body . . . It circulates in, around and even through us, both individually and collectively.'

Bond (2009) describes an approach to the education of deaf-blind children, which she calls Dance and Play. She suggests that current practice in this field relies on physical action through which 'the child is encouraged to learn that he [*sic*] can influence the other person: interaction has begun' (Bond 2009: 405, citing Aitken). Adults, as in effective interactions between young babies and carers, follow the child's lead and make use of rhythmic movement, and sound which may be perceived for this group of children through vibration.

- Music is also of great value in supporting communication with young children in the early stages of learning English as an additional language. Vocabulary is rendered memorable in song; sounds are often exaggerated and can therefore be more readily identified, and actions support the meaning. In common with storytelling, the high level of repetition (which would be unacceptable in everyday conversation) supports the development of understanding.

Creativity and music

Finally, but by no means of least importance, music has a role or function in supporting the development of creativity (see also Duffy, Chapter 8). The early development of individual babies (Trevarthen 1998) and that of the species as a whole (Lewis-Williams 2002; Mithen 2005) owes much to music and the physical action that accompanies it. The playfulness of music and dance appears to have a vital function. The evidence from recent work on creativity seems to indicate that the biological function of play, music and dance is to support the development of creativity that enables our remarkable brains to develop flexibly (Pound 2003, citing Papousek).

Music and play

Having considered the functions of music it is now important to link music and play. Music is not just important in its own right: it can make a unique contribution to playful learning. Papousek (1994) suggests that the voice is the baby's first plaything and, in the development of humans, dance was probably the precursor or herald of our humanity. It is likely that we were unable to use our voices to sing or our hands to play instruments before we had risen up on to two legs. Since Storr (1989: 12) suggests that 'human beings danced before they walked', is it possible that the playful, emotional excitement and physical exuberance that we now associate with dance caused us to rise up on our hind legs?

In Figure 9.1, links are made between music and the learning that is associated with play.

Statements about play (based on EYFS 4.1)	Links with playful music making
Children's play reflects their wide-ranging and varied interests and preoccupations	When children make up songs, dances and instrumental pieces, their explorations reflect not only their interests but their knowledge. This will inevitably have a cultural bias – drawing on the music they hear (and see) at home and in the community.
Children have to experience play physically	Physical action is an essential part of young children's learning. Music, like play, allows children to explore what they can do – but although play-based action such as rough-and-tumble play and dance may have similarities, movement in response to music involves higher-order thinking (Panksepp and Trevarthen 2009).
Children may play alone and with others	Music making involves interaction with others. Improvised musical conversations in pairs or groups, as well as regular singing times, enable children to develop a sense of group cohesion. Opportunities to find a quiet place where a child can really explore what a particular instrument or sound maker can do, or to listen to a favourite piece of music, are also of immense value. In addition, music making requires self-discipline and negotiation with others – both important learning.
In their play children use the experiences they have and extend them to build up ideas, concepts and skills	Most children have ample opportunity to practise familiar songs, but generally the amount of time given to explore sound freely is insufficient to enable children to develop or extend musical ideas or skills. In addition to whole- or small-group periods of music making, children need time and space to 'play about' with sounds. In theory, music areas should provide this as part of continuous provision, but all too often the music area gathers dust because adults lack confidence in using the resources. Time to practise and explore is as vital as time for role play or block play. A large area for music making, space to dance and a mirror to see the effect of your movements are essential. So too is the engagement of adults confident enough to support exploratory music and dance.

Children have to experience play emotionally; while playing, children can express fears and relive anxious experiences	The common experiences of children who go on to become high musical achievers include important lessons for early childhood educators: • early musical stimulation • opportunities for long periods of engagement in musical activity • family support • an early emphasis on having fun with music, and • opportunities to express feelings through music (Sloboda 1994, cited by Pound and Harrison 2003). The latter is not often explicitly considered by early years practitioners. Much of the music we use with young children is bland. If emotions are mentioned at all, they tend to be of the happy-clappy variety.
In play children can try things out, solve problems and be creative	Exploration, creativity and problem solving are intrinsic to playful music making. Music making and dance offer what Odam (1995: 19) describes as a 'unique schooling for the brain' – using as it does both sides of the brain, and requiring both spatial and temporal understanding. Playing with sounds, listening to music, responding in dance, painting or other creative media all contribute to creativity and imagination.
Play enables children to take risks and use trial and error to find things out	The traditional emphasis in education on getting it right has led generations of adults to claim that they can't sing, or can't play because they can't read music. It's time to reclaim the play in playing music and to encourage children (and adults) to take musical risks, having a go at picking out a well-loved tune, drumming like the drummer who came to perform, or playing the recorder like your big brother.

Figure 9.1 Music, learning and play.

How can we make music education in the early years more playful?

The essence of play is its exuberance – music shares this but often practitioners shy away from allowing playing music to achieve its full potential. Of the many possible or desirable changes, I have selected three as of particular importance. These are musical improvisation, song writing and physical engagement. Renewed emphasis on these three things could not only transform music education but offer an increased focus on creativity in the early years.

1   Improvisation is frequently associated with jazz musicians but, in fact, it has a firm place in most musical traditions, including western classical music. It fulfils the role of play – in promoting the rehearsal of ideas, exploring boundaries, drawing on and transforming familiar themes. It can be the doodling that leads to the masterpiece or the transitory chatter. Just as learning to talk involves play, alone and with others, so learning to musick needs to involve playful improvisations – alone and with others. We do not think of spoken conversation as of less value than printed words – different but with different functions. We do, however, refer to improvised music – the 'talk' of music (Harrison and Pound 1996) – often in a disparaging tone as being just 'made up'. In fact we should be encouraging children to engage in musical chatter cooperating with others, to take risks, and to make up songs and music (Gratier and Apter Danon 2008).

2   Singing is widely promoted as making learning easier, and as energising and enthusing learners (www.singup.org). However, although children as young as 2 years of age can be heard improvising songs as they engage in other forms of play, song writing is often ignored. By statutory school age this spontaneous and creative music making has generally disappeared. Davies (cited by Pound and Harrison 2003) has identified three types of song produced by children: story songs; songs that follow a known structure (or frame songs); and what she terms secret songs. She believes that with more active encouragement children would continue to make up songs and that creative development would be enhanced. As Hildebrandt (1998: 68) reminds us, we don't always appreciate children's invented songs as music. Although we strive to honour children's creativity in all areas of development, sometimes music gets lost in the process.'

Cameo 9.3

Staff at one children's centre began to collect children's invented songs. Sometimes they picked out a song to teach to other children and at other times they typed the words to accompany a display. A number of children, some as young as 2, were often creating secret songs. In general these did not follow the normal structure of a song or really tell a story. They were very often a sort of running commentary on what was happening, often sung on a few notes with long-drawn-out phrases and word repetition. Many children made up frame songs – based on known songs or tunes – changing the words. Staff at this centre were particularly good at making up songs of this sort – including children's names or familiar events in known songs – and this encouraged children's own song writing. Small-world play was often accompanied by story songs. Sandeep, for example, accompanied play with farm animals with his song:

> *The horse is in the field,*
> *He's eating all the grass,*
> *He's treading on the rabbit and*
> *Hitting all the sheep.*

3   Physical engagement is an essential part of all learning. As the neuro-scientist Susan Greenfield (1997) tells us, if we did not move we would not need a brain. Sadly, the importance of the body is not always acknowledged (see Knight, Chapter 12). Ross (2004: 173) asserts that 'progress through the educational system brings with it increasingly less time and permission for the physical participation of the body. The student body's presence in the classroom from kindergarten to twelfth grade gets quieter and quieter until it is effectively mute.' This might be read as suggesting that all is well in the early years. In fact, as Tobin (2004: 111) points out, 'the body is disappearing in early childhood education'. Not only, he claims, has there been a kind of moral but misguided panic about physical contact with children, but the emphasis 'on academic over social development' has had the effect of drastically reducing the amount of time that children spend in physical activity, creating 'an imbalance which favors the brain over the body and skill acquisition over feelings and more complex thinking' (Tobin 2004: 123).

While acknowledging that some similar pressures are beginning to create some similar responses in Japan, Walsh (2004: 97) highlights the importance given to physicality in Japanese early childhood education. In Japanese culture young children are viewed as essentially and importantly physical. Their physical development is central to early schooling. Many Japanese early childhood educators believe that intellectual development requires a balanced body and that physical play aligns the body.

Walsh suggests that physical competence gives children a sense of agency – of being able to take risks, to explore, and to control their bodies and environment. He reiterates Tobin's view that this has been lost from much early childhood education, citing Japan as 'a last best place in early schooling across the world' (Walsh 2004: 107).

Music, with its inherent physicality, offers an important mechanism for reclaiming the body in early childhood education. Bowman (2004) describes the way in which arts educators have embraced Multiple Intelligence Theory (see Gardner 1999). Although this has helped to underline the importance of the arts, it has, in some respects, been counterproductive. Music educators have missed opportunities to develop understanding of the links between physical and cognitive development. This, Bowman contends, means that we have failed to 'highlight the co-origination of body, mind and culture' (2004: 46) and to 'create a model of education in which music's role might be seen as a continuation and enhancement of precisely what makes all our intellectual achievements possible' (Bowman 2004: 34) – namely the body.

More recent research (Panksepp and Trevarthen 2009) supports this particular view of music – indicating that although spontaneous physical activity and that occurring in response to music may look similar they are driven by different areas of the brain. Rhythmic movement occurs in response to the brain's analysis of the music – requiring higher-order thinking.

For young children, it is a physical impossibility for them to listen to music without moving. Early childhood educators can take two simple steps to re-embody music education, making it more playful. First, we can ensure that music areas have enough space for children to move freely, with or without instruments, and that mirrors are available so that children can see what their bodies look like when they are moving. This is difficult in many classrooms where there is a shortage of space – but we can at least try to make it possible sometimes. Second, we can offer more musical opportunities outside. While physical development does not have to happen outdoors, the space and freedom it can offer make it more likely that gross motor activity will occur. There are, in addition, opportunities to explore loud sounds and natural sounds.

Conclusion

While it is true that 'in their play children learn at their highest level' (EYFS 4.1) it seems likely that, in musical play, learning is at an even higher level. Like play, music is of fundamental importance in human development and learning. Unlike some other forms of play, since it involves different areas of the brain, it offers a bridge between 'physical exuberance and rationality' (Panksepp and Trevarthen 2009: 112). Early childhood educators have a grave responsibility to ensure that the benefits that playing music offers are made available to young children, by teaching it playfully.

Questions to set you thinking

1   What steps do you need to take to make music in your setting more playful?
2   What do you need to do to help parents appreciate both the long-term and the short-term benefits of musical activity?
3   What support do you need to feel sufficiently confident in your own musical ability to intervene successfully in children's musical play?
4   What spontaneous opportunities do you provide for child-initiated 'musicking'?

References and further reading

Bond, K. (2009) The human nature of dance. In S. Malloch and C. Trevarthen (eds) *Communicative Musicality: Exploring the Basis of Human Companionship*. Oxford: Oxford University Press.

Bowman, W. (2004) Cognition and the body: perspectives from music education. In L. Bresler (ed.) *Knowing Bodies, Moving Minds: Towards Embodied Teaching and Learning*. Dordrecht, the Netherlands: Kluwer Academic Publishers.

Cross, I. and Morley, I. (2009) The evolution of music: theories, definitions and the nature of the evidence. In S. Malloch and C. Trevarthen (eds) *Communicative Musicality: Exploring the Basis of Human Companionship*. Oxford: Oxford University Press

Devi, S. (1990) *Figuring*. London: Penguin.

Donnachie, I. (2000) *Robert Owen: Owen of New Lanark and New Harmony*. East Linton: Tuckwell Press.

Eliot, L. (1999) *Early Intelligence*. London: Penguin.

Exley, H. (1991) *Music Lovers' Quotations*. Watford: Exley.

Fernald, A. (1992) Human maternal vocalisations to infants as biologically relevant signals: an evolutionary perspective. In J. Barklow, I. Cosmides and J. Toobly (eds) *The Adapted Mind: Evolutionary Psychology and the Generalisation of Culture.* Oxford: Oxford University Press.

Gardner, H. (1999) *Intelligence Reframed.* New York: Basic Books.

Gratier, M. and Apter-Danon, G. (2008 The improvised musicality of belonging: repetition and variation in mother–infant vocal interaction. In S. Malloch and C. Trevarthen (eds) *Communicative Musicality: Exploring the Basis of Human Companionship.* Oxford: Oxford University Press.

Greenfield, S. (1996) *The Human Mind Explained.* London: Cassell.

Greenfield, S. (1997) *The Human Brain: A Guided Tour.* **London: Weidenfeld and Nicolson.**

Hargreaves, D. (2004) Keynote lecture, National Association of Music Educators Conference London, 17–19 September.

Harrison, C. and Pound, L. (1996) Talking music: empowering children as musical communicators. *British Journal of Music Education*, 33(3): 233–242.

Hildebrandt, C. (1998) Creativity in music and early childhood. *Young Children*, 53(6): 68–74.

Lewis-Williams, D. (2002) *The Mind in the Cave.* London: Thames and Hudson.

MacGregor, H. (1998) *Tom Thumb's Musical Maths.* London: A&C Black.

Mithen, S. (2005) *The Singing Neanderthals: The Origins of Music, Language, Mind and Body.* London: Weidenfeld and Nicolson.

Odam, G. (1995) *The Sounding Symbol: Music Education in Action.* Cheltenham Nelson Thornes.

Panksepp, J. and Trevarthen, C. (2009) The neuroscience of emotion in music. In S. Malloch and C. Trevarthen (eds) *Communicative Musicality: Exploring the Basis of Human Companionship.* **Oxford: Oxford University Press.**

Papert, S. (1980) *Mindstorms.* Brighton: Harvester Press.

Papousek, H. (1994) To the evolution of human musicality and musical education. In I. Deliege (ed.) *Proceedings of the 3rd International Conference for Music Perception and Cognition.* Liege: ESCOM.

Pound, L. (2002) Breadth and depth in early foundations. In J. Fisher (ed.) *The Foundations of Learning.* Buckingham: Open University Press.

Pound, L. (2003) Creativity, musicality and imagination. Symposium paper presented at the 13th Annual EECERA Conference, 3–6 September.

Pound, L. and Harrison, C. (2003) *Supporting Musical Development in the Early Years.* **Buckingham: Open University Press.**

Powers, N. and Trevarthen, C. (2009) Voices of shared emotion and meaning. In S. Malloch and C. Trevarthen (eds) *Communicative Musicality: Exploring the Basis of Human Companionship.* Oxford: Oxford University Press.

Ross, J. (2004) The instructable body: student bodies from classrooms to prisons. In L. Bresler (ed.) *Knowing Bodies, Moving Minds: Towards Embodied Teaching and Learning.* Dordrecht, the Netherlands: Kluwer Academic Publishers.

Siegel, D. (1999) *The Developing Mind*. New York: Guilford Press.

Small, C. (1998) *Musicking: The Meaning of Performing and Listening*. New England: Wesleyan University Press.

Storr, A. (1989) *Solitude*. London: Collins.

Tobin, J. (2004) The disappearance of the body in early childhood education. In L. Bresler (ed.) *Knowing Bodies, Moving Minds: Towards Embodied Teaching and Learning*. Dordrecht, the Netherlands: Kluwer Academic Publishers.

Trevarthen, C. (1987) Sharing makes sense: intersubjectivity and the making of an infant's meaning. In R. Steele and T. Treadgold (eds) *Essays in Honour of Michael Halliday*. Amsterdam/Philadelphia, PA: John Benjamin.

Trevarthen, C. (1998) The child's need to learn a culture. In M. Woodhead, D. Faulkner and K. Littleton (eds) *Cultural Worlds of Early Childhood*. London: Routledge/Open University.

Walsh, D. (2004) Frog Boy and the American Monkey: the body in Japanese early schooling. In L. Bresler (ed.) *Knowing Bodies, Moving Minds: Towards Embodied Teaching and Learning*. Dordrecht, the Netherlands: Kluwer Academic Publishers.

10 Science and play

Alan Howe and Dan Davies

Summary

In this chapter we explore ways in which young children learn scientific concepts, attitudes and skills through play, and how science can contribute to a rich early years curriculum. We focus on a number of key ideas including the relevance of recent research on play in science rich contexts, the role of the practitioner, science in the Foundation Stage, the place of ICT in early science, learning for the environment and how assessment can inform planning of an appropriate play-based curriculum. We offer practical advice for the practitioner on how to promote children's scientific learning, based on principles that emerge from theories about how children learn through play.

Introduction

Bruce (1994) identifies three main views of childhood that have informed educational thought through the last century: empiricism, nativism and inter-actionism. The empiricist view is essentially a deficit model of childhood that emphasises gaps in knowledge and skills, which teachers need to 'fill'. This notion of 'filling gaps' has been prevalent in much science education to date. Nativism suggests that children's development is biologically pre-programmed and there is little that educators can do, so we believe that an interactionist account offers keener insights into children as scientists. This account (Norman 1978) explains children's development in terms of interactions between their own mental structures, the environment and the ideas of other people.

Interactionism is consistent with the prevalent social-constructivist per-spective of learning in science. Social-constructivism draws particularly on the work of Bruner and Vygotsky to explain that learning in science depends on what learners already know and how they can build on this through social interaction with others. These existing concepts are likely to be 'alternative' to the 'scientifically correct' view but provide children with sufficient working understanding for their needs. For example, a child may think a puddle 'disappears' during a warm day because it soaks into the tarmac, rather than have any concept of evaporation. It is these alternative frameworks (Driver 1983) that provide the foundation for future learning.

Cameo 10.1

Returning home from a trip to Longleat Safari Park, Ewan (5) and May (4) set up a 'train safari' using a Brio set and their toy animals. After an hour of play, their park had been populated with the following groups, as described by Ewan:

- cold water and 'normal water' animals *including dolphins, fish, polar bears, starfish and water-living dinosaurs*
- African animals *including elephants, zebras, giraffes and hippos*
- jungle animals *including chimps, caterpillars, a toucan and frogs*
- desert animals *including snakes, cacti, camels and scorpions*
- lake animals *including lizards, crocodiles, turtles and flamingos*
- flying birds *including vultures and owls*
- farm animals *including horses, bulls, a fox and a selection of insects.*

When dad tried to intervene by suggesting some animals might be placed in different categories, Ewan and May were clear this needed to be considered carefully: 'The desert is too hot for the polar bear, but the farm animals could go to Africa as long as they weren't hunted by the animals or people there.' Ewan thought the snails could live in the desert, but only if they were African snails (like the one in the glass box in his classroom).

In this cameo, the children demonstrate a sophisticated concept of animal classification during their play. They are encouraged to rethink their classification of animals through play by the adult as a sensitive 'more knowledgeable other' who attempts to scaffold learning through questioning (see also Kitson, Chapter 7). In this case, the intervention shows Ewan is able to draw upon what scientists might call 'ecological knowledge' in relation to habitats and food chains, and explain to the adult that animal classification is a complicated idea. It would seem the adult was wise to leave the children to continue their play.

We shall see that the role of the adult is crucial in this interactionist account of learning; the child will learn in a social context, and interactions with 'more knowledgeable' people will be vital encounters along the way to scientific learning, whether the encounter serves to develop children's understanding or enables them to articulate it.

Current research on play in science-rich contexts

Two strands have emerged in recent research on children's scientific play; the first concerns the role of play in concept formation. In a recent study of play in two early childhood settings in Australia (Fleer 2009a), children were observed making links between their own 'everyday' concepts and more 'scientific' concepts, moving from 'disorganised heaps' of materials to more 'complex thinking', particularly where the adults in the setting were focusing on the concepts rather than the materials themselves. This is a process of progression within play-based learning, which Johnston (2008) has called 'emergent science'. Johnston (2009) explored the observational skills of children between 1 and 3 years of age while playing with a collection of toys. This indicated that young children's observations are stimulated by sound and movement, and lead to both fantasy play and play based on their previous knowledge. Kallery *et al.* (2009) have examined young children's learning of the concept of floating and sinking through both play-based and more didactic approaches in Greek early years settings. They concluded that approaches that help children to make links between their exploratory (play-based) findings and scientific phenomena (in this case, the objects that were floating and sinking, and the materials they were made of) were much more effective than formal teaching.

In recent research on the role of young children's repetitive (schematic) play in concept formation, Schwartz (2008) argues that:

> The archetypal movements and rhythms underlying activities like sweeping, stirring, kneading and washing – gestures which have formed the bodies and wills of human beings for countless generations – are rapidly disappearing in the lives of modern children.
>
> (p. 137)

Her observations in early years settings in which children were encouraged to engage in such movements, led her to conclude that they were developing an 'inner grasp' of the laws of physics, particularly forces – through their direct experience of pushing and pulling.

Another current theme in the research literature is the role of talk in play and its contribution to children's view of themselves as scientists. Johnston's work cited above (Johnston 2009) also highlights the importance of social interaction in play, encouraging more scientific play and observations, and enabling children to negotiate social boundaries. This strand of research involves a shift from a 'cognitive' view of teaching and learning towards a more 'socio-cultural' one. What a socio-cultural view of science education acknowledges is that there is a close relationship between cognition, identity and cultural values (Aikenhead 1996). Children in a classroom or play setting will each bring a set of cultural ways of knowing and relating to one another, which will affect their perceptions of what happens in that space, which is itself loaded with cultural norms and values – for example, the shared understanding that play is important. The way that children and teachers communicate their own cultural assumptions and meanings is through *dialogue*. Bakhtin (1981) argues that all speech is dialogue, since every utterance has the implication of response, either internally to the mind of the speaker or from a listener. Children talking in a role-play scenario such as a doctor and patient are involved in an 'inter-mental process' through which they are 'co-constructing meaning' (Mercer and Littleton 2007) about, say, aspects of the human body, what a doctor does, the relationship between doctor and patient, etc. – all mediated through their own cultural experience of visiting a doctor's surgery and their cultural expectations of what goes on in the classroom role-play area.

Pedagogy: the practitioner's roles in enabling 'scientific' play

To maximise the potential for 'science-rich' epistemic play, we need as practitioners to create the conditions and provide the resources children will need. Children can be prompted into new patterns of play by presenting them with materials in new ways – for example, by changing the contents of the water tray to promote new thinking. A 'sparkly water tray' containing a range of objects small and large, some of which float, some sink, some reflect and some refract the light creating changing colours, leads to a range of questions and observations such as: what do these things do when they get wet? This wet mirror is a bit like the one in our bathroom that gets 'steamy'. Is this the same tinsel that was on the Christmas tree? Can I stick the wet sequins to my arm? Why do some sequins float and some sink? Similarly, the provision of interesting resources in the setting role-play area can make all the difference to the scientific potential of ludic play. Broadhead and English (2005) suggest that pre-themed role-play areas may actually have less potential for stimulating cooperative play and higher-order learning than practitioners assume. Their research has focused on the setting up in reception classes of open-ended role-play areas or 'whatever you want it to be places'. Two key features of these are:

1   play resources that can be used for a variety of purposes
2   extended play periods with regular access so children can become 'expert players'.

A word of caution is needed here. The notion that, simply by providing a set of resources within a stimulating environment, children will spontaneously 'discover' scientific principles has been discredited (Harlen 2000). Even non-directed, child-initiated activities need to be part of a carefully planned sequence, and the value of any experience we set up should be judged on the basis of its potential future pathways. For example, a water tray activity in which carefully chosen objects float at different levels may be more productive than one in which all have equal buoyancy, depending on the prior experience and observation skills of the children.

We need also to remember that it is not just the indoor environment that we need to plan for. Our outdoor spaces need to include resources that children can use to explore physical phenomena such as the flow of water, perhaps by providing a range of containers, pipes, tubes and funnels (see Knight, Chapter 12). Children will mimic adult behaviour whether it is in the contexts of play or 'real life'. Visitors to the classroom or visits to workplaces can be used to provide new knowledge and ideas about how adults interact and behave. These experiences can in turn stimulate play: a visit to a local garden centre can subsequently involve children in setting up a 'garden centre' area where they can play the adult roles they witnessed during the trip. As practitioners we can also model the scientific attitudes we might wish the children to adopt – for example, by handling seedlings carefully and returning to them regularly to observe, measure and monitor water and light levels.

In addition to providing for science-rich play, we may further enhance children's learning through sensitive intervention (see Kitson, Chapter 7). Intervening in children's play can have several purposes (Edgington 1998):

- to encourage imitation (e.g. to demonstrate appropriate use of equipment)
- to broaden knowledge and introduce specialist vocabulary (e.g. sitting in the dentist's chair and asking, 'Can you look at my filling?')
- to challenge and extend thinking (e.g. by introducing incongruity such as the teacher in role as a crying police officer who is afraid of the dark).

Another function of dialogue between adult and child during play is to help children engage in 'possibility thinking': '. . . a continuum of thinking strategies' from 'What does this do?' to 'What can I do with this?' (Craft 2002). The kinds of open, exploratory talk that facilitate possibility thinking do so because they create what Maine (2009) calls a 'dialogic space of possibility' in which the gap between intention and interpretation allows for provisional meanings and multiple possibilities.

As practitioners, our sensitivity to instances of scientific learning, and ability to take it forward through dialogue, are highly dependent upon our own attitudes towards science and confidence in handling scientific concepts. Fleer (2009b: 1069) found that without a mediated scientific framework for using materials in play-based contexts, children generated their own imaginary, often non-scientific, narratives for making sense of the materials provided. This conceptual focus arises from the teacher's philosophy about scientific *learning*, which Fleer found to be more significant in their practice than their level of scientific *knowledge*.

One further type of play in which practitioner intervention can be significant is what Hutt (1979) calls 'games-play', where the focus is on rule making and following. This can provide a bridge between early exploration and more formalised scientific enquiry. For example, in previous writing (Davies and Howe 2003), we suggest 'playing the scientist game' with young children, including a set of 'rules' or steps to be followed. The rules are expressed in terms of questions that guide the process of scientific enquiry:

☉	What have we noticed?
⍰	What are we going to find out?
☁	What do we think will happen?
☞	How did we do it?
🗩	What did we find out?

The shapes used for each stage in the game are intended to convey something of what that particular step involves. Some teachers make a display or mobile of the shapes for the classroom, or even use giant versions on the floor for children to move between when playing the scientist game. 'I've moved to the think cloud so now I'm predicting what will happen' is a kinaesthetic way of remembering the process. Armed with magnifying aids and note pads, children can be encouraged to be scientists as they make observations, perform 'investigations' and report back their findings. This is an example of 'guided exploration' by practitioners who are modelling scientific behaviour themselves.

Expert practitioners are able to see the everyday through a child's eyes – the shape of a snail trail, the flow of sand, the smell of an apple – and these 'commonplace' observations can promote questions: 'Where is the snail now?' 'Does the sand feel wet?' 'Does an apple core smell different to a whole apple?' By modelling questions, we can show children how to put their natural curiosity into words, which can then form the basis of the rules for the scientist game. This kind of structured games-play is moving children towards the kinds of scientific activity they will experience as they move into the statutory years of schooling.

Curriculum: science and the Early Years Foundation Stage

The *Statutory Framework for the Early Years Foundation Stage* (DCSF 2008) supports the idea that practitioners should make effective use of unexpected and unforeseen opportunities for children's learning. This is good news for early years science educators who believe that the best science begins with children's curiosity and that therefore the child's interests should determine the content. It is also, we believe, appropriate that science is not a 'subject' in the EYFS. However, it is perhaps unfortunate that science is so closely identified with the learning and development area 'knowledge and understanding of the world', which is said to form the foundation for later work in science, design and technology, history, geography and ICT, a message reinforced by the progression outlined in the recent *Independent Review of the Primary Curriculum* (Rose 2009). Science-rich play can provide appropriate contexts for all six areas of learning and development. For example, children's well-being, together with their 'personal, social and emotional development' can be enhanced by thinking about what keeps them healthy – for example, when sharing fruit together or role playing 'hospitals' or 'restaurants'. Any kind of active outdoor play can be enhanced by asking children to listen to their breathing when they've been running around, or talking about why they're feeling hot and sweaty.

There is a close relationship between 'communication, language and literacy' and science. Black and Hughes (2003) suggest that the construction and use of narrative is a vital part of coming to understand the world. Scientific understanding has been passed down through cultures by making use of narrative. This approach is ideally suited to EYFS practice, where children encounter stories, songs, rhymes, fantasy and scientific phenomena daily. Children can be encouraged to tell the story of what they have done, what they have found out or what they plan to do. They can play with new language that they learn (the names of dinosaurs or trees) or invent vocabulary to describe the properties of materials. In turn they can be told stories about how things came to be as they are. Children will wish to follow up stories with their own questions or play around with their own ideas; this is the beginning of the scientific skill of hypothesising, as well as developing their language abilities.

Clearly, a narrative approach to science in the early years is supported by a socio-cultural understanding of children's learning. Talking about what we have found out is probably the most important phase of the 'scientist game' (see above) yet is sometimes neglected through lack of time or the stress of tidying up. Harlen (2000) places great importance on speech as reflection upon what we have learned; we often understand better when we try to explain to others. Some children may lack confidence in verbalising their ideas; this is where a prop such as a puppet can be invaluable, since they do not have the status or authority of the teacher and so may be seen as more approachable and less judgemental. Simon *et al.* (2008) found that the use of puppets to tell stories and initiate scientific discussion could 'legitimise certain kinds of talk that do not normally feature within a teacher's repertoire, such as claiming to be confused or ignorant about a situation'. This resulted in an increase in the time that children used talk involving reasoning, and a decrease in the time that they talked about practical and procedural matters; an increase in the teachers' use of argumentation and a decrease in the extent to which they gave information to children; and, perhaps most importantly, an increase in the teachers' use of story and narrative and an increase in the extent to which teachers offered encouragement.

Children's 'problem solving, reasoning and numeracy' can be combined by using the learning potential from collections of objects that lend themselves to description and classification, central to science at all levels. Such collections should include natural materials for children to explore. For example, a collection of pebbles, shells or sticks carefully selected to include a range of shapes, sizes, textures or colours will lend themselves to individual and small-group play. Children may want to order the objects in patterns, line them up, roll or rotate them, or make them into pictures depending on their schematic interests (Nutbrown 1999). These actions will lead to the development of ideas about shape, space, colour, cause and effect. Different collections will appeal to different interests – papers and flexible materials for wrapping, mechanical toys for cause and effect schemas – so variety of provision is essential.

Sorting games may be an appropriate next step to developing children's mathematical reasoning: 'How many ways can you sort this collection?' Sorting can also be used to develop questioning skills: Does it float or sink? Is it hard or soft? Does it stick to a magnet? And as a way of introducing children to concept areas of science such as the properties of materials, where children are encouraged to test for the criterion they suggest. Less curious children may be encouraged to sort objects by a practitioner modelling this behaviour. Children's 'physical development' can be encouraged by using scientific equipment such as magnifying glasses, 'bug boxes', liquid droppers and beakers. Science is at the heart of 'creative development' through its emphasis on epistemic play and 'possibility thinking' (see Duffy, Chapter 8). Although statutory frameworks do not always make it easy to identify the potential for science and creativity in early years practice, it is only necessary for the observant practitioner to look around the setting at what children are doing to realise the huge scope for these dimensions to be made more explicit across the curriculum.

The *Independent Review of the Primary Curriculum* (Rose 2009), currently due for implementation in September 2011, seeks to smooth the transition between the EYFS and KS1 by reframing the curriculum from 12 subjects to six learning areas, and stating that 'the value of play to children's learning and development should be made explicit in any revisions to the primary curriculum' (Rose 2009). The new learning area of 'scientific and technological understanding' ensures that science is fully integrated with design and technology in the 'early phase' (ages 5–7) but in the middle (7–9) and later (9–11) phases there are separate statements for each subject. The requirement to teach scientific knowledge and concepts through enquiry has become explicit throughout, lending extra weight to the importance of epistemic play and 'the scientist game' in the early years (see above). For example, the first statement in the proposed programme of learning requires children to 'explore and observe in order to collect data and describe and compare their observations and findings' (QCDA 2009). This suggests a direct progression from informal exploratory play to more systematic enquiry, a continuum we would endorse, with the proviso that children need to keep playing throughout the primary years!

ICT and learning: the uses of new technologies in the development of scientific skills

There continues to be lively debate about the desirability of young children using ICT. Some argue that new technologies can transform learning and, therefore, teaching (Papert 1993; Loveless and Ellis 2001), while others call for a halt to the introduction of computers to preschool settings, to allow a 'refocus' on the essentials of childhood, which include play and hands-on experiences (Plowman and Stephen 2003). The debate seems particularly relevant to science, where educationalists stress the importance of a pedagogy that values first-hand experience and interactions; yet information technology is playing an ever more central role in the 'real' world of science. As the discussions continue, practitioners attempt to incorporate ICT into their provision, often with little guidance or training, and hand-me down resources from later primary classrooms.

Eagle *et al.* (2008: 35) identify one of the recurring problems with ICT provision for early learning:

> [We] argue that most designs of digital technologies for the early years are, implicitly at least, aimed at supporting individual interactions with technology. They are designed for the individual child, interacting in a fairly solitary fashion with the software.

Plowman and Stephen (2003) observe that the conventional reliance on screen-based information presents a barrier to interaction for preschool children that could be overcome by products designed with interfaces that are more appropriate and accessible to young children. As we have seen, we subscribe to the view that children learn through interactions with the physical world and with other people. This suggests ICT-based resources must at least facilitate these interactions and would clearly be most valuable if they made possible observations, sensations and experiences that were otherwise unattainable.

Furthermore, McFarlane and Sakellariou (2002) remind us that in order to find a meaningful role for ICT in science education it is necessary to return to fundamentals and identify the objectives of that education. If we believe it is important to encourage children to explore and investigate that physical and living world in order that they might begin to notice and explain phenomena and understand emerging patterns of order and predictability, then ICT should be harnessed to those ends.

Fortunately a number of new resources have become available to schools that do have such potential. Technology that allows children to capture images of moments and changes over time clearly has great potential to enhance learning. Digital cameras and microscopes, coupled with large-screen projection, can enable children to observe materials and organisms in incredible detail. A 'blown up' photo of a money spider or woodlouse, a short video of a rabbit feeding or a bird flying can be made and reviewed by children with relative ease (Feasey and Gallear 2001). Awe-inspiring videos can be accessed via YouTube or 'view again' websites that show the natural world in amazing detail. Webcams and time-lapse video from zoos and parks can introduce children to new species and types of animal behaviour. Feasey and Still (2006: 84) report that children can be highly motivated by access to digital imaging, including the digital microscope, that images can promote discussion, new observations and a 'wow' factor associated with these new discoveries.

Learning for the environment

The use of digital images and videos is no replacement for using the outdoors as an integral part of the learning environment. It is outside the classroom that children are most likely to have the opportunity to conduct scientific exploration through all the senses, and perhaps develop a sense of awe and wonder at our natural world (see Knight, Chapter 12). It is apparent that we are moving into an era where the very future of the planet is a concern of us all, not least educators of young children. Along with this concern comes a responsibility: to prepare children with an understanding of environmental concepts such as sustainability and conservation. White (2004: 6) suggests the task starts with the development of an appreciation of the natural world: 'We need to allow children to develop their biophilia, their love for the Earth, before we ask them to save it.'

This sentiment echoes that of scientist and champion of the environmentalist movement, Rachel Carson: 'The more clearly we can focus our attention on the wonders and realities of the universe about us the less taste we shall have for the destruction of our race' (cited in Lear 1999: 94).

White (2004) asserts that research is clearly substantiating that an affinity to and love of nature, along with a positive environmental ethic, grow out of children's regular contact with and play in the natural world. Robertson (1978) identified that a 'Nature Nursery' programme (consisting of play-based 'free-choice' and exploratory activities, mostly outdoors unless the temperature dropped below minus 20 degrees Celsius) made a measurable and persistent change in the attitude of children towards their environments. Sobel (cited in White 2004) believes that developing children's empathy with the natural world should be the main objective for early years education.

Play and assessment

To gain a holistic overview of a child's scientific concepts, skills and attitudes, observation should be carried out over a range of science-related activities in a variety of social contexts, e.g. when the child is with an adult, a group of peers or working independently. Sometimes the activities might be teacher-initiated as this can provide a broader range of experiences than children may encounter on their own. At other times the observed activity should be something the child has initiated herself, because it is when she is fully engaged and interested that she is likely to demonstrate her most creative behaviour and deep understanding (see Papatheodorou, Chapter 17).

Angela, teaching a reception class, had set up a display of magnets for the class to explore in their first term at school. On one occasion she worked with groups of children to focus their attention on the display and assess their understanding. Angela played alongside the children while another adult made notes about the interactions in a 'floorbook' using a different-coloured pen to record each child's ideas. A floorbook is a large-format 'home-made' book of plain pages, made of sugar paper or flip-chart paper in which an adult or the children write and draw ideas, observations, predictions, questions and explanations. With young children the book is compiled on the floor so the group can all have a good view and opportunity to contribute. It can be completed during one session or revisited during a number of sessions. In analysing the information gathered from the play with magnets afterwards, it became apparent to Angela that children in the group had responded quite differently. For example, Louise made a number of comments indicating the kinds of observations she was making during her exploration:

- The big magnets stick to each other.
- They are wobbly (two 'polo-mint' magnets on a dowel); they won't stick.

From these and other comments it was clear that Louise was on her way to reaching the Early Learning Goals for exploration and investigation, and would benefit from encouragement to find out about a wide range of things that interested her. Damien made the following observations:

- When I stuck a magnet to another magnet they stuck really hard.
- The can has metal on the back.

Yet most of his utterances were questions:

- What happens when you spin [the magnet]?
- What's under [the display] sticking to the magnet?
- What happens when you slide them on each other?

These indicated to Angela that Damien was achieving the following Early Learning Goal: 'Ask questions about why things happen and how things work' (DCSF 2008). She anticipated that he would benefit from support to be more systematic in his explorations in order to satisfy his curiosity.

Ellie made little comment during the session, although she was engrossed with the resources. Rather than make notes of what she said, the observer had sketched some examples of the ways in which Ellie had arranged the magnets – in 'trains' and 'ropes'. It was clear to Angela that she would need a lot of encouragement during the year to put her ideas into words and express them confidently in a group.

Another powerful tool for recording science play is the digital camera. Pictures can be taken by adults and children and used in a range of ways. Pictures can record the activities or the events that seem of interest: the tower or shadows we made, the pet that visited or the way we played. Children can review what they have made, seen or done during the day. These pictures can be shared with parents to promote a discussion about children's attitudes to science, including curiosity, perseverance and enjoyment in their scientific play.

Questions to set you thinking

1 How do we lay the foundations for a developing scientific literacy and appreciation of the natural world?

2 What skills, knowledge and attitudes does a practitioner require to facilitate children's scientific learning?

3 Is there place for an affective dimension to children's learning in science?

4 Can new technologies enhance children's learning about their 'natural' environment?

References and further reading

Aikenhead, G.S. (1996) Science education: border crossing into the subculture of science. *Studies in Science Education*, 27(1): 1–52.

Bakhtin, M.M. (1981) *The Dialogic Imagination* (trans. C. Emerson and M. Holquist). Austin: University of Texas Press.

Black, P. and Hughes, S. (2003) Using narrative to support young children's learning in science and DandT. In D. Davies and A. Howe (eds) *Teaching Science and Design and Technology in the Early Years*. London: David Fulton Publishers.

Broadhead, P. and English, C. (2005) Open-ended role play: supporting creativity and developing identity. In J. Moyles (ed.) *The Excellence of Play* (2nd edn). Maidenhead: Open University Press.

Bruce, T. (1994) Play, the universe and everything! In J. Moyles (ed.) *The Excellence of Play*. Buckingham: Open University Press.

Bruner, J.S. (1996) *The Culture of Education*. Cambridge, MA: Harvard University Press.

Craft, A. (2002) *Creativity in the Early Years*. London: Continuum.

Davies, D. and Howe, A. (eds) (2003) *Teaching Science and Design and Technology in the Early Years*. London: David Fulton Publishers.

Department for Children, Schools and Families (DCSF) (2008) *The Statutory Framework for the Early Years Foundation Stage*. Nottingham: DCSF Publications.

Driver, R. (1983) *The Pupil as Scientist?* Milton Keynes: Open University Press.

Eagle, S., Manches, A., O'Malley, C., Plowman, L. and Sutherland, R. (2008) *Perspectives on Early Years and Digital Technologies*. Available online at: http://www.futurelab.org.uk/resources/documents/opening_education/ Early_Years_report.pdf (accessed 30 October 2009).

Edgington, M. (1998) *The Nursery Teacher in Action: Teaching 3, 4 and 5-Year-Olds*. London: Paul Chapman.

Feasey, R. and Gallear, B. (2001) *Primary Science and ICT*. Hatfield: ASE.

Feasey, R. and Still, M. (2006) Science and ICT. In M. Hayes and D. Whitebread (eds) *ICT in the Early Years*. Maidenhead: Open University Press.

Fleer, M. (2009a) Understanding the dialectical relations between everyday concepts and scientific concepts within play-based programs. *Research in Science Education*, 39(2): 281–306.

Fleer, M. (2009b) Supporting scientific conceptual consciousness or learning in 'a roundabout way' in play-based contexts. *International Journal of Science Education*, 31(8): 1069–1089.

Harlen, W. (2000) *The Teaching of Science in Primary Schools* (3rd edn). London: Paul Chapman.

Hutt, C. (1979) Play in the under-fives: form, development and function. In J. Howells (ed.) *Modern Perspectives in the Psychiatry of Infancy*. New York: Brunner/Mazel.

Johnston, J. (2008) Emergent science. *Education in Science*, 227: 26–28.

Johnston, J. (2009) Emergent observation: observational skills of children aged one to three years of age. Paper presented at the European Science Research Association Conference, Istanbul, 31 August–4 September. Available online at: http://www.esera2009.org/fulltextpaper.asp (accessed 22 October 2009).

Kallery, M., Psillos, D. and Tselfes, V. (2009) Typical didactical activities in the Greek early-years science classroom: do they promote science learning? *International Journal of Science Education*, 31(9): 1187–1204.

Lear, L. (ed.) (1999) *Lost Woods: The Discovered Writing of Rachel Carson*. Boston, MA: Beacon Press.

Loveless, A. and Ellis, V. (2001) *ICT, Pedagogy, and the Curriculum*. London: RoutledgeFalmer.

McFarlane, A. and Sakellariou, S. (2002) The role of ICT in science education. *Cambridge Journal of Education*, 32(2): 219–232.

Maine, F. (2009) In pursuit of meaning: an enquiry into children's language use in the co-construction of meaning from texts. Unpublished PhD thesis, Bath Spa University.

Mercer, N. and Littleton, K. (2007) *Dialogue and the Development of Children's Thinking: A Socio-cultural Approach*. Abingdon: Routledge.

Norman, D. (1978) Notes towards a complex theory of learning. In A.M. Lesgold (ed.) *Cognitive Psychology and Instruction*. New York: Plenum.

Nutbrown, C. (1999) *Threads of Thinking: Young Children Learning and the Role of Early Education* (2nd edn). London: Paul Chapman.

Papert, S. (1993) *Mindstorms: Children, Computers and Powerful Ideas* (2nd edn). New York/London: Harvester Wheatsheaf.

Plowman, L. and Stephen, C. (2003) A 'benign addition'? Research on ICT and pre-school children. *Journal of Computer Assisted Learning*, 19(2): 149–164.

Qualifications and Curriculum Development Agency (QCDA) (2009) *Primary Curriculum Review: Consultation Responses*. London: QCDA.

Robertson, J.S. (1978) Forming preschoolers' environmental attitude: lasting effects of early childhood environmental education. Unpublished BSc thesis. Montreal: McGill University

Rose, J. (2009) *Independent Review of the Primary Curriculum: Final Report.* Nottingham: DCSF Publications.

Schwartz, E. (2008) From playing to thinking: how the kindergarten provides a foundation for scientific understanding. *European Journal of Psychotherapy, Counselling and Health*, 10(2): 137–145.

Simon, S., Naylor, S., Keogh, B., Maloney, J. and Downing, B. (2008) Puppets promoting engagement and talk in science. *International Journal of Science Education*, 30(9): 1229–1248.

White, R. (2004) *Young Children's Relationship with Nature: Its Importance to Children's Development and the Earth's Future.* Available online at: http://www.whitehutchinson.com/children/articles/childrennature. shtml (accessed 30 October 2009).

11 Mathematics and play

Rose Griffiths

Summary

Teaching maths through play has many advantages. Play can increase the child's motivation to learn by providing sensible and enjoyable contexts, and by allowing children to direct their own learning. An emphasis on using and applying maths with young children can build the confidence of children and the adults who work with them. This chapter includes many practical examples that illustrate how this can be done, and demonstrates links between children's learning at school or nursery, at home and in the world around them. Some examples were teacher-initiated, and some child-initiated. I emphasise that children need time to experiment to see that maths can be enjoyable and useful. Making and doing, talking and listening, with writing and drawing used in a purposeful way, provide a better route to understanding in maths than premature formal methods of working.

Introduction

Sadly, mathematics and play seem to be mutually exclusive activities to many people. As one teacher said to me, 'If I enjoy doing something, then I know it can't be maths. I was never any good at maths when I was at school. I hated it.' Like many others, she assumed that it was her own lack of ability that caused her difficulties with the subject. She had never considered the possibility that her feelings of inadequacy may have stemmed from the methods that were used to teach her.

There are, unfortunately, many ways of teaching mathematics badly. Nearly 30 years ago, the Cockcroft Committee (DES 1982) set up in response to concern about the standards of mathematics teaching in England and

Wales, considered that many teachers used too narrow a range of both mathematical content and teaching styles. The Committee also echoed the concern of many employers and teachers that children (and adults), when faced with real-life, practical problems, often had difficulty in making effective use of the mathematical skills they actually possessed.

This emphasis on the importance of children being able to use and apply mathematics was evident in successive versions of the *National Curriculum* (see DfEE/QCA 1999). Subsequently, the statutory framework for the *Early Years Foundation Stage* (DfES 2007: 14) states that, 'Children must be supported in developing their understanding of Problem Solving, Reasoning and Numeracy in a broad range of contexts in which they can explore, enjoy, learn, practise and talk about their developing understanding.'

Providing children with opportunities to use and apply mathematics is not always easy: it can be difficult to provide 'real life' experience within the classroom, and teachers need to be wary of presenting contexts that oversimplify the real world, without acknowledging the pretence to children. For example, you cannot buy a teddy for a penny in an ordinary shop but I have seen a classroom shop where this was possible. The teacher's desire to make the arithmetic manageable had undermined the link to the real world, and made it more difficult for children to come to understand the value of coins in terms of what you can really buy with them. Using prices in whole pounds would have been more helpful: £1 teddies are more realistic!

Hughes *et al.* (2000) outline the situation like this:

> . . . it may be helpful for teachers to think in terms of a continuum. At one extreme, there are activities that are basically classroom exercises, and where the 'real-life' content is minimal . . . At the other extreme are activities that are firmly rooted in real life, and where the constraints of the classroom have been reduced as far as possible. In practice, activities at this end of the continuum are likely to be much messier and harder for the teacher to control: however, they may have greater value in promoting application.
>
> (p. 115)

How can children learn mathematics successfully through play? First, I shall explore some of the advantages of learning maths through play, and, second, offer a range of examples of successful play activities that promote the development of mathematical skills and understanding.

The advantages of learning mathematics through play

There are five key factors that I believe are worth exploring: purpose and motivation; context; control and responsibility; time; and practical activity. All of these can be seen when children are playing at home (see Griffiths 2008) as well as being evident in effective educational settings.

Purpose and motivation

All of us learn better when there is a clear purpose to what we are doing. When children (or adults) play, a clear and significant purpose is enjoyment, and fun is often sufficient to encourage us to concentrate on a task for long enough for learning to occur (see Whitehead, Chapter 5).

Sometimes we teach children skills and then look for ways of practising them, but sometimes it is much more effective to use problems that children are interested in, to motivate them to learn new skills in order to use them immediately. For example, we can ask children to practise drawing straight lines with a ruler – or we can begin work on making stripy patterns and then talk to children about improving their skills at using a ruler, to help make their patterns.

Context

One of the things that makes maths a difficult subject to learn is the fact that some elements of mathematics are very abstract. Paradoxically, this abstraction is also what makes maths such a powerful tool. Ways need to be found of helping children to see the links between concrete and abstract ideas (Hughes 1986). This can often be done using a starting point that makes human and practical sense to children in a context provided by play. A context that makes sense to children will also be one that makes sense to the staff working with them (no matter how little confidence those adults have in their own mathematical ability) and to the children's parents or carers at home (see Fabian and Dunlop, Chapter 15).

Control and responsibility

Many adults find it much easier to encourage children to make their own decisions when they are playing than when they are in a more formal learning situation. Allowing and positively prompting children to take control of their own activity is a very important aspect of teaching mathematics (see Parker-Rees, Chapter 4). It is difficult to become more skilled at problem solving, investigating or discussion if the teacher is always telling children what to do and how to do it. Children who are used to organising themselves in play and learning activities are more likely to become confident and creative mathematicians than those who are continually 'spoon fed'.

Time

Time for mathematical play provides children with a welcome and valuable opportunity to repeat things and gain mastery over actions and ideas, to raise questions, to discuss things with their peers and to clarify ideas, free from pressure to progress too quickly to the next mathematical concept. (Time for playful and creative approaches is also a theme in Chapter 8 by Bernadette Duffy.) Everyone needs time for new ideas to be assimilated. This is especially important with those aspects of maths that are hierarchical, where understanding each new idea depends on having understood its precedents.

Practical activity

Play ensures that the emphasis rests on practical activity, not written outcomes. For children to increase their mathematical understanding, it is important that their written recording should serve a purpose that is useful to each child, and is linked to activity and discussion. Written recording for its own sake will not help children with understanding. As Hughes (1986: 170) asserts, 'If they cannot tell how many bricks result from adding five bricks to nine, then there is no advantage to be gained by writing down the problem as "9 + 5 =": this gets them no nearer the answer.'

Thinking about these five key factors may be especially helpful for adults who do not feel very confident with maths themselves. Liz, a teacher of Year 1 children, expressed her own anxieties: 'I want to let the children learn through play but I worry that there's not enough maths in what they are doing, so I ought to be doing something more formal.'

This raises the following two possibilities.

1   Adults may not always recognise the mathematics in a play-based activity and may need time to analyse it carefully, preferably with a supportive colleague. For example, a teacher who was concerned about the mathematical value of playing with a railway layout was reassured when she realised the children were, among other things, gaining experience of comparing distances, using straight, curved and parallel lines, discussing position and movement, using diagrams and building in three dimensions.

2   The activity may *not* provide much opportunity for mathematical learning and it may need planning again to make mathematical activity more central and more explicit. For example, a teacher who had

hoped that playing in a pretend shop would lead to sorting, categorising and counting soon realised that this was not actually happening. Although the shop was full of things to sell, there was generally only one or two of each item – unlike a real shop where, for example, there would be 10 or 20 tubs of margarine, not just one or two. The teacher increased the amount of sorting and counting the children could do by providing a larger number of a smaller range of items.

Playing *with* children obviously provides educators with time to discuss children's own ideas and, in addition, gives opportunities to share information and to teach them in a more direct way. For example, some mathematical facts are rules or agreements that people have established in the past, such as:

- we call a shape with exactly three straight sides a triangle
- this is how we write the number five: 5
- when we count things, we count each thing once; we don't miss any out or count any twice.

Children might eventually realise that these things are true by observing other people, but it can be more straightforward for learners to be given this kind of information as and when they need it or want it.

Some mathematical facts, however, are ones that children need to be able to work out for themselves, if they are to gain understanding and are to be convinced by them. For example:

- when we count a group of things and we do not add any or take any away, then there will still be the same number when we count them again
- 3 add 5 makes 8.

Frequent use may lead to children knowing facts like '3 + 5 = 8' off by heart but, if they forget, they should be able to work each fact out again from scratch because they understand the process. Play can provide the variety, repetition, motivation and interaction with peers and adults that is needed to establish both understanding and fluency in an enjoyable way.

Helping children learn mathematics through play

Play can give children the confidence to tackle quite complex ideas. The role of the teacher is to suggest new possibilities, to give information, to support children's ideas and to encourage discussion.

The rest of this chapter will focus upon examples of play-based activities that were both enjoyable and mathematically useful. They include both teacher- and child-initiated activities, something emphasised throughout this book. The examples are grouped under two main headings: 'Play and counting' and 'Play and shape and space'.

Play and counting

Learning to count groups of objects or events accurately takes a surprisingly long time for young children, and counting underpins children's understanding of arithmetic. For example, if a child cannot count ten objects consistently, then it makes little sense to ask her what four add six makes, since she is likely to get a different answer each time she tries this question. But as soon as a child is confident about counting a group of, say, six objects, and knows that the number will still be the same if he counts them again, then he is ready to think about any problems involving addition or subtraction within that range.

Children who are learning to count need frequent practice in a variety of contexts in which they are genuinely interested in finding out how many objects there are. There is no incentive to count accurately if you really do not care whether there are eight or nine counters! Children also need someone else to check their counting sometimes while they are learning, but that does not always need to be an adult.

Teddies' teatime

Children helped to set up the home corner as the bears' house and made a variety of food for the teddies to eat. It was important to make a good quantity, so that there was enough to count when a group of children played together. The children cut cookie shapes from salt dough for their teacher to bake at a low temperature until they were hard enough to play with. Jam tarts were made in the same way, with a small-sized cutter and 'jam' painted on after they had been baked, using red or orange acrylic paint. Corrugated card became sandwiches and crackers, and a variety of beads and bricks were used to represent nuts and fruit.

Some children needed no prompting at all to count as part of their play; others started to do so only after watching and listening to the adult or other children. For example, Kerry mostly used none, one or two: 'What do you want, Blue Bear? Two cakes?' Anna set herself much more complicated tasks: 'I don't know about these jam tarts, if I can give them all five each or if there's not enough.'

Sitting with children who are playing and talking often gives us the chance to review their achievements and think about what they might benefit from doing next, in a way that is more accurate than more formal methods of assessment.

Counting actions

One important context for learning to count is when children want to count how many hops, kicks or other actions they have done. Counting actions or events may be more common at home than in educational settings, and often seem to encourage children to try to count to higher numbers than when they are counting objects. My own observations of children counting at home included many examples of this (Griffiths 2008: 51):

> Achayla, aged 4, only counted to a maximum of five with toys or household objects (because that is all there were), but counted confidently to twenty when she was hopping. When she was on the swing in the garden, she extended her counting using her own version of the counting sequence: '37, 38, 39, 50, 51, 52, 53, 54, 55, 56, 57, 58, 59, 30, 31 . . .'

Photograph 11.1   Achayla counts while she is swinging.

Monsters in the bath

The adult made four cards showing monsters having a bath (see Figure 11.1). Monsters love playing with sponges, and these were made by cutting two sponge kitchen cloths (one blue, one orange) into small pieces. Children played with the cards and sponges in a variety of ways. Some children wanted time to play on their own to start with, without any suggestions from an adult or their peers. Others wanted an idea to get them started.

For counting practice, the first step was to choose a number that the child needed to practise counting. Suppose it was six. Just for the first go, the adult would count six sponges on to one card to show what was wanted. Then the child would give the other monsters six sponges each, too. The most popular way of playing was in a pair, when each child had four monsters in the bath cards, and they rolled a dice or picked a card from a pile of number cards to choose which number to count. When they had given their own monsters their sponges, they would count each other's to check. In the course of one turn of the game, each child had counted the practice number eight times.

Children could also make up sums for each other: 'Monster had four blue sponges and five orange ones. How many did she have altogether?' or 'Monster used to have ten sponges but she's lost two. How many has she got now?'

Some children liked using the little sponges to wash monster's face or to polish the bath taps, and some little sponges turned up in the bath in the dolls' house! Children liked drawing or painting pictures of monster, and some wrote captions for their pictures or wrote on a number to say how many

Figure 11.1   Monsters in the bath game.

sponges there were. They wanted to represent the maths they had done on paper, and they did so in ways that made sense to them, which only gradually moved closer to using numerals and other symbols.

As they gained in experience, when children made up problems for each other about monster and her sponges, they found they could solve them without needing to re-enact the whole problem. Using play-based materials had helped them imagine the scene 'in their head' – the beginnings of mental arithmetic. Using a calculator alongside their game, to check or reassure them, was also useful. It provided them with a real reason to learn to recognise each written number and the symbols +, – and =, so that they could press the right keys on the calculator, and that gave them a model to write down – for example, 2 + 3 = 5.

Mobile phones and remote controls

Young children who are used to organising themselves, taking the initiative and improvising or making props for their own play will often surprise the adults around them with their ambition, ingenuity and skill.

Photograph 11.2   Avan and his dad playing at phoning Pingu.

Gemma and Kyle (aged 4 and 5) decided to use small boxes to make 'mobile phones', and asked their teacher to show them how to write a 2, 6, 7 and 9. (Between them, they already knew how to do 0, 1, 3, 4, 5 and 8.) Interestingly, Kyle positioned his numbers in the order of his mum's phone number, but Gemma realised that the numbers should go in order, 1, 2, 3, and so on. They also used calculators as pretend mobile phones and tried hard to learn which number was which to phone each other up. When their teacher found an old mobile case (with numbers intact), they noticed that the calculator and the mobile had their numbers in a different arrangement and spent some time discussing whether one of them was 'wrong' or whether it did not matter what order the numbers were in. Their motivation to learn how to read and write numbers was high because they wanted to *use* them.

Dylan (aged 4) was good at number recognition. His motivation was cable television – he wanted to use the remote control to choose Channel 608, or 144, or 102. I suspect he would soon be telling the time very competently, too, as he told me, 'This programme is on again at five thirty, so I'm going out to play in the garden now, and I'll watch it later.' When he started school, would his teacher recognise the skills he already had or would it be assumed these were things he still had to learn?

Dogs and bones

Children who have used counting games like monsters in the bath sometimes come up with ideas of games they can make themselves (see Figure 11.2). 'Dogs

Figure 11.2   Dogs and bones game.

and bones' was Kelly's idea. She drew and cut out one dog, and fixed it to another piece of card so that it would stand up. Her friend Jo (aged 5 – a year younger than Kelly) made the other dog, and both children cut 'bones' from little pieces of card.

At first the children used the bones in the same ways as monsters. Then they invented a simple new game: they took it in turns to throw a dice on behalf of each dog, and gave the dog that number of bones, so that each dog gradually accumulated more and more. Every now and then they counted to see how many bones each dog had altogether. When they ran out of bones they made some more, and only stopped playing when each dog had such a large pile that they were finding it difficult to count them.

I was keen to use Kelly and Jo's own context to explore division, using problems where they had to share different numbers of bones between the two dogs. This was prompted by watching a children's television programme where two puppets were sharing five apples between them. 'One for you and one for me. One for you and one for me. Oh, there's one left over!' said the puppet, 'What shall we do?' The 3 year old who was watching television with me shouted excitedly 'Cut it up! Cut it up!' The puppet, sadly, ignored this possibility, and said, 'We'll have to put it back in the bowl.'

Why was the writer of this programme apparently so frightened to introduce halves as an obvious solution to a real problem? We should not have such low expectations of children when presenting ideas in a context that makes sense to them. Fractions may be difficult to deal with when the expectation is one of calculating with them using pencil and paper, but this does not mean we should ignore them at earlier stages.

So I talked with Kelly and Jo about sharing bones fairly between their two dogs. It was agreed that, if we had four altogether, each dog should have two bones. But what if we had five bones: how could the dogs share the extra bone? Kelly thought the dogs should just take it in turns and have a lick each, but Jo said they wouldn't like that because they might want to crunch it up. Then Kelly produced scissors and snipped it in half! The children were told that a half is written like this – ½ – and were given a blank dice with the numbers ½, 1, 1½, 2, 2½, 3 written on the faces. At first, the children counted up parts of bones separately: 'This dog's got four and a half and a half', so I showed them that it is possible to fit two halves together and count it as one bone. They played their dogs and bones game again, with adult help at first on how to say the numbers. They had no difficulty in counting out the right quantity, with the aid of scissors if appropriate. After a few sessions of playing on their own, they were happy to work out in their heads the answers to questions such as: 'If your dog had three and a half bones, and you gave him two more bones, how many bones would he have altogether?'

Board games

In theory, many board games should encourage children to count, match and follow rules. In reality, children often play these games without gaining much in terms of mathematical experience. For example, when children play in a group, those who most need counting practice frequently have their pieces moved for them by more experienced players, or they are told where to move to. If the main purpose of the game is to become the 'winner', there can even be good logical reasons for counting badly! Cooperative games encourage children to explain things to each other.

Playing boards made by drawing grids with a permanent pen on pieces of plastic table covering or large pieces of card are a good start. The most popular board I have made was a rectangle of four squares by eight, where each square measured 10 cm. (One of the advantages of making your own game is that it can be made to a large scale.) The simplest way of using this board was for 'race games'. For example, four plastic people, animals or toy cars were lined up, and one or two children took turns to throw a dice and move the pieces to see which one would get to the end first.

Variations are plentiful. Using the same board, one group of children made 'ghosts' from cotton wool and had ghost races. Taking up the idea, a second group invented a new version where toy people raced, each with a ghost just behind them. For each turn, a dice was thrown twice – once for the person, once for the ghost – and the person had to try to get to the end before the ghost caught them. The children experimented with different rules to give the toy people a reasonable chance of escaping. After a great deal of discussion, they decided that giving them one extra throw of the dice to start was best.

Numbers were made for the board by writing them on separate 3 cm squares of card, which children could fasten on to the main board for themselves using Blu-tack. Sorting the numbers into order and deciding where to put them is quite challenging for many children, but it helped them understand the layout of numbers on other board games. We used these numbers, along with cardboard cut-out snakes, and ladders made by gluing lollipop sticks together, to make our own snakes and ladders games. Before playing, agreement had to be reached as to where to fasten the snakes and ladders: it was possible to have only ladders, but the children usually decided it was more fun to have at least one snake.

Play and shape and space

Many activities, including board games, that children enjoy use shape, pattern, movement and position. Building, threading, sewing, printing, dancing and climbing are just a few examples. Children learn more when they have problems to solve than when they are just asked to name shapes or describe what someone else has done: they need to use and apply their growing mathematical knowledge.

Towers for tortoises

Katie sometimes made small piles or lines of wooden bricks but she never seemed to be very confident or enthusiastic about building. The turning point came after she had spent some time talking about how (especially at age only 4 years) it is possible to see much more when you stand on a chair. At that time, Katie often played with two wooden pull-along tortoises, which we decided must sometimes get fed up because they could only see people's ankles. Katie decided to build them a tower, to give them a different view. Katie's building now had a definite purpose and she returned to the problem several times over the next few days. At first she did not want anyone else to copy her or help her, but then she relented and enjoyed working with other children, getting ideas from them in return. For example, she started to think about ways of making bridges so that the tortoises could get from one tower to another. She learned by trial and improvement, becoming quicker, more skilful and more imaginative with her constructions. In quite a short space of time, Katie's new confidence with wooden bricks encouraged her to be more adventurous and thoughtful with other construction toys.

Sleeping bags

Talking with a group of 5 and 6 year olds, I discovered that they had all, at some time, slept in sleeping bags. They were very keen to take up the suggestion that they could make little pipe-cleaner people and sleeping bags for them (see Figure 11.3). When they had each made a person, we discussed sleeping bags before they started to make them. How big should they be, and what shape? They decided that a sleeping bag is cosiest if a person can stretch out and still have her shoulders covered, but it should not be so big that the person disappears completely inside it. Most sleeping bags that the children had seen were rectangular, and most had patterns on them.

Cutting out a rectangle proved to be more difficult than most of the children had thought. Trying to judge how big to make the rectangle so that it would be the right size for their person once it was folded over was challenging, too, and called for a great deal of trial and improvement. (One child decided that changing the sleeping bag to fit the person was much too hard, so she cut her person's legs shorter instead!) The children were reminded not to fix their sleeping bags together with sticky tape until after they had decorated

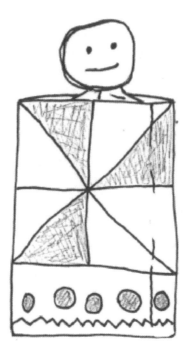

Figure 11.3   Sleeping bag game.

them. They used a variety of designs, sometimes like ones they had seen themselves. Some drew on pictures (dogs, fairies or racing cars); others did spots, stripes or geometric patterns. Some of the children made tents from folded card, or chalets from small boxes, but many preferred to make another little person and another sleeping bag, the second time much more expertly than the first. They enjoyed playing with the things they had made, and they had developed their knowledge of shape, size and pattern.

Fish and chips

It is important to remember how much children learn outside school or nursery, and how they can link their play in an educational setting with the real world.

Michelle (aged 3 years) was playing in the 'fish and chip shop' at her nursery. When her first customer came, she shovelled a portion of plastic chips on to a sheet of white paper and pulled the paper around them. As she handed them over, all the chips shot out of the front and fell to the floor. Michelle kicked them to the side with her foot, said, 'You can't eat them, they're dirty' and served another portion. This time, she wrapped the paper the other way round, and this time the chips fell out of the side. Michelle gave up at that point and skipped off to play in the sand.

Two weeks later, I visited again and saw Michelle in the 'chip shop' again. She served a portion of chips, wrapping them diagonally side to side then rolled front to back, as though she had worked in a chip shop all her life. I talked to her mum when she came to collect Michelle. 'She's been driving me mad – we walk home past the chip shop, and I have to take her in and hold her up so she can see what the lady does, how she wraps up the chips. And she's been wrapping up her toys at home, too. I've said to her, we'll have to have pass the parcel for your birthday, won't we!' It seemed evident that Michelle had not seen her initial problem with wrapping as a 'failure' but as a prompt to find out more from an expert and to experiment for herself.

Wrapping involves many complicated mathematical ideas that children can work on intuitively, including size, shape, surface area, position and sequencing. Michelle's teacher made sure that Michelle had a chance to talk about her new skill, and to think about *why* this way of wrapping works. As Michelle said, 'I did it before, and chips fell out because there was holes. Now I do it and they can't get out.'

Gymnastics

Sometimes children's spontaneous play from lunch or play times gives them ideas they want to pursue when they come back into the classroom. So it was with Emma and her friend, who had been playing 'gymnastics' during the lunch break. Emma wanted to count up how many different gymnastics positions she had tried. She tried describing them and counting at the same time, but lost track after just two or three, and said impatiently, 'Oh, give me some paper, I'll write them down and count them.'

Representing something from real life (i.e. in three dimensions) on to paper (in two dimensions) can be quite difficult to do, but Emma managed very well. Before she did each new drawing, she checked to make sure she had not already drawn herself like that before. She numbered her drawings as she went along, and was very pleased to find 15 positions altogether (although I have my doubts about number 12 – see Figure 11.4). Emma's concentration was remarkable – except if you realised how much she wanted to know the answer to her own question.

Physical activity is an important part of learning and, in particular, in learning about shape and space – there is usually no reason to record what you do with pencil and paper. Just as with number work, children's written work in shape and space is most likely to be successful if the children can see a purpose in it for themselves. It should build on practical activity and play, and never become an end in itself.

Figure 11.4 Emma's gymnastics.

Conclusion

Maths and play are very useful partners. If we want children to become successful mathematicians, we need to demonstrate to them that maths is enjoyable and useful, and that it can be a sociable and cooperative activity, as well as a quiet and individual one. We must be careful, too, to remember that play is not just a way of introducing simple ideas. Children will often set themselves much more difficult challenges when we give them control of their learning than if it is left to adults.

Questions to set you thinking

1   How can you support colleagues who lack confidence in teaching maths (or improve your own confidence, if needed)?

2   Could you introduce some new and more varied ways for children to practise counting in your setting, where children will be keen to be accurate because they are interested in the materials or contexts provided?

3   How often can children in your setting follow their own line of mathematical enquiry? How can you make sure this is valued and encouraged?

4   What links do you make at the moment between learning at home and in your setting? How could you strengthen these links?

References and further reading

Department for Education and Employment (DfEE)/Qualifications and Curriculum Authority (QCA) (1999) *The National Curriculum*. London: DfEE/QCA.

Department for Education and Skills (DfES) (2007) *The Early Years Foundation Stage: Setting the Standards for Learning, Development and Care for Children from Birth to Five*. Nottingham: DfES.

Department of Education and Science (DES) (1982) *Mathematics Counts*. Report of the Cockcroft Committee. London: HMSO.

Griffiths, R. (2008) Family counts. In I. Thompson (ed.) *Teaching and Learning Early Number* (2nd edn). Maidenhead: Open University Press.

Hughes, M. (1986) *Children and Number*. Oxford: Basil Blackwell.

Hughes, M., Desforges, C. and Mitchell, C. (2000) *Numeracy and Beyond: Applying Mathematics in the Primary School*. Buckingham: Open University Press.

12 Forest School: playing on the wild side

Sara Knight

Summary

This chapter starts with the premise that we are seeing the reintroduction of wilder outdoor play, and that there is understandable reluctance on the part of some practitioners to engage with this. However, there is a range of encouragements from government sources, and many reasons why risk taking and outdoor play are important. This chapter describes one initiative for wilder and riskier play, Forest School, and discusses why risk taking and outdoor play is important for the under-5s. The author suggests ways in which practitioners can develop their own skills. The chapter covers some of the safety issues, and makes suggestions for creating riskier outdoor play in settings, including ways to deal with mud, wet and cold.

Introduction

It seems that the twenty-first century is offering us the opportunity to reconnect young children with their natural environment. After two decades of 'don't do' we are beginning to hear 'please do'. This brings to mind a summer's barbeque in the late 1990s, just before I went to Wales to train as a Forest School leader. I looked at a friend's son, aged about 3, sitting on the ground under a large bush with an arm round the host's dog, holding a stick in his other hand. I thought, 'That feels right. And that is the experience I want other children to have.' Ten years on and we are beginning to get there. Sticks, small boys and dirt go together again.

It is unfair to expect a generation who either did their training or their schooling in the 'don't do' era to be able to accept the 'please do' dictum without a debate about why these things feel so right and what their true value might be. When I take trainee practitioners out for a walk in induction week at university and they refuse to eat the blackberries on the bushes because they are dirty, I know that I have a long way to go. We are missing at least one generation of children who were sent out on a Saturday morning as I was. 'Go and play,' said my mother – and we did, travelling miles on our bikes, or crawling along in the tunnels created by bushes over ditches, coming home filthy *and fitter*. No one knew where we'd been, what we'd done, which was just as well sometimes. We learned to keep ourselves safe; a theme to which I'll return later.

We are now being encouraged to facilitate outdoor experiences for children and to give those outdoor experiences equal but different value to indoor experiences. There is a plethora of new books (e.g. Knight 2010) giving help and support in 'how to' ways, but it will take time and effort to build confidence and commitment among practitioners. Perhaps a quote from a recent Forest School trainee with the Green Light Trust (see 'Useful websites' at the end of this chapter) will act as encouragement:

> I trained as a teacher just as the National Curriculum was being introduced into primary schools. Despite my best intentions, and without me really recognising that it had happened, what had once been a vocation was now a chore, a stressful, unpleasant, daily slog . . .
>
> And then I went to Forest School. And my life changed. Six days later I left the course determined to continue what I had learnt and experienced there, not only in the workplace but also throughout my life.
>
> I just want to say that the combination of solid theory, learning new skills and the chance to reflect and be child-like outside in the wood renewed my spirits and restored my faith in myself and the children I teach.

The exhortations of officialdom

It started with the academics and writers, as all good revolutions do. People like Robinson (2001) pointed out that removing creativity from schools by making the curriculum too prescriptive was stifling learning (see also Duffy, Chapter 8). I will argue that it is easier to be creative outside than inside. Lindon (2003) voiced the concerns of many that wrapping children in cotton wool was wrong. Palmer's (2006) popular polemic focused attention on the relationship between modern life and modern problems. Gill (2006) has described ours as a 'risk-averse' society and pointed out the possible consequences. To be fair, the English government was not far behind. In 2003, the *Every Child Matters Framework* (HM Treasury 2004) launched a new perspective on the care and welfare of children that has influenced all practitioners. This is widening the perspective of professionals. For example, teachers have to think about children's well-being, and health visitors have to think about the school. The 2007 *Children's Plan* and the revised 2008 *ECM Framework* have subsequently heightened the focus on the environment as a key contributor to health and well-being. The *Outdoor Manifesto* (DfES 2006) signalled government recognition of the importance of experiential learning for all ages. The new website for the manifesto (www.lotc.org.uk) is developing support materials for people working with all ages outdoors. Building on the *Growing Adventure Report*, the Forestry Commission has produced guidance materials downloadable from www.forestry.gov.uk/england-play, which can help planners and headteachers to design better play spaces. Play England, the recently established national organisation for play, funded by the Big Lottery Fund and an integral part of its Children's Play initiative, is working closely with local authorities and the voluntary sector to transform public play space and play services.

It was exciting to see outdoor provision given prominence in the revised *Early Years Foundation Stage Curriculum for England* (DCSF 2007), particularly after the devastating report from the United Nations Children's Fund (UNICEF 2007) earlier in the year, ranking the UK bottom of all industrialised countries in its assessment of child well-being. Evidence from research on my own particular area of Forest School (Knight 2009) has linked the right kind of outdoor experiences to benefits linked to well-being (more on this below). All these publications increase the pressure on practitioners to focus their attention on what they provide outside for their children.

Considering the fears and concerns of practitioners

Many practitioners find this pressure daunting. They are balancing it with what seems to be the equal but opposing pressure to keep children safe, to protect them from the vagaries of that self-same environment. In addition, the practitioners are often without the cultural foundations of being outside themselves, as there are few over-50 year olds still working routinely with young children, and anyone younger than 50 will have felt the stultifying effects of 20 years of 'don't do'. This means that, although I can tell you that you cannot catch a cold simply by being outside and getting wet in the rain, and intellectually you can believe me, still deep inside you there will be a fear that perhaps I am wrong.

To allay these fears and concerns will take time and effort. For example, in Essex, early years advisers have been organising trips to early years settings in Denmark, where practitioners can see practice that is very different, where children are supported to use sharp tools (inside and outside), where there are tea lights at child height (inside) and where babies sleep in their prams outside in all weathers (a practice common in this country until the 1960s). But the response among the sceptics could be that in Denmark they do things differently and you couldn't do them like that here (see Chapters 17 and 18 for more on cultural differences).

The Health and Safety Executive website has a monthly myth on its website. Figure 12.1 shows the one for March 2009. Many of the issues raised on the poster are discussed below, but I include it here to show two things. One is that many of our fears are based on myths that, in turn, are based on poor

Great health and safety myths

The myth Health and safety rules take the adventure out of playgrounds

The reality We're all for playgrounds being exciting and challenging places. Children should have fun in them, get fit, develop social skills and learn how to handle risks.
What's important is to strike the right balance – protecting children from harm while allowing them the freedom to develop independence and risk awareness. Exciting and challenging playgrounds do this, poorly maintained or badly designed ones don't.
Health and safety laws don't stop children having fun but ill-considered and overprotective actions do.

HSE Go to www.hse.gov.uk/myth/index.htm to find out more   No 24 March 2009

Figure 12.1 Myth: health and safety rules.

information. The other is that there is support from the appropriate govern-ment agencies for anyone wanting to be more adventurous. You can download these myths as posters and I recommend them.

The poor information that feeds the fears of practitioners includes the idea that our children are at risk and, in particular, at risk from the external environment. Children today are safer than they have ever been and the acci-dents that do happen are more likely to occur indoors than out. Look at the HSE statistics if you do not believe me. And children are more at risk from harm from the people they know than they are from strangers. In addition, Criminal Record Bureau (CRB) checks only uncover things a person has done and been caught doing, not the things they might do or have not been caught doing.

It is analogous to the labelling on foodstuffs. These show sell-by and use-by dates. Generally, these are dates that guarantee that no manufacturer will ever be liable for prosecution because they are so conservative as to be verging on the ridiculous. And, because of them, vast numbers of the population have stopped trusting their eyes and their noses. I know when a fruit juice is going off, because it goes fizzy. I know when milk goes off, because it smells and is lumpy. My life experience will protect me from most of the foodstuffs that will do me harm, but not from the odd E. coli bug that no label protects me from and my nose and eyes cannot spot. Poor information could mean that I would throw food away unnecessarily because of labels on packaging but put myself at risk by not trusting my eyes, nose and taste buds when eating. And there would still be a risk, albeit a reasonable one, that the odd bug could escape both the labelling and the human checks. The labels that are supposed to protect me could, were I to rely on them, de-skill my ability to keep myself safe. In the same way, making the environment that children operate in too safe prevents them from learning to keep themselves safe. But no environ-ment can be completely risk free and so everyone needs to learn to use their eyes and noses.

Forest School examples

In my recent book (Knight 2009), I look at the impact of Forest School on outdoor learning in the UK early years sector. Forest School is one way of working outside, stemming from a visit made to Denmark by the nursery nursing department at Bridgewater College in 1994. It has been developed, by them initially and latterly by others, and is a popular initiative now available in most areas of the UK. To find out what is happening locally, look at the Forest Education Initiative (FEI) website and then for local cluster groups. Most Forest School practitioners join FEI cluster groups as a good way of accessing funding and support. Alternatively, go on to the Institute for Outdoor Learning website, as it has a Special Interest Group for Forest School.

Children participating in Forest School will go to a wild space, usually a wood, for at least a half-day a week for at least 10 weeks. In that space they will engage with the environment in a way that is age/stage appropriate but as child-initiated and child-led as possible (see Howe and Davies, Chapter 10). The leaders will be trained Forest School practitioners who are familiar with making the space as safe as possible, and who will have set up the expectations of the children and the other adults in ways to facilitate what is, with early years groups, creative free play. Taking risks is considered to be central to the process but, as I will discuss below, risks are different things to different people. One obvious risk is that we go to Forest School in all weathers except high winds. Getting hot and cold, wet and dry, are early risks children learn to manage – possibly rather better than some practitioners!

For children who are unused to such an environment it usually takes two or three weeks for them to overcome the initial risk of being in the wood and be ready to explore and play more creatively. That is facilitated by the experience taking place over time. This fits with the process of forming neural pathways in the brain. It is like creating a pathway across a field. The first walker only dents the grass. Only by subsequent feet treading the same path will the path become permanently established. Once it has been established, then even if it falls out of use, the faint trace of its existence will be visible to archaeologists hundreds of years in the future. Forest School aims to make big changes to children's lives. When children have experienced Forest School in the Foundation Stage they are more socially adept and have better dispositions

Photograph 12.1 Storytelling space in the snow.

to learning than children from similar origins who have not. As the HSE poster in Figure 12.1 says, 'Children should have fun . . . get fit, develop social skills and learn how to handle risks.'

Other benefits from participation in Forest School resonate with the drive to build better partnerships with parents. In my book, I cite findings from Worcestershire, where members of the local Bangladeshi communities have welcomed Forest School as linking the children to the more environmentally attuned culture of Bangladesh. Many settings report better communication with hard-to-reach families, who find they have something they can talk to practitioners about. And male carers seem to feel more able to contribute to outdoor activities than they do in indoor, more feminised spaces.

This is not the only way to enable wilder play outdoors. As I have said, there are many books making excellent suggestions for relieving the monotony and sterility of some paved, or even grassed, play areas. All of these will assume that practitioners already understand the need for riskier, wilder, play. One strong advocate is Richard Louv, whose organisation, Children and Nature (see 'Useful websites' at the end of this chapter) originates in North America but can offer ideas to us.

Why risky, wild play? What risks for under-5s?

Taking risks is essential to being a human being and we all do it all the time. It is just that we do not focus on the risks in all activities. Eating breakfast is risky – if the milk I pour on my flakes is sour I am exposed to potentially harmful bacteria, so I take an unconscious risk that it is edible, based on what I know about milk and how I have stored it. To know what I know I have pushed the limits of milk storage occasionally, and reaped my due rewards. 'Assessing and managing risk is a skill that needs to be developed, practised and refined if we are not to succumb to overwhelming anxiety or to recklessness' (Tovey 2007: 103). I do not expect a 3 year old to know what I know about storing milk. But if I deprive him of the opportunity to put the milk away in the fridge or to leave it on a sunny table in the summer, he will not have the opportunity to start that learning process.

This is the experiential learning process recognised by the *Learning Outside the Classroom Manifesto* (DfES 2006). It is the responsibility of practitioners to enable the children in their care to take the risks that are appropriate to them, so that they can learn experientially. One of the first risks we encourage children to take is to trust their own care and well-being to strangers, namely the practitioners in nurseries. We do not shy away from doing this, as we understand that it can be managed in a positive way, and that all children will need to separate from their main carer at some point (see Fabian and Dunlop, Chapter 15). The key phrase is 'to take the risks that are appropriate to them', recognising that we are all different and have had different prior experiences. Our natures equip us differently and our nurture gives us different opportunities. When taking a group of 4 year olds into a wood, I do not expect them all to react in the same way, although they all live within 10 miles of each other. Some will find just going into a wood sufficient of a risk, if they are not accustomed to walking along shady paths with nettles and brambles to negotiate. I would do those particular children a great disservice if I cleared those obstacles from the path before they arrived. Equally, I would be setting them up to fail if I did not point them out and talk about them as we walk.

Each practitioner needs to enable every child to stretch themselves physically, emotionally and intellectually. Usually, these things are interlinked. A baby sitting with a treasure basket will be gaining pleasure from exploring physically the natural objects which will in turn develop their conceptual understanding of those objects. A young child learning to balance on a log is using their physical skills and their intellectual knowledge of the nature of the log, and may be challenging themselves to be brave and try this new skill. Why I am suggesting that this is done outside is to counter some of the symptoms of 'nature deficiency disorder', as Louv (2008: 2) calls it.

We are seeing an increase in physical and mental health problems such as obesity, allergies, depression and unwanted behaviours. Many of us believe that these problems are linked to a disconnection between children and their natural environment. That this disconnection exists was highlighted by a survey undertaken in 2009 by the National Trust, which found that only 53 per cent of children surveyed could identify an oak leaf. Out of 17 questions, 11 were related to the natural world, 6 to the fictional world: more children could answer the 6 questions correctly than any of the 11.

Learning to take risks safely, whether that is climbing trees or running under them, prepares children for adulthood when the risks may be more critical. It is a better learning environment than the choices that children who have been deprived of risky play may opt for later, such as playing 'chicken' on busy roads. As Sir Digby Jones pointed out to headteachers in 2005, without risk today there are no entrepreneurs tomorrow. Climbing trees and running under them establishes habits of fresh air and exercise that, if established before children are 7, are likely to stay with them for life. These activities also help to foster respect and love for the environment, which will be important in the future fight against global warming and pollution. Without wild natural play we are potentially depriving our children of a large part of their future.

Safe as possible

As a responsible Forest School practitioner, I undertake risk assessments before I take children into the woods. It is a complex process, but not difficult. I assess the space, the likely activities, the competence of the children, any particular needs, and such like. My objective is not to eliminate risk but to create an opportunity that is as safe as it needs to be to enable those children on that day to take some chances. By taking chances they will learn and develop their skills. The paperwork I generate demonstrates to anyone accompanying me, be they OfSTED inspectors, headteachers or parents, that the risks are reasonable and the experience managed.

All settings have their own risk-assessment procedures. Introducing wilder and riskier play is not about ignoring them; it is about using them to protect the children and adults in your setting as far as reasonably practical (Health and Safety Executive 2006). It can even be an empowering process when you realise that a part of managing the hazards is to make others aware of their share of the responsibility for their own safety. Safety and risk taking are all about trust and shared responsibilities. When I light fires with 3 year olds, it is after we have spent time, usually weeks, building up a shared trust, and a shared understanding of how this thing is done, what the rules are, and what happens if they are not adhered to. It is their responsibility to adhere to the rules as it is mine to set them.

Another aspect to trust is to give children credit for choosing the activities that are relevant to them at any given time. In Forest School we try to hand over control to the children as much as we can. This may take time by the time children are of school age as they are becoming used to being organised and told what to do next. But younger children generally will establish their

Photograph 12.2   The author lighting fires with 3 year olds.

own agenda within a week or two. I took a mature student – an experienced practitioner – with me to visit a Forest School one day. We walked with the children from their setting to the wood in an orderly crocodile but once there they immediately scattered around the base camp area and were quickly engaged in deep and meaningful play. The student asked 'Who told them what to do?' No one, or at least only the little voice in their heads. They had purpose and intent, and were busy learning: about the environment; about themselves; about each other.

Once practitioners get used to this phenomenon they quickly realise that here is a wonderful opportunity to carry out observations and, when invited, they can join in and extend the play. This includes introducing tool use and the aforementioned fires. In this, Forest School is something akin to the Reggio Emilia approach, in that it is the children's interests and discoveries that lead the action and often inform activities back in the setting. This is the creativity of Forest School, which becomes a space as wide as children's imagination and as deep as their invention 'without barriers or expectations' (Else 2009: 93).

Making settings wilder

Not everyone can access Forest School and for the under-2s this may not be the best way to experience wilder and riskier play. It is, therefore, worth considering what it is that you can do to make your own settings wilder and riskier. The first step is to want to and to convince your colleagues that they want to.

The most effective way to make a big, deep change in yourself or a colleague is to experience the difference. Visit a setting where the outdoor play is of a kind that will really challenge you. Observe what happens when the children are there. Observe the adults and what they do. You will not be able to copy them exactly but you can start to develop the skills and experiences that will give you the confidence to make changes. My experience of Forest School is that the practitioners who come on training courses or visit Forest School in action may not have the confidence to go back straight away and launch into full-scale replicas of what they have seen, but they may change one thing and then another, and so on.

Another approach is to invite someone in to look at your premises. Recently I visited a day nursery to 'open' its willow igloo and, while I was there, we discussed how it could become wilder and riskier. It had a grassed play strip on two sides and a sloping path on a third. What it did own was the access to the adjacent primary school playing field, and the school was about to have work done there. We discussed the possibility of negotiating that access in exchange for digging a trench across one of the strips, thereby creating two slopes and the potential for a bridge. Instantly, one of the play areas would have greater physical challenges and opportunities, including scrambling, balancing and rolling.

For young children, differences in height do not have to be huge to create an interesting difference; half a metre is a good start. It can also help to make water even more interesting as it can now flow. Guttering added to large building blocks helps to inspire the civil engineer in us all. Garden centres now have siphons at reasonable prices to help water go up as well as down. Water is not just natural, it is elemental, and experimentation with it can have many outcomes, including mud, wet sand, washed stones, and so on.

I have mentioned treasure baskets as possibly the first encounter for babies with natural objects such as fir cones (Goldschmied and Jackson 2003). Play spaces can contain baskets of natural objects, that slightly older children will spend hours investigating and sorting. For example, stones, cones and shells all come in varieties of colours and sizes. This is instinctive maths, although it does not need this label to validate inclusion. One of the wilder aspects of this kind of play can be to persuade colleagues that objects can usefully migrate into the sand, water or mud for experimental purposes.

It is inevitable that children will get dirty if their play is wilder and more adventurous. They may well experience being muddy, wet and cold. Indeed, your setting may be the only opportunity they have to have that experience, so it is very important that it should happen. I was out with a group of 4 year olds in heavy rain when one of them pointed out to me that she was getting wet. 'Yes,' I said. She realised that I was giving her permission to experience rain and, instead of looking worried, proceeded to roll in the long grass, covering her waterproofs with grass seeds and water. After a gloriously wet hour we all returned to the nursery and peeled off the wet layers. Not a lot was left that was dry, so we raided the spare clothes box to its depths, bagging up the wet clothes to go home with some tired, happy and oddly dressed children. They were no longer in any doubt that if we get wet we do not swell up and pop (my favourite line to my students) but can dry off and resume normal life when appropriate to do so. It is not a cause for concern but a celebration of our climate, as our country would not look the same without it.

Experiencing the weather will require management, including the education of carers and colleagues. Setting up an area adjacent to the access point with wellington boots and waterproofs is a good starting point, including larger sizes for staff, who will be more willing to take their turn outside if they have the appropriate attire. Waterproofs can be an appropriate item to seek funding for, as local charities and organisations such as the Forestry Commission like to have something specific as the focus for bids for grants. The saying in Forest School circles is that there is no such thing as unsuitable weather, only unsuitable clothing.

Conclusion

All settings are being required to think about their outdoor provision. Not all settings can access something like Forest School. I do believe, however, that all settings can provide riskier and wilder play for their children. More than that, we have a duty to do so. Children need risks in order to develop the ability to keep themselves safe. Children need wilder experiences to engage with the natural world in order to become better world citizens. Children need to experience the awe and wonder of the natural world in order to grasp the enormity of what life has to offer them.

Questions to set you thinking

1   Is there a Forest School facility in your area? How can you find out? (Clue: see the 'Useful websites' section below!)
2   Do the children in your setting get sufficient opportunities for the kind of real freedom to be themselves and engage in wilder and riskier play such as that in Forest School settings?
3   Is there anything holding *you* and your team back from encouraging wild, risky play outdoors for young children?

References and further reading

Department for Children, Schools and Families (DCSF) (2007) *Early Years Foundation Stage Curriculum for England*. London: DCSF.

Department for Education and Skills (DfES) (2006) *Learning Outside the Classroom Manifesto*. Nottingham: DfES.

Else, P. (2009) *The Value of Play*. London: Continuum.

Gill, T. (2006) *Growing Adventure: Final Report to the Forestry Commission*. Available online at: http://www.forestry.gov.uk/england-play (accessed 9 August 2009).

Goldschmied, E. and Jackson, S. (2003) *People Under Three: Young Children in Day Care*. London: Routledge.

Health and Safety Executive (2006) *Five Steps to Risk Assessment*. Available online at: http://www.hse.gov.uk (accessed 9 August 2009).

HM Treasury (2004) *Every Child Matters*. London: HM Stationery Office. Available online at: http://www.dcsf.gov.uk/everychildmatters (accessed 9 August 2009).

Jones, Sir Digby, cited by Haplin, T. (2005) Children must learn to embrace risk, heads are told. London: *The Times* Online. Available online at: http://www.timesonline.co.uk/tol/news/uk/article387910.ece (accessed 9 August 2009).

Knight, S. (2009) *Forest Schools and Outdoor Learning in the Early Years.* London: Sage.

Knight, S. (ed.) (2010) *Risk and Adventure in Outdoor Play.* London: Sage.

Lindon, J. (2003) *Too Safe for Their Own Good?* London: National Children's Bureau.

Louv, R. (2008) *Last Child in the Woods* (2nd edn). USA: Alonquin.

National Trust (2009) *Wildlife is Alien to a Generation of Indoor Children.* Available online at: http://www.nationaltrust.org.uk (accessed 9 August 2009).

Palmer, S. (2006) *Toxic Childhood.* London: Orion.

Robinson, K. (2001) *Out of Our Minds: Learning to be Creative.* Chichester: Capstone.

Tovey, H. (2007) *Playing Outdoors.* Maidenhead: Open University Press.

United Nations Children's Fund (UNICEF) (2007) *Report on Childhood in Industrialised Countries.* Details downloadable from: http://www.unicef.org.uk (accessed 9 August 2009).

Useful websites

Children and Nature: http://www.childrenandnature.org

Forest Education Initiative Forest Schools: http://www.foresteducation.org/forest_schools.php

Green Light Trust: http://www.greenlighttrust.org

Institute for Outdoor Learning Forest Schools: http://www.outdoor-learning.org/membership/forest_schools_sig.htm

Play England: http://www.playengland.org.uk

PART 4

Play, pedagogy and culture in early education

13 The developmental and therapeutic potential of play: re-establishing teachers as play professionals

Justine Howard

Summary

There is a growing appreciation that education should be concerned with the whole child and not just the development of skills and knowledge (Grotewell and Burton 2008). Early years curricula that centralise play are consistent with this. The freedom and choice afforded to children in play promotes confidence, esteem and well-being, and as a result it has powerful developmental and therapeutic potential. Specialist courses in play include play therapy, playwork, developmental and therapeutic play, and hospital play. The majority of these courses are of at least one year's duration. Teachers and learning assistants receive markedly less training in play, despite the fact that children spend a great deal of their time in the school environment. *Teachers and classroom assistants are arguably the most important play professionals in children's lives.* This chapter argues that play has developmental and therapeutic potential regardless of the context in which it takes place and that, as such, it is vital that early years educators are equipped with a sound understanding as to *why*, and *in what ways*, play is such a powerful medium. It identifies the fundamental characteristics of play that render it valuable from a developmental and therapeutic perspective, and explains how play serves to support children's development using the challenge-resource model. It suggests that understanding why play is important to children's development is an essential starting point for all play professionals and that this has the potential to free early years educators from curriculum constraints, empowering them to develop informed play practice.

Introduction

Although play in early childhood has come under the spotlight over the past few decades, the consideration of play among scholars has persisted for centuries. The Greek philosopher Plato (427–347 BC) is said to have claimed that *you can discover more about a person in an hour of play than in a year of conversation.* We have a long-standing fascination with children's play and we have devoted considerable time to researching what is often described as children's natural occupation.

Providing systematic accounts of children's play from the perspective of *what* children play and *when*, has proven relatively easy. Without doubt, when we watch children playing there is evidence that their play affords them opportunities to develop gross and fine motor skills, to interact and converse with others, to explore the properties of objects or to demonstrate problem-solving capacity. Without doubt, observations of children's play demonstrate it changing in form, content and complexity over time. However, is describing change and opportunities for development in play really enough to justify its prominent place within policies surrounding early childhood? Children learn in a variety of ways – for example, by rote, observation, modelling and imitation. Do children really need to play in order to learn and develop? As a strong advocate of the developmental and therapeutic potential of play, I certainly do not wish to question its importance. However, determining *why* play is a unique mode of learning and development for children is a very difficult task. Not all of the developmental value inherent in play is easily observed and, as a concept, it has proven to be relatively elusive in terms of isolation as a causal variable (see Chapter 1). I have used the following exercise to demonstrate this point with students for many years (see Figures 13.1 and 13.2).

Figure 13.2 offers an example of what you may come up with.

- Observe a child or a group of children engaged in a play activity.
- Write a brief a description of this activity, and note down the learning or development you think is happening during the play.
- Next, go through your list and ask yourself the following question. Could children develop this skill without being engaged in play activities? The aim here is that you are trying to isolate something that children gain from play that can't be gained elsewhere.

Figure 13.1   An activity to set you thinking (1).

The play activity: a brother and sister are playing with the Lego blocks. They are each working on individual models (one is building a house and the other is developing a repeating pattern). Both are using the same box of Lego.

Learning opportunity	Area of development	Is this unique to play?
Taking turns with each other	Social	X
Colour recognition by selecting blocks	Cognitive/intellectual	X
Learning new words	Language/communication	X
Negotiation about pieces	Social	X
Fine motor skills via picking up and placing blocks	Physical	X

Figure 13.2 Example of possible outcome to the activity in Figure 13.1.

What did you find?

Invariably, there will be no unique learning opportunities left on your list (or at least very few)! Children can develop skills in multiple contexts, including those that are formal. For example, in Figure 13.2, children can learn to take turns in general conversation and are constantly perfecting their fine motor skills. They will use everyday experiences such as a walk to the shops, to learn about themselves, others and the world around them. Play is not necessarily essential for these things to develop. However, all is not lost, and this activity results in deep and critical thinking. My students often become defensive about play and a lot of healthy debate ensues! A common response is 'OK, so children may be able to develop these skills in lots of different ways, but there is something special about learning when it happens in play, something different.' Let's start to investigate what this special thing might be and why it might be frequently overlooked.

Understanding play

Cohen (2006) suggests that, since the 1950s, our motivation to study play has derived from three perspectives: cognitive, societal and emotional. Cohen associates different professional contexts with these areas. Play from an educational perspective is associated with cognitive development, play therapy with emotional development and the playwork movement with societal development. Traditionally, these perspectives have also differed in terms of whether they tend towards considering play as a way of *being* or as a way of *becoming*

(Sturrock *et al.* 2004). The cognitive approach has been more commonly associated with the way in which play contributes to children *becoming* competent learners. The societal and emotional approaches, however, have tended towards considering play for play's sake, and emphasise how *being* is inextricably linked to *becoming*. Their focus has been on the process of play and the qualities that render it valuable for development. Of course, developmental issues are not so easily divided and the boundaries between each of these areas are blurred. There is a distinct tendency, however, to build our knowledge base from the body of literature that is most closely associated with the work in which we are engaged. Specific texts are dedicated to play work, play therapy and play in early years education. Crucially, however, once we engage in critical thinking about play and begin to consider play as a disposition or approach to a task rather than merely an observable behaviour, similarities begin to emerge.

The developmental and therapeutic potential of play

Accounts of play from a developmental perspective can be divided into those that focus on the way play develops over time and those that consider how play promotes particular aspects of children's development. Parten (1932) identified how children's play becomes increasingly social, where initial play activity is largely solitary, progresses to parallel where children work alongside but not with one another, until, finally, children engage in full cooperative activity. A similar social trajectory is stressed in the more recent work of Broadhead (2004). Piaget (1952) identified how children's play progresses from that which is sensory in nature, towards object play as skill in symbolic representation emerges, followed by more complex play with rules. Rather than being concerned with the development of play from a social perspective, however, Piaget suggested that these different forms of play were consistent with the development of children's thinking skills.

A further body of research has sought to identify specific learning outcomes via play (e.g. Sylva *et al.* 1976; Pepler and Ross 1981). However, an important problem associated with trying to provide evidence for the developmental potential of play is that it is a difficult concept to define (Moyles 1989; Garvey 1991). Without a definition, we have been unable to isolate play as being causal and it has been argued that previous studies have failed to show that it is specifically play (rather than any other experience) that is influencing children's development. Even studies of children who are deprived of play face problems in this regard as, often, being deprived of play is coupled with other forms of deprivation such as malnourishment, inadequate parenting or poor housing conditions. Significant advances have been made in providing evidence for the developmental potential of play as a result of research that has investigated children's own perceptions of what constitutes play activity (Howard 2009, 2010).

Research into children's perceptions of their own play has revealed that they define play according to where, when and with whom the activity takes place (Karrby 1989; Wing 1995; Howard 2002). My work has systematically elicited children's perceptions of their own play using photographs of classroom situations, and has consistently revealed that children use personal choice and control in order to define play (Howard 2002; Howard *et al.* 2006). Crucially, the same research also shows that these perceptions are not static. Children develop an understanding of what it means to play based on their experiences. For example, children who experience directed activities at the table and free play on the floor or teacher involvement in formal activity but not often in play, pick up on these cues and use them to categorise future play events (so activities where an adult is present or activities that occur on a table are not considered to be play). Children perceiving an activity as play or not play has a significant influence on how they behave and perform during problem-solving tasks. Using children's own perceptions to create practice conditions, McInnes *et al.* (2009) have shown that children who practise a task under playful conditions (voluntary, on the floor and with no adult present) show more purposeful problem-solving strategies, more independence and are far less distracted than those who practise under formal conditions (directed activity at the table with an adult present). Whitebread (2010) has also found increased frequency and sophistication of meta-cognitive events in play where adults are not present. However, adult interaction is arguably an important feature of quality early years environments (Siraj-Blatchford and Sylva 2004). Understanding children's perceptions allows us to maximise on learning via play rather than learning disguised as play: play *as* pedagogy rather than play *for* pedagogy. Teachers are pivotal in creating and maintaining the conditions for play and, with careful consideration, can be accepted as play partners (Payler 2007; Westcott and Howard 2007; Rogers and Evans 2008; Howard and McInnes 2010). Being sensitive to choice and control in play enables practitioners to support children's development in activities that they themselves perceive to be play, while at the same time injecting a sense of playfulness into more purposeful activities. Starting with a fundamental understanding as to the nature of play allows practitioners to maximise on the potential of children's playful disposition.

Just as there appears to be contention between play *for* pedagogy and play *as* pedagogy, there exists a similar contention in relation to play *for* therapy and play *as* therapy (see also Georgeson and Payler, Chapter 2). The naturally occurring therapeutic value of play is probably best associated with non-directive play therapy (Axline 1969). Axline proposes that, in their play, children are able to work through challenges, developing and experimenting with strategies for problem solving, learning about themselves and others (McMahon 2009). In this approach it is essential that children are in control of the play activity, and the adult role is to provide and maintain a genuine, warm and accepting environment (see Goouch, Chapter 3). The play activity is chosen by the child and they are in complete control over the emergent narrative. Care is taken to ensure a sense of permissiveness, and adult interaction takes the form of reflection. No praise or judgement is offered as this would be suggestive that certain elements of play might be more desirable than others. In this approach, the therapist is not conducting psychotherapy in the traditional sense but is acting as a partner, witnessing and valuing children's play. It is here that we can begin to see how developmental and therapeutic potential are inextricably linked. If we offer opportunities that are defined by children as play based on freedom, choice and control, we create an environment that facilitates both intellectual and emotional growth (Whitehead, Chapter 5).

Despite being best known for his work in the field of cognitive development, even Piaget recognised the therapeutic potential inherent in child directed play and is said to have remarked 'We can be sure that all happenings, pleasant or unpleasant, in the child's life, will have repercussion on her dolls.' Similarly, Bruner (1983) suggested that when children are in direct control of their play, they are afforded a unique opportunity to think, talk and be themselves.

While we have readily accepted the work of these theorists in relation to teaching and learning, their insight into children's emotional health has been largely ignored. Ecclestone and Hayes (2008) talk of the dangerous rise of therapeutic education and, certainly, it would be dangerous to unnecessarily expose vulnerabilities, to emphasise emotional development at the expense of educational achievement or to claim there is a need to teach children how to be happy (Oakshott 2008). However, far from creating a culture of children who require therapy, attending to children's emotional and intellectual needs via play would appear to increase resiliency and lessen this likelihood. A play-based curriculum that focuses on emotional well-being builds on the inherent value of play. This is not articulated well within curriculum documentation, however, which tends to emphasise what kind of play experiences teachers *should* provide, rather than a clear rationale as to *why* play is important.

As is argued by Hyder (2005), the vast majority of children, even those who face significant challenge, may not need therapy if they have the ability, and opportunity, to play. Play serves as one of these many resource pools, and empowers children to meet intellectual and emotional challenge with lower levels of anxiety. This lower level of anxiety leads to an increased sense of well-being, emotional security and subsequent improved task performance. The inherent value of play from a developmental and therapeutic perspective is shared. My challenge-resource model of play is presented in Figure 13.3.

Figure 13.3 illustrates how the relationship between play resources available and complexity of task determines the level of anxiety/challenge experienced by a child and the potential support required.

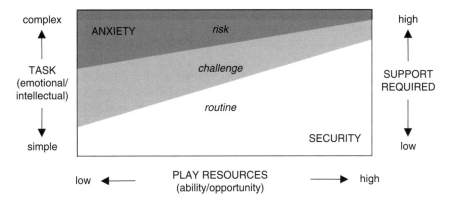

Figure 13.3 The challenge-resource model of play.

A holistic approach to education

A holistic approach to education that emphasises emotional well-being is evident in the experiential curricula developed by Laevers (Laevers *et al.* 1994; Laevers 2000). This suggests that an enriched, experiential learning environment stimulates developmental and therapeutic processes that manifest in optimal personal growth. Recent developments in early years curricula in the UK have also begun to emphasise children's emotional health, proposing that this is core to achievement across other developmental domains. The Welsh Foundation Phase Curriculum states that children's well-being is at the heart of early learning experiences and that children generally learn better when they are happy in themselves (DCELLS 2008: 4). Play is seen as a key way to support children's emotional and intellectual growth, and early years educators are pivotal in the development of playful learning experiences both in terms of the environment they provide and the nature of their interactions with the children.

This philosophy is consistent with the literature surrounding the fundamental characteristics of play and the maintenance of children's playful disposition. It is also not entirely new. Zachry (1929) argued that children's emotional and intellectual development were so intertwined that 'success in one was contingent on success in the other' (p. 272), and Maslow's hierarchy (1947) clearly identified the significance of meeting emotional needs in a bid for self-actualisation. However, up until now there seems to have been a resistance towards the integration of ideas from the field of counselling and therapy into education (Mayes 2009). Given that we are now more aware as to the nature of play and the qualities that render it powerful from both a developmental and therapeutic perspective, perhaps it is time to reconsider this reluctance. Perhaps it is unavoidable that teachers must function as therapists to some extent 'not in the formal sense of conducting therapy ... but in the practical sense of being alert and responsive to psychological needs' (Basch 1989: 772).

One way forward might be to reconceptualise what is meant by the term therapeutic. Rather than being solely related to a person's engagement in therapy, the term therapeutic would appear to encompass a much broader range of restorative behaviour. We can reflect on our own recreational activities to highlight this point (see Figure 13.4).

- What kinds of activities are you involved in outside of your work or study life? Do you go swimming or to a craft class? Do you love cooking or reading books?
- What are your reasons for being involved in these activities?
- In what ways do you think these activities are important to you?
- How would you feel if you weren't able to do these things?

What did you find?
When asked about our recreational activities (essentially our adult 'play'), we tend to focus almost exclusively on therapeutic potential.

Some of the previous responses this activity has provoked include:
  'I just find it really therapeutic: it's a release from the pressure of life'
  'it's not something I have to do and I don't have to be great at it'
  'it provides me with an escape from work'
  'it makes me a more balanced person, it reminds me I'm not only a mum, a wife or a nurse, I am me too'
  'it makes me feel good about myself'
  'I get rid of all my anger and anxiety'

Figure 13.4   An activity to set you thinking (2).

The importance of play training

Wood (2007) suggests there is a contention between play for the sake of play and play for the purposes of education. However, I propose that this contention is fuelled by the fact that classroom practice has largely been driven by accounts that describe the *what* and *when* of play, rather than the *why*. As we have seen, there are qualities inherent in play that render it powerful from a developmental and therapeutic perspective, and these cannot necessarily be isolated. With curriculum emphasis on emotional health and well-being, we are beginning to see a shift away from the *teacher-master* conception to the *teacher-therapist* conception (Shalem and Bensusan 1999, cited in Mayes 2009), and it is vital that early years educators are treated as play professionals and are afforded the training necessary to prepare them for this role. Despite their spending the most time with the most children, teachers and learning assistants receive markedly less training in the field of play than other professionals (Howard 2009).

Soles *et al.* (2009) argue that teachers have such a vital role in supporting children's mental health and identifying when intervention might be required, that training must be amended to include more emphasis on typical and atypical development. Play-based curricula have the potential not only to illuminate such issues but also offer the potential for healing and development. From an educational perspective, to maximise on the potential of play, 'early childhood educators need a sophisticated pedagogical repertoire that is grounded in contemporary theories and research evidence' (Wood 2007: 318). As we have seen, contemporary research evidence based on listening to children's voices, highlights particular features of play that render it valuable, and these features are those that render it valuable from both a developmental and therapeutic perspective.

Theoretical understanding and levels of training in play, however, have repeatedly been highlighted as a challenge to implementing play-based curricula in the early years (Bennett *et al.* 1997; Moyles *et al.* 2002; Howard and McInnes 2010) and this challenge was evident long before education became so heavily focused on emotional health and well-being. Teachers have faced the dilemma of having to balance their intuitive belief in the value of play with parental pressure towards academic achievement and the need to document learning outcomes (Palmer 2006). They have felt as though they were driving a curriculum van (Edwards and Knight 1994) rather than being guided by any real philosophy of learning. It is hardly surprising that many have articulated a lost sense of professionalism (Moyles 2001). The following case study describes the Effective Play Practice in the Classroom (EPPIC) training programme (Howard and Alderson 2010). It demonstrates what can be achieved when professionals are afforded the opportunity to develop a fundamental understanding as to the nature of play via experiential learning, reflective practice, and sharing knowledge and experience.

Case study: About the EPPIC programme

The Effective Play Practice in the Classroom (EPPIC) training formed part of a large Welsh Assembly government-funded project that was designed to support practitioners in promoting children's emotional health and well-being. EPPIC is an intensive six-day training that has at its core, the challenge-resource model of play. Considering the challenges practitioners have described when implementing play within previous curricula, the training was designed to ensure that the benefits of the Foundation Phase were maximised. The training ran one day per week for a six-week period and was largely experiential, requiring involvement in practical tasks, reflection on personal experiences of play in childhood and critical reflection on current classroom practice. The topics covered through the training included the following.

- *What is play*? Theories of play, its developmental function and inherent characteristics.
- *The playful classroom*: understanding why children's perceptions of play are important and learning how to gauge children's views using photographs.
- *The role of the adult in children's play*: the value of being a play partner, enabling children's choice and control.
- *Creative play practice*: identifying the benefits of different play types and the way in which these might feed into the curriculum.
- *Inclusion and diversity in play*: understanding the importance of cultural difference in play and facilitating play for diverse groups.
- *Record keeping and assessment:* identifying the need for additional support or referral via play, and utilising play for assessment and planning.

The EPPIC course was designed to:

- increase practitioners theoretical understanding as to the nature of play and introduce them to research that links play with learning and development
- highlight the affective qualities of play that make it a unique and valuable form of learning, healing and development
- enable practitioners to confidently defend play-based practices
- demonstrate how play might be used for assessment and recording purposes across all areas of learning within the Foundation Phase
- raise awareness about the power of play from recreational, therapeutic and educational perspectives
- equip practitioners with the practical skills and confidence to become involved with children in their play.

Thirty practitioners from one local authority in Wales took part in the first EPPIC training. This included 15 nursery and reception class teachers and 15 classroom assistants. The eventual aim of the authority is for all early years practitioners to have received the training. We measured whether the aims of EPPIC were met, via a pre- and post-training questionnaire and a sample of interviews.

Knowledgeable, confident and professional practitioners

Prior to EPPIC, practitioners reported low levels of training in play. Surprisingly, some practitioners had received no play training at all (e.g. 'I've learned it all on the job really') and the most common type of training reported related to the Foundation Phase curriculum. Before training, the average practitioner rating of their theoretical understanding was low and the way practitioners described the benefits of play was heavily linked to how play could be used as a tool for delivering the curriculum. Few theorists were referred to (e.g. 'I seem to remember Piaget and Vygotsky'). Following training, however, practitioners' ratings of theoretical understanding significantly increased and the range of material drawn on to justify play practice was broad, focusing on intellectual, social and emotional development. Practitioners showed a much deeper understanding as to the inherent value of play (e.g. 'Play is a catalyst for emotional well-being and that's why it promotes learning' or 'Children are more playful in a happy environment where they feel safe to explore').

Practitioners left the programme more confident in their ability to defend play practice, and felt empowered in their role as a teacher (e.g. 'I understand the principles and educational value of learning through play, I can back up my beliefs and opinions'). They described feeling far less constrained by the need to measure or set up activities that met curriculum objectives. Practitioners also reported an increase in their own playfulness. Prior to the training, practitioners attributed levels of playfulness in their classroom solely to the children (e.g. 'The group I have this year aren't really playful at all' or 'Sometimes they are moody or tired'). After training, however, they were much more aware of how the experiences they provided and the way in which they interacted, influenced how children functioned in their class (e.g. 'I am more aware of how playful I am now, I try to show the children I am having fun too' or 'The children seem more playful on the floor so I have tried to take directed activities down to that level; it seems to work'). A crucial finding was that not only did practitioners become more involved with children in their play after the training, but that this involvement was more likely to be as a play partner, rather than as a teacher, modeller or guide (e.g. 'I wait to be invited to play and am more of a partner than a director now' or 'I try and go with the flow, I let the children tell me what to do, it really shows them that I value their play and their ideas').

Practitioner reflections

> Before the training I mainly thought of play as an opportunity to increase intellectual development, however EPPIC raised my

awareness of the importance of play for children's emotional development too. Many changes have been made in my classroom as a result of the training, the routine has been altered to include more time for free play, the staff are now aware about the importance of observations and we often follow the principles of the non-directive approach giving children freedom and control. Children view us more as 'playmates' rather than 'teachers' now because we've allowed them to take ownership of their play. Both the children and the staff have benefited and I am certainly more confident.

(Reception class nursery nurse)

The best thing was understanding more about why children play, and how it helps their learning. I can see now how play fits in the Foundation Phase. My practice has changed. Now I'm not afraid to hang back and observe the children while they are playing. I feel I have learnt more about the children from doing this and I know them better as a result. I have noticed a difference in the children too. I have made a big effort to become a play partner with them and as a result, over the last few weeks I have noticed that they are more frequently asking me to join in their play and they are enjoying it when I do!

(Reception teacher)

Since the training I've become much more aware about why play is important. I've found the ideas from non-directive work (giving children freedom, choice and control) really valuable. I'm much more involved in the play now. We are also starting to use photographs to see how children feel about the activities we are offering them and we also use the involvement scale. It's really reassuring to see that the activities children see as most playful are also the ones they're most heavily involved in. I feel much more confident about justifying why children need to play now.

(Nursery/reception teacher)

Conclusion

This chapter has considered *why* play is important for children's emotional and intellectual development. Identifying the fundamental characteristics of play has highlighted the vital role of early years educators as play professionals and the need for this professional status to be recognised. The chapter suggests that a play-based curriculum promotes resilience, self-esteem and flexibility of thought that can enable children to meet intellectual and emotional challenge as empowered individuals. Focusing on play *as* pedagogy frees practitioners from the constraints of providing activities that simply look like play and allows them to share in children's activities as play partners. With this freedom, however, comes the need to acknowledge that play *as* pedagogy and play *as* therapy are inextricably linked. Far from suggesting that all teachers must act as therapists or that all children are in need of therapy, the chapter simply asks us to consider whether, if we truly believe in the power of play (defined by children themselves via their perception of freedom, choice and control), we are prepared for how this might manifest in their play from both a developmental and therapeutic perspective. It urges us to re-establish early years educators as play professionals and empower them to be driven by a philosophy of play.

Questions to set you thinking

1   How far do I understand the theoretical grounding of a play-based curriculum?
2   Do I understand *why* play supports children's emotional and intellectual development? .
3   Am I truly offering children freedom, choice and control in their play?
4   How playful are the play experiences in my classroom?
5   What is my role in children's play? Am I happy with this role?

References and further reading

Axline, V. (1969) *Play Therapy*. New York: Ballentine Books.
Basch, M. (1989) The teacher the transference and development. In K. Field, B. Cohler and G. Wool (eds) *Learning and Education: Psychoanalytic Perspectives*. Madison: International University Press.
Bennett, N., Wood, L. and Rogers, S. (1997) *Teaching Through Play*. Buckingham: Open University Press.
Broadhead, P. (2004) *Early Years Play and Learning: Developing Social Skills and Cooperation*. London: Routledge.
Bruner, J.S. (1983) Play, thought, and language. *Peabody Journal of Education*, 60: 6–69.
Cohen, D. (2006) *The Development of Play*. London: Routledge.
Department for Children, Education, Lifelong Learning and Skills (DCELLS) (2008) *Revised Curriculum: Foundation Stage*. Available online at: http://wales.gov.uk/topics/educationandskills/curriculumassessment/arevisedcurriculumforwales/foundationphase/?lang=en (accessed 30 December 2009).
Ecclestone, K. and Hayes, D. (2008) *The Dangerous Rise of Therapeutic Education*. London: Routledge.

Edwards, A. and Knight, P. (1994) *Effective Education in the Early Years*. Buckingham: Open University Press.

Garvey, C. (1991) *Play* (2nd edn). London: Fontana.

Grotewell, P.G. and Burton, Y.R. (2008) *Early Childhood Education: Issues and Developments*. New York: Nova Science Publishers.

Howard, J. (2002) Eliciting young children's perceptions of play, work and learning using the activity apperception story procedure. *Early Child Development and Care*, 127: 489–502.

Howard, J. (2009) Play, learning and development in the early years. In T. Maynard and N. Thomas (eds) *An Introduction to Early Childhood Studies*. London: Sage.

Howard, J. (2010) Making the most of play in the early years: understanding and building on children's perceptions. In P. Broadhead, J. Howard and E. Wood (eds) *Play and Learning in Early Childhood: Research into Practice*. London: Sage.

Howard, J. and Alderson, D. (2010) Early years practitioners as play professionals: findings from the Effective Play Practice in the Classroom (EPPIC) project. *Educational and Child Psychology*, 27(2): forthcoming.

Howard, J. and McInnes, K. (2010) Thinking through the challenge of a play-based curriculum: increasing playfulness via co-construction. In J. Moyles (ed.) *Thinking about Play: Developing a Reflective Approach*. Maidenhead: Open University Press.

Howard, J., Jenvey, V. and Hill, C. (2006) Children's categorisation of play and learning based on social context. *Early Child Development and Care*, 176(3/4): 379–393.

Hyder, T. (2005) *Play, War and Conflict*. Buckingham: Open University Press.

Karrby, G. (1989) Children's conceptions of their own play. *International Journal of Early Childhood Education*, 21(2): 49–54.

Laevers, F. (2000) Forward to basics! *Early Years: An International Journal for Research and Development*, 20(2): 20–29.

Laevers, F., Vandenbussche, E., Kog, M. and Depondt, L. (1994) *A Process-oriented Child Monitoring System for Young Children*. Belgium: Centre for Experiential Education.

Maslow, A. (1947) A theory of human motivation. *Psychological Review*, 50(4): 370–396.

Mayes, C. (2009) The psychoanalytic view of teaching and learning. *Journal of Curriculum Studies*, 41(4): 539–567.

McInnes, K., Howard, J., Miles, G.E. and Crowley, K. (2009) Behavioural differences exhibited by children when practising a task under formal and playful conditions. *Educational and Child Psychology*, 26(2): 31–39.

McMahon, L. (2009) *The Handbook of Play Therapy and Therapeutic Play*. Abingdon: Routledge.

Moyles, J. (1989) *Just Playing: The Role and Status of Play in Early Childhood Education*. Buckingham: Open University Press.

Moyles, J. (2001) Passion, paradox and professionalism in early years education. *Early Years: An International Journal of Research and Development*, 21(2): 89–95.

Moyles, J., Adams, S. and Musgrove, A. (2002) *Study of Pedagogical Effectiveness in Early Learning (SPEEL)*. London: Department for Education and Skills Research Report No. 363.

Oakshott, H. (2008) Pupils taught how to be happy. Headline article from *The Sunday Times*, 7 September.

Palmer, S. (2006) *Toxic Childhood*. London: Orion.

Parten, M. (1932) Social participation among preschool children. *Journal of Abnormal and Social Psychology*, 27: 242–269.

Payler, J. (2007) Opening and closing interactive spaces: shaping four-year-old children's participation in two English settings. *Early Years: An International Journal of Research and Development*, 27(3): 237–254.

Pepler, D.J. and Ross, H.S. (1981) The effects of play on convergent and divergent problem solving. *Child Development*, 52(4): 1202–1210.

Piaget, J. (1952) *The Origins of Intelligence in Children*. New York: Norton.

Rogers, S. and Evans, J. (2008) *Inside Role-play in Early Childhood Education. Researching Young Children's Perspectives*. Abingdon: Routledge.

Soles, T., Bloom, E., Health, N. and Kargiannakis, A. (2009) An exploration of teachers' current perceptions of children with emotional and behavioural difficulties. *Emotional and Behavioural Difficulties*, 13(4): 275–290.

Siraj-Blatchford, I. and Sylva, K. (2004) Researching pedagogy in English preschools. *British Educational Research Journal*, 30(5): 713–730.

Sturrock, G., Russell, W. and Else, P. (2004) *Towards Ludogogy, Parts I, II and III. The Art of Being and Becoming through Play*. Sheffield: Ludemos.

Sylva, K., Bruner, J.S. and Genova, P. (1976) The role of play in the problem-solving of children 3–5 years old. In J.S. Bruner, A. Jolly and K. Sylva (eds) *Play: Its Role in Development and Evolution*. Harmondsworth: Penguin.

Westcott, M. and Howard, J. (2007) Creating a playful classroom environment. *Psychology of Education Review*, 31(1): 27–34.

Whitebread, D. (2010) Play, metacognition and self-regulation. In P. Broadhead, J. Howard and E. Wood (eds) *Play and Learning in the Early Years: Research into Practice*. London: Sage.

Wing, L. (1995) Play is not the work of the child: young children's perceptions of work and play. *Early Childhood Research Quarterly*, 10(4): 223–247.

Wood, E. (2007) New directions in play: consensus or collision? *Education 3–13*, 35(4): 309–320.

Zachry, C.B. (1929) *Personality Adjustments of School Children*. New York: Scribner Sons.

14 Building friendship through playful learning in the early years

Pat Broadhead

Summary

This chapter identifies the development of friendships as a seldom considered but key aspect of educator responsibility in an early years setting. It examines and illustrates how friendship is linked both to identity development and to high-order intellectual engagements between interacting and cooperating peers across the early years. Such engagements are clearly a crucial site for learning for young children. The chapter looks at aspects of playful pedagogy and considers how the 'whatever you want it to be place' might stimulate the development of friendships and the potential for intellectual challenge by allowing children to bring their own thematic interests and cultural experiences into their early years setting and to jointly engage in playful explorations of these with peers, with newly emerging friends and with well-established friends.

Introduction

The study of, or reflections on, friendship within the early years educational literature is quite rare. Many texts, of course, talk about the importance of children developing social skills and of children's activities within 'peer groups' but seldom of friendship as an integral and developing part of their playful engagements with peers. Friendship is so much more than the development of social skills or being active within a peer group; it is an integral part of the young child's growing sense of culture and identity, just as it is also for young people and adults. It is also often the case that, where friendship is considered in relation to young children's playful experiences in their early years settings, it may be associated most predominantly with outdoor play, especially as children move beyond the Foundation Stage and on into Key Stage 1; as something not within the orbit of the educator to understand or nurture. In this chapter, I want to explore and consider how central the concept of friendship might be to children's learning processes in early years settings both in the classroom and in the outdoor classroom.

For many years, I have been researching how children become sociable and cooperative in their play in educational settings and the links with learning (Broadhead 1997, 2001, 2004, 2006, 2009, 2010a, 2010b). The research is based on observations of children playing together in traditionally available activities – places where they might be more likely to interact with one another such as the sand, water, role play, large and small construction, and small world activities. Many of these observations, over the years, have been undertaken with practitioners as co-researchers. We follow our observations with post-observation reflections that are informed by the practitioner's greater knowledge of individual children, their recognised interests and play preferences, and by my own wider experience of observation and interpretation and of the related literature on play and learning. This chapter draws on a range of cameos taken from this research and used to illustrate how friendship-building links with curriculum and pedagogical development in early years settings through facilitating open-ended, playful learning experiences.

Play and friendship in the *Early Years Foundation Stage* (EYFS)

Play is more substantially evidenced within the EYFS (DfES 2007) for children aged from birth to 5 years than it was in the previous curriculum for children aged from 3 to 5 years (DfEE 2000). We are informed (para. 1.16) that play underpins the delivery of all the EYFS, and (para. 1.17) that play underpins all development and learning for young children. Paragraph 1.20 lists what children might achieve through play but, unfortunately, the list makes no reference to friendship development. Children are identified as 'unique individuals' (para. 1.24) but not substantively as social beings who can make and share meanings with peers as well as with facilitative adults. In some cases, play seems to sound rather like a vehicle for curriculum delivery by adults rather than an opportunity for children to understand the world around them in the company of similarly and collaboratively engaged peers. There is a short, welcome section in the *Principles into Practice* Section 2.1, 'Respecting each other', on 'Friendships', which briefly reiterates the emotional value of friendships and the inherent sense of fun they carry; but no mention of the capacity of young children to set and solve increasingly complex problems together when working with trusted and familiar peers; the intellectual dimension and potential for shared experiences of cognitive challenge that arises from friendship-based interactions is lacking as is the sense of helping children to understand their own characters and personalities in relation to the development of their relationships with other children.

In some contrast to the EYFS, the *New Brunswick Curriculum Framework* in Canada (Department of Social Development 2008), has a related publication entitled: *Well-being, Professional Support Development* (Ashton *et al.* 2008). I want to quote an insert from p. 29, provided by a Children's Centre practitioner within this curriculum document. For me, this captures an inherent commitment to a much deeper engagement with the complexities of friendship as interconnected to character and personality, even for very young children.

Sam, in focus in the extract, is aged 4 years. This Canadian curriculum encourages the use of Learning Stories, as discussed by Carr (2001) and Whitehead (in this volume, Chapter 5). Learning Stories focus on the child as a learner in specific contexts rather than on their achievement or otherwise of de-contextualised objectives and skills. Instead of the mechanics of ticking achievement or noting 'failure', Learning Stories provide a more holistic and natural picture of the child's strengths and development as observed in situ. The use of Learning Stories also aims to encourage children to 'think about and display their learning' (Cowie and Carr 2004: 97) to, in effect, become partners in the assessment process, as this practitioner invites Sam to do, below. In this slightly edited reflection, we can see the practitioner actively engaging with this greater complexity in her intention to support the development of positive relationships and hence friendships between Sam and his peers. She helps Sam to see his strengths and deems it a privilege to do so.

Cameo 14.1

As human beings, we are made up of a mind, a body and a spirit. As educators, we often tend to focus on the children's minds and their physical bodies, but what about who they are as people? . . . To ignore the child's personality or character de-values who they are as people, which is crucial to how they see themselves and how they relate to others. Learning Stories provide an opportunity to share even the very heart of a child.

In this case [here, she is referring to a previously recorded observation] Sam acted kindly . . . He has such a heart to help others and I wanted to bring this part of Sam to light . . . Sam has a real passion for superheroes. He would pretend-fight his enemies. Heroes do fight enemies and I didn't want to discourage Sam's passion to be a hero by dictating how a hero should behave . . . I took Sam aside and we sat on the stairs . . . I told him that I had noticed how many times he reached out to others to help or comfort. I connected Sam's passion for heroes with Sam's character. I told him that helping others is a big part of what makes a hero a hero.

I could see in his face that he had really grasped that lesson. What a privilege to be able to encourage and speak into the life of a child. To me, this is what teaching is all about. (Jill McGuigan)

Interestingly, the *Rose Review* (2008) has opened up wider debates around play and learning in KS1 and 2, and also the relevance of active learning approaches and child-initiated enquiry in these older-age classrooms. The *Review* draws directly on Vygotskian theory and, from para. 2.69 onwards, makes several references to 'play-based learning' and the relevance of this, especially within KS1; a very new development for curriculum provision in England (as Angela Anning points out in Chapter 1). If pedagogical restructuring were to follow on from the implementation of a revised curriculum, group work may begin to emerge yet again in primary schools, as a more common pedagogical approach and, along with it, debates about group dynamics, social interactions and friendship groupings may also emerge as a basis for supporting collaborative and interactive commitment among older children. Of course, older children are developing more sophisticated strategies for making and keeping friends than are younger, early years children, but we should not underestimate the capacities of younger children, and we should recognise the inherent challenges for all children of making and keeping friends within an educational setting and the need for it to be acknowledged as important within pedagogies of practice.

Why is friendship important for children in an early years setting?

My own research has built on Vygotsky's work and those who have taken and developed Vygotskian theories. Vygotsky argued that learning is a social process and that play is a principle activity for children in relation to building knowledge and understanding of the world in all its aspects (Vygotsky 1978). He maintained that younger children learn best when actively engaged alone and with peers, and while making meaning in a well-resourced environment (Yelland *et al.* 2008). This environment should be structured so as to recognise both their intellectual and their cultural interests. It should allow the child to immerse in their learning both socially and culturally within their 'zone of proximal development', this being the learning space into which they may move with assistance from expert others – some of whom may be adults and some of whom may be children – their peers and friends (Vygotsky 1978).

In terms of progress within and beyond the zone, Vygotsky reiterates the importance of these expert others. While the educator is a very important 'expert other' in terms of knowing where the child is in the learning process in order to move them forward (also known as scaffolding, see Wood *et al.* 1976) other children can also be expert others (Gallimore and Tharp 1990; Broadhead 2004) when they play with peers whom they know well and regularly expose them to their own skills and abilities and, through language, their own ways of thinking about the problems and creative experiences with which they are engaging. And these are the sorts of things we tend to do with friends rather than with strangers or acquaintances. If we accept Vygotskian theory relating to the social and cultural dimensions of learning, then as educators, this gives us particular responsibilities in building and developing a learning environment that not only helps children to develop their social skills and their personality but that actively supports children in the ability to build and maintain friendships as an important part of their individual learning processes and engagements with intellectual challenge.

Studies also tell us that children's play is more complex and intellectually challenging when they are playing with friends (Howes 1994); they tell us, too, that cooperative play is more sustained when engaged in by friends (Hartup 1996; Green *et al.* 2003). In part, this may be because, through their friendships, children begin to recognise cultural similarities in the extent to which 'others' are like themselves in terms perhaps of the interests they have and the things they like to do, and are learning to do well through practice, repetition and re-engagements in a learning environment where they are allowed to explore and experiment together on a regular basis. The more familiar children are with one another – and this includes quite young children of 3 or 4 years – the more likely they are to be able to resolve their conflicts and continue their play. In my own research (Broadhead 2009), I have argued that conflict resolution among familiar peers can often help the play to progress to greater levels of cognitive challenge with associated high levels of problem solving and with quite complex uses of language. In the next section, I want to use some of my observations to illustrate some aspects of *friendship-in-action* within the learning process and also friendship-in-development, which I will look at first.

Friendship-in-development

Friendships are 'made', which implies the passage of time. Educators are often heard saying to children 'We are all friends here.' It's understandable why this phrase is used; the adult is trying to denote a sense of community to the child, perhaps a sense of togetherness and shared responsibility. However, there is a danger of conveying a false sense of community, or indeed no sense of community at all, to a child who has not yet made any friends, perhaps because they are new to the setting (see Fabian and Dunlop, Chapter 15). Young children are in the process of learning what a friend is, which is why we often hear them asking: 'Are you my friend?' or 'You're my friend, aren't you?' As well as seeking to make a social relationship, the child is also building their concept of 'friend' and of how friends behave, of what friends do and of why they might want a friend. All this has to be learned and an early years setting is, potentially, an excellent place to learn this.

In any community, only some of the members are actually friends because a friend, as the dictionary tells us, is 'a person one likes and chooses to spend time with'. When young early years children enter their early years community they may know none of the other children so the notion of 'all being friends here' is, in effect, a nonsense just as it is for any adult newly entering a work community where they know no one.

Friendship is not a contrivance to manage human behaviour; it is a state of being, and by no means necessarily a permanent state. As children become older, they have core friends and contingency friends that they fall back on; we are a social species and children without friends are seldom happy children (Factor 2009).

In a recent publication, I reflected:

> At the heart of any successful relationship – for adults or children – is the right to make choices from a range of possibilities. The ability to make choices is a skill and has to be learned; this means it has to be practised and a good early years' environment is one where children get lots of practice appropriate to their developing abilities and knowledge. Much of this, of course, they do through play and much of their playful learning comes through their engagements with others – hence the need for a capacity to develop good relationships.
>
> (Broadhead 2010b)

Consider this next cameo, based on a recent observation in an early years unit, and begin to consider what kinds of choices Nadia and Roxanna are each making in their own small but important ways.

Cameo 14.2

Nadia and Roxanna are both new children in the unit, having been here as afternoon part-timers for about three weeks. Nadia is already confidently exploring the environment and interacting with adults. She plays alongside other children sometimes but not yet with them. Roxanna is often observed quietly walking around the unit. She watches other children and watches adults interact with other children but seldom approaches adults or children. She will sometimes go to a table and use the materials to draw or play but does not seem to want to interact with others.

Today, a tape of Abba is playing by a raised stage area. Nadia goes to it immediately, climbs on the stage and begins to dance, smiling at others but not speaking. Roxanna goes over and watches Nadia as she dances, she smiles but does not make eye contact with Nadia. Nadia does not seem to notice and continues to dance to the music. Roxanna copies Nadia's actions and Nadia looks at her, studies her for a moment and then smiles and makes eye contact. Both girls smile and the eye contact is intermittent over a very brief period. Nadia finishes her dancing and goes outside. Roxanna goes to watch her but does not go through the door to the outdoor area.

Nadia returns a few minutes later and goes back to the dancing. Roxanna sees her immediately and goes over to be near her (but not on the stage) and copies her dance movements. The eye contacts and smiles begin again and are more pronounced and more 'connected' now. Nadia stops and goes outside again. Roxanna follows her and this time goes through the doorway and follows Nadia into the outdoor area. She watches as Nadia begins to run around the area pulling a piece of rope behind her. Roxanna gets a piece of rope and runs after Nadia.

We cannot know if this is the beginning of a friendship between these two new, young entrants to the unit but consider what the signs of an emerging friendship might be and what an observer-practitioner might do to facilitate the emerging potential for friendship between two girls who are not yet using much language to communicate either with adults or with other children in this relatively unfamiliar setting. Consider what the educator in the 'Sam' vignette did (Cameo 14.1). Would it be helpful, do you think, having observed this interaction, to speak to Nadia and Roxanna together about their actions and interactions?

Carlina Rinaldi, Director of Schools implementing the Reggio Emilia approach, has also reflected on the relationship between the growth of cognitive development and social relationships. Like Vygotsky's notions of expert others as being both adults and peers, she considers how the adults need to form good relationships with the children and also need to create a learning environment where children can be active in and supported in their friendship building. Rinaldi (1998) emphasises the links between the social, the intellectual and the growth of a strong self through resolution of peer conflict, something I have noted above as evident in my own research into the development of sociability and cooperation in young children. Nadia and Roxanna have the potential of many months in the setting before them. There's no knowing who might be the 'expert other' in the friendship if it were to form, although at the moment it seems to be Nadia with her early confidence in evidence. In concluding this section, however, I would want to emphasise the importance of educators understanding, nurturing and expanding such possibilities by recognising the potential of the importance of this emerging social relationship between Nadia and Roxanna.

Friendship-in-action

In this final section, I want to draw on two related cameos to explore more explicitly the links between friendship, intellectual engagement and playful learning. These cameos are based on observations, over a two-month period, of two boys. The lead teacher in the unit, Andy, has substantially developed ideas around 'open-ended role play' or 'the whatever you want it to be place', as discussed in Broadhead (2004, 2010a). In brief, the idea of an open-ended role-play area grew out of joint research with five early years teachers undertaken some time ago (Broadhead 2004). We had each used the same observational schedule in paired observations within each of their early years settings. This schedule is known as the Social Play Continuum (SPC). Andy had taken an early interest in this work and began by developing 'the whatever you want it to be place' in his Year 1 class. He subsequently moved schools and we lost touch, but when our paths crossed again several years later he had developed these ideas quite considerably in the outdoor area and was looking to expand them also indoors. We are currently engaged in joint research of the indoor and outdoor space and its impact on children's play, and these two cameos come from that research. They focus on Hughie and Josh in outdoor play.

Cameo 14.3: May

Hughie and Josh have made a small enclosure with plastic milk crates, no more than 2 metres square. Hughie also has a small wooden box, a pine cone and a stone on the wall that forms one edge of the enclosure, and is using them within one corner of the enclosure, arranging and rearranging them very carefully. Josh is moving around in and out of the enclosure collecting various small items from indoors and outdoors – a fork, a bucket, a spade, some leaves – and returning with them to the enclosure. Josh says something to Hughie about 'the toilet'; it appears quite serious and seems to relate to the area around the collection of objects that Hughie is engaged with in one corner; Hughie focuses on this area for much of the play. Hughie spends time collecting soil with a spoon from a little pile just outside the enclosure, placing it carefully in an aerosol top and taking it to his collection of objects on the wall. Josh has been to fetch water in the bucket he found earlier. He then goes and 'sits' on the toilet, quite absorbed; Hughie laughs at him as if sharing a joke and Josh laughs as well; it seems very amicable and jointly understood as genuine humour. Hughie has found a piece of paper, which he takes to his collection of objects. Josh pours the water he has fetched into the 'toilet' and Hughie watches and then pretends to clean the imaginary toilet as if with his hand. There are two 'doors' in the construction and Josh, who often leaves and returns to the enclosure, is very careful to 'open' and 'close' these by moving the selected crate to one side and back again. Josh goes to dig in the soil as Hughie returns to the corner where all the action is taking place. He carefully manipulates small piles of soil and looks carefully at stones and pieces of paper. Josh has found a woodlouse in the soil and examines it carefully but does not say anything to Hughie about it; Hughie remains very preoccupied and busy around the 'toilet' area. Their interactions are brief and infrequent but their goals are clearly shared.

I had filmed this play and we played the film back to Josh and Hughie later. As we watched, I asked Hughie if this is their house. He nods and says: 'That's the toilet. I'm putting bleach down the toilet to make it clean.' They continue to reflect as they watch the film and Hughie says: 'I'm still cleaning the toilet.' Josh then remarks: 'I flush the toilet.' Hughie responds: 'I need a stick to clean the toilet' and then 'I got the paper to wipe inside the toilet.' Hughie looks at me as we watch and then says, as if for my understanding: 'That's the sink there.' As they watch the film, they have a quiet conversation with one another about 'wiping your bum when you go to the toilet'. They smile as they talk to one another but it is also clear that they both share an understanding of the seriousness of this to them. Josh (who was the one who often left and re-entered the enclosure through the 'doors') then turns and says: 'The crates keep falling down so you have to be careful.' When I ask, they say this is the first time they have played at this together.

We can see in this cameo that Hughie and Josh have some shared pre-occupations around toilets and, in my experience of observing children, I have found this to be a common theme among young children in free play as they master the complexities and responsibilities of changing toilet habits at this stage in their lives; it seems an integral part of their identity. As Andy watched the video, he was able to recognise the continued interest in this theme from the boys as he had observed them on many occasions, engaged in aspects of domestic play together in the small enclosed spaces they had created. They enjoyed one another's company and spent a lot of time together in their shared play themes. In the May vignette (Cameo 14.3), the domestic theme seemed of more importance than the space in which it was played out, which was quite small but clearly adequate for their purposes. By July (Cameo 14.4), their design skills had developed considerably and seemed, for Hughie at least, to be of more importance than the domestic play. This next cameo reflects more widely than their specific play captured on film in order to illustrate the substantial developments in play and some elements of how friendship can influence the interaction between an expert other (Hughie) and his friend (Josh).

Cameo 14.4: Two months later

When the film begins, the play space is already well developed although, over time, Hughie continues to refine it further. The boys have used milk crates to create an entrance hall or corridor that is about 10 feet long. It leads into a large enclosure that measures roughly eight feet square. The entrance to the enclosure for Hughie and Josh, and for other children who now come and go and engage with the boys in a range of ways, is always via the 'door' at the end of the corridor; everyone understands the rules around entering and leaving the enclosure. The enclosure clearly has rooms, although these are not boundaried in any way. There is a bed that Hughie and Josh get into for conversations, a kitchen area where cooking is ongoing; discussions about watching TV both in bed and elsewhere in the enclosure. Josh is very preoccupied with a particular construction that looks like a window (they have hung a plastic container about two feet by four feet on the wall). Josh seems to spend a lot of time cleaning this area, whereas Hughie leaves the enclosure quite regularly to fetch other things into the area and to develop the area. He seems to be working to an internal image of what he wants although of course it is difficult to be sure of this. Josh shows no sense of matching what he sees around him to some internal image of possibilities; his main preoccupation is with the 'window'.

Josh still seems preoccupied with replicating domestic themes whereas Hughie is interested in design and construction, and this has been evident at other times in his play where he often takes the lead in deciding what he wants to build and what he might use to build it. One day he worked with a student teacher to build a telescope; he had visited a real telescope the previous weekend. Josh watched this play throughout, but clearly did not know what Hughie had in mind – until it was finished – and they could look through a wide tube into the sky – then Josh understood what Hughie was trying to achieve. The fact that Josh stayed around, however, suggested that he already understood that his friend Hughie always had good ideas that were worth taking an interest in.

Their filmed enclosure play came to an end through the intervention of other children. They were building a 'course' around the playground for a long line of children to follow (10–15 children were engaged in following the obstacle course). The course builders needed more materials and began to take them from Josh and Hughie's enclosure. At first they tried to resist this but when Hughie saw what they were doing, he stopped the resistance and began to watch the course builders.

Josh continued to defend his resources a little longer but as he noticed Josh's loss of resistance he looked at what Josh was looking at and then allowed the children to take the materials.

The boys are now building on a bigger scale although it seems to be Hughie that is leading this. Hughie seems less interested in domestic themes but happy to engage in them alongside Josh, who also engages in the domestic aspects far more extensively when Hughie moves back to design and development of the structure. Hughie seems the expert builder but in other ways is a less confident player in engaging with other children. Josh seems to have more conversations with children who come into the enclosure and talks to them about what he is doing, encouraging them to join him. It seems that each boy has something to offer the other – hence perhaps their choice to be friends and to play together so intensively and deeply. The open-ended play materials allow each of them to pursue their immediate interests in joint endeavour. Neither of them seems particularly concerned about the requirement to end their play because of other children's interventions. Hughie in fact seems very interested in what they are doing and, after initial resistance, Josh capitulates, perhaps because he notes Hughie's interest and apparent unconcern, perhaps because he knows, from his many daily experiences in accessing these materials, that he and Hughie can replicate their play again and again if they wish.

Conclusion

I have tried to illustrate in this chapter how central the development and exploration of friendships are to young children within educational settings and to their opportunities for learning within and from their early years environment. The chapter has shown that open-ended play materials, to which children can return again and again on a daily basis, have some real potential for building social relationships and for enabling these to develop into friendships that have problem setting, problem solving and joint learning at their heart. The concept of the expert other is central to this, but we have seen here that the expert other can be the emerging friend or the established friend.

The friendships illustrated in the cameos have focused on play materials that have no predetermined thematic function attributed to them. The materials serve as tools to support children's meaning making in relation to their own self-identity and being within the world they inhabit. The resources or tools are sufficiently open ended to match with interests and experiences from which the children are trying to draw in order to consolidate their understanding of how the world works and of their own place within it.

Questions to set you thinking

1   What do you think Sam (in Cameo 14.1) has learned about himself, and how might this affect his future contacts with other children in the class?
2   How might these characteristics and personality traits assist children like Sam in building friendships in the future?
3   What kinds of learning opportunities does a child like Sam need in his ongoing intellectual and social development?

References and further reading

Ashton, E., Hunt, A. and White, L. (2008) *New Brunswick Curriculum Framework for Early Learning and Childcare: Well-being, Professional Support Document*. Brunswick: Early Education Centre.

Broadhead, P. (1997) Promoting sociability and co-operation in nursery settings. *British Educational Research Journal*, 23(4): 513–531.

Broadhead, P. (2001) Investigating sociability and cooperation in four and five year olds in reception class settings. *International Journal of Early Years Education*, 9(1): 23–35.

Broadhead, P. (2004) *Early Years Play and Learning: Developing Social Skills and Cooperation*. London: RoutledgeFalmer.

Broadhead, P. (2006) Developing an understanding of young children's learning through play: the place of observation, interaction and reflection. *British Educational Research Journal*, 32(2): 191–207.

Broadhead, P. (2009) Conflict resolution and children's behaviour: observing and understanding social and cooperative play in early years educational settings. *Early Years: An International Journal of Research and Development*, 29(2): 105–118.

Broadhead, P. (2010a) Cooperative play and learning from nursery to year one. In P. Broadhead, J. Howard and E. Wood (eds) *Play and Learning in the Early Years: From Research to Practice*. London: Sage Publications.

Broadhead, P. (2010b) Making relationships. In J. Johnston and L. Nahmad-Williams (eds) *Supporting Development in the Early Years Foundation Stage*. London: Continuum.

Carr, M. (2001) *Assessment in Early Childhood Settings: Learning Stories*. London: Paul Chapman.

Cowie, B. and Carr, M. (2004) The consequences of socio-cultural assessment. In A. Anning, J. Cullen and M. Fleer (eds) *Early Childhood Education: Society and Culture*. London: Sage Publications.

Department for Education and Employment (DfEE) (2000) *Curriculum Guidance for the Foundation Stage*. London: QCA Publications.

Department for Education and Skills (DfES) (2007) *The Early Years Foundation Stage*. London: DfES.

Department of Social Development (2008) *New Brunswick Curriculum Framework for Early Learning and Childcare*. Presented to the Department of Social Development by the Early Childhood Research and Development Team, University of New Brunswick.

Factor, J. (2009) 'It's only play if you get to choose.' Children's perceptions of play and adult interventions. In C. Dell Clark (ed.) *Transactions at Play. Play and Culture Studies*. New York: University Press of America, Volume 9: 129–146.

Gallimore, R. and Tharp, R. (1990) Teaching mind in society: teaching, schooling and literate discourse. In L.C. Moll (ed.) *Vygotsky and Education: Instructional Implications and Applications of Socio-historical Psychology*. Cambridge: Cambridge University Press.

Green, V.A., Cillessen, A.H.N., Berthelsen, D., Irving, K. and Catherwood, D. (2003) The effect of gender context on children's social behaviour in a limited resource situation: an observational study. *Social Development*, 12: 586–604.

Hartup, W.W. (1996) The company they keep: friendships and their developmental significance. *Child Development*, 67: 1–13.

Howes, C. (1994) *The Collaborative Construction of Pretend*. Albany, New York: State University of New York Press.

Rinaldi, C. (1998) Projected curriculum constructed through documentation – Progettazione. An interview with Lella Gandini. In C. Edwards, L. Gandini and G. Foreman (eds) *The Hundred Languages of Children. The Reggio Emilio Approach – Advanced Reflections*. Westport: Ablex Publishing Corporation.

Rose, J. (2008) *The Independent Review of the Primary Curriculum: Interim Report*. Crown copyright. Available online at: http://publications.teachernet.gov.uk.

Vygotsky, L. (1978) *Mind in Society: The Development of Higher Psychological Processes*. London: Harvard University Press.

Wood, D., Bruner, J. and Ross, S. (1976) The role of tutoring in problem-solving. *Journal of Child Psychology and Psychiatry*, 17: 89–100.

Yelland, N., Lee, L., O'Rourke, M. and Harrison, C. (2008) *Rethinking Learning in Early Childhood Education*. Berkshire: Open University Press.

15 Personalising transitions: how play can help 'newly arrived children' settle into school

Hilary Fabian and Aline-Wendy Dunlop

Summary

This chapter explores issues affecting children who arrive at school – either collectively or individually – when classes are already established, for example mid-way through the school year, and considers the importance of play in supporting children in such atypical transitions. Moving schools can be both an exciting and an anxious time for children; they face new experiences and opportunities, and the transition to a new school will often bring a complete change of routine and culture, as well as new friends and teachers. It identifies ways in which a collective approach to each child's needs, viewed within the context of the family and local community, can assist children in settling into school. This personalised approach requires a parental–educator shift, whereby understanding of the expectations of learning through play can be a pivotal process in children's successful inclusion in school.

Introduction

The majority of children start school or transfer to another class as a group at the beginning of the school year, but there are some who join the class, either on their own or as a small group, part-way through a term with no introduction to help them settle into the school. Advance notice to schools is not always possible and some children – for example, refugee or armed forces children – arrive unannounced. Lave and Wenger (1991) state that each child's individual learning comes into existence in a context of interactions between the child and the surrounding objects and people. While embedded in and tied to specific situations, this suggests that learning is fundamentally a social process: with 'legitimate peripheral participation' (Lave and Wenger 1991), offering a way for newcomers and the existing community to share know-ledge, activities, practices and artefacts as well as to learn about each other's identities. This calls for a transition approach that supports the individuality of children within a shared process, so taking account of what the individual child brings to the school or classroom community they are entering and equally calling upon that receiving community to embrace the newcomer's contribution – creating what Lave and Wenger describe as a 'learning curric-ulum', rather than a 'teaching curriculum'.

This seems to be a useful concept to adopt in reflecting on children's participation in the activities provided in new and unfamiliar settings: at first they may be and feel, to be, 'on the edge' but gradually they develop changes in their involvement. Broström (2003) raises serious questions about why some children feel 'suitable' more quickly than others in new school environ-ments; he speculates that for some children their learning may be more context bound than it is for others. By personalising this process, 'different interests', 'diverse contributions' and 'varied viewpoints' (Lave and Wenger 1991: 99) can flourish. Play has the qualities that could enable the child in transition to participate, to use what they have learned in a previous setting and to expand to embrace the more complex thinking that may be required as they accommodate the new (Fabian and Dunlop 2005; Broström 2007).

While transitions are normative there may be advantages for all 'transi-tioners' if their experience is personalised in some way – through even small recognitions of their individuality, through a range of props and through play, and this may be achieved in cooperation with parents, educators and out-of-school services, e.g. school psychological services. However, there are more vulnerable groups that can also be identified for whom transitions may go beyond the usual challenges and demands, and where play and playful learning as tools for transition are less than available to them, perhaps by virtue of cultural norms and differences, language or disability, but neverthe-less may create a more recognisable bridge than more formalised classroom activities.

What measures are taken to personalise a child's introduction to a new classroom if they are transferring from another school or even from another country? Some newly arrived children might have experienced a school with a different curriculum or pedagogy: others might arrive in a traumatised state with no understanding of the local language. Sometimes these children are not just 'traversing physical and emotional worlds but stepping, within a few streets, from culture to culture, into an almost wholly English-speaking environment' (Barratt-Pugh 1994: 122).

A further aspect about transition for these children is the way that parents from countries where the curriculum is taught in a formal manner may be helped to understand the use of 'play for learning' in early years classrooms. In addition, teachers are likely to find it helpful to become informed about the child's past experiences of learning through play so they can use this to plan their teaching. This raises questions about how to make transition appropriate for each individual child by using a collective, collaborative approach, involving them and their parents, to address their needs and create a personalised transfer.

According to the Department for Children, Schools and Families (DCSF) there are five components of a personalised approach to learning: assessment for learning; effective teaching and learning strategies; curriculum entitlement and choice; school organisation; and strong partnership beyond the school. In Scotland the principle of personalisation is linked to choice: 'the curriculum should respond to individual needs and support particular aptitudes and talents. It should give each young person increasing opportunities for exercising responsible personal choice' (Curriculum Review Group 2004: 14).

Throughout this chapter the aspect of personalising school organisation with regard to transition is explored, such as effective pastoral care; leadership and management of the settling-in process; networks and collaboration with parents for supporting learning and pupil inclusion. However, the main focus throughout each of these issues is the way in which play and play-based pedagogy can be incorporated to make the transition process successful for each child and their family.

Mobility cameos

A growing number of pupils transfer between schools part-way through a phase, not necessarily leaving or joining at the end of a year or the end of a term. This so-called 'pupil mobility' is defined by the Office for Standards in Education (OfSTED) as 'the total movement in and out of schools by pupils other than at the usual times of joining and leaving' (OfSTED 2002: 1).

Some refugee children may have witnessed atrocities or lost parents, and require emotional support. Some parents and children arrive with little or no English. For example, Patryk was introduced to others in the class but was unable to understand what they were saying or what work he was supposed to do. He said:

> On the first day I sat on the carpet and cried. I spoke to the teacher in Polish but she couldn't understand. Sam and Ben gave me a teddy bear but I threw it on the floor. I felt very sad – I had friends in Poland, but here I had no one. I got five blue tickets for pushing and kicking children at playtime. But one English boy tried to say hello to me in Polish and we played football. Then everyone wanted to be my friend. I stopped feeling scared and thought school was cool.
>
> (Hamilton 2009)

He not only had little understanding of English when he first arrived but was also very frustrated about the lack of friends. However, it is also clear that play – in this case, football – and using his own initiative or agency, assisted him in making new friendships (see also Broadhead, Chapter 14, on the importance of friendships).

Trying to adjust to another culture and pedagogy can sometimes provide tensions. Take the following example from a Polish parent:

> In Poland there is more discipline. In Poland, school is very strict. Children work hard and have a lot of homework. School is a place to learn, not play. Play is done at home. Children just have a desk and chair, no toys. Teachers speak louder. They have a distant relationship with children. Children need to be strong in Polish schools. When I went to school I was scared to go. My children are never scared. School here is colourful and cosy. School here is like a family.
>
> (Hamilton 2009)

The family in this cameo clearly have expectations of school that do not include play. How are teachers going to persuade parents that play can help second-language children as doing things that are fun in a context where they can interact with their peers makes it easier for them to absorb a new language? Not only do newly arrived children have difficulties in understanding how school works but crossing cultures can sometimes mean that they become confused about values.

Children who have experienced frequent moves but who may feel relatively secure in the process because for them transitions are a way of life, may arrive brimming with confidence and capable of very quickly assessing what the new situation requires of them, even when they arrive singly and mid-term. Children from services families are such an example, as they tend to be more mobile than most. A teacher in the north of Scotland reflects on her experience of services children:

> We have an army camp in our school catchment area, so families come and go – sometimes staying for several years, sometimes for only a few months at a time. It's not always easy for children who make frequent moves, but I recall one little girl who joined us aged 7 having already attended four different schools in as many different countries. She was very quick to know the names of all in the class; she watched continuously to pick up on our routines and practices; she asked for help when she needed it and joined in at every opportunity with groups of children in the class. She also picked up the intonation of the local accent and tuned in to our local culture. Over the years I have learned to respect such children's experience

and to make room for them to share their different experiences with our local children . . . But not all are such competent transitioners as Susie was.

In Susie's case, her family worked hard to provide continuity; her mother shared with the class teacher that, every time the family made a move, as a teacher herself she made a point of coming into school again within a few days of her children starting school to ensure they were placed in an appropriate class and to find out if the particular teacher needed any further information. Susie's brother Paul was not such a socially orientated child and the family moves left him far more vulnerable than his sister, threatening to have a longer-term impact on how he viewed and coped with change, as well as on his sense of achievement and his actual levels of attainment.

More emphasis is needed on transition as a process rather than transition as an event. For parents of incoming children how much they are enabled to participate may depend heavily on the invitation and support of professionals and the services around the family. Parents, too, may be struggling with the changes that have led to a move, to a choice of school, to coming home after some years abroad, to being in a country where their first language is unknown, to recovering from trauma and, in some cases, exile.

Children coping with the new situation may need expected support but they are also likely to need some help or encouragement with the 'horizontal transitions' that occur across the school day from activity to activity (Ostrosky *et al.* 2002). A case study into transitions issues undertaken in a primary school to explore the impact of the school's transition policy on the experiences of school entrants and the sensitivity shown by practitioners and parents to children entering school for the first time, used a combination of storytelling and puppet play to support children to make sense of their own feelings, actions and environment in the transition to school (Misfud 2009). Such playful personalisation of the experience of transition generates new understandings about how children themselves experience transitions, that it can be an 'arduous task' (p. 62) and that 'the nature of children's transition experiences will play an important part in developing [them] as learners' (p. 63). The child's voice in this process can inform and transform the immediate experience but can also be informative for the development of school policy and practices.

Thinking about transitions

An exploration of educational transitions studies reveals some principal thrusts in thinking about transitions. Studies that address school readiness, school preparation, adaptation to school, adjustment to school and the learning of school culture, lead to models that focus on the strengths and difficulties of the child or young person who is in transition from one setting to another. These studies may be viewed as intra-personal in nature, with the success and effectiveness of transition resting on the individual competence (or perceived competence) of the child or young person, whose individual development forms the boundaries for successful or less than successful transition. Included here are studies that address psychological aspects of transition, such as identity, self-esteem and competence (see Papatheodorou, Chapter 17). Such a view of transitions could be dubbed 'development without context'.

On the other hand, there is a set of studies that focus on context and the capacity of systems to adapt and change in order to accommodate the transitioning child, by embracing ideas of environmental change, teacher adaptation, curriculum adjustment and attuning relationships. These studies could be classified as 'context without development' in that they tend to consider links between policy and practices, structures, standards and benchmarks. However, a further set of studies brings together development and context, and addresses their interrelatedness. These studies could be classified as 'development in context' as they take account of both the inter-personal and the socio-cultural (Dunlop 2009).

Thinking about play: what does it mean for our newly arrived children?

There seems no doubt that children learn through, and are motivated by, play (Bruner *et al.* 1976; Vygotsky 1978; Moyles 2005; see also Howard, Chapter 13). Learning through play and first-hand experience engages children with others and helps with developing relationships. Children construct social knowledge in social situations and learning is facilitated when they are interacting in meaningful ways with their peers, often through their own self-initiated play (Moyles 2008). Play, therefore, becomes one of the most important aspects in helping children to acquire an understanding of customs, rules and power relationships. It is the mechanism that helps children to cope with the changes in their world – a process known as the human capacity for 'adaptive variability' (Brown 2006). Play can be used to provide appropriate frameworks in which children can attempt to work things out for themselves – for example, through role play – thereby gaining confidence in being and in doing (see also Howe and Davies, Chapter 10 in this volume). Through play, children come to understand themselves and the world about them, while building new concepts.

Learning through play provides the conditions for developing confident, strategic thinkers and increased self-belief. One way of developing confidence is to encourage children to play in situations where there is no 'right or wrong' – for example, home corner, sand play, water play. 'Allowing learning and play events to take their full, natural time, increases confidence in both doing and being' (Taylor 1999). Football helped Patryk in the playground just as Susie quickly learned the Scottish playground games at her new school. But children who are newly arrived are also likely to recognise play equipment in the classroom such as building bricks and have some idea what is required of them. Natalia said that on 'the first day the English girls in my class came and talked to me. They knew I couldn't understand, so they used their hands to mime and helped me by showing me things to play with' – equipment and games that she knew well from previous experience. Play is about doing, and by 'doing' with others she was able to begin to learn English. So we can see that the curriculum can be designed to incorporate play in terms of resources on offer as well as the context provided by the teacher. However, the setting up of play areas and activities does not, in itself, produce good language development – they also require the involvement of adults and the planned use of dramatic contexts that make sense to children (see Kitson, Chapter 7).

Play not only helps children to develop, but play props can also be used as symbols to help children learn the procedures of the classroom. The teacher can use a toy to indicate to children the transition to the next activity – for example, by holding up a teddy dressed appropriately, such as in PE kit, to show the focus of the next lesson. This can be particularly helpful to those children who do not speak the language.

One responsibility of education is to give children the emotional nourishment that will support their well-being (see Goouch, Chapter 3). Play is recognised as being healing and calming for children who have faced difficult or negative experiences (Barber 2008; Howard, Chapter 13), so opportunities that provide expressive activities such as play dough, role play and messy play are likely to help children work through their feelings and come to terms with their past. Children who are secure, attached and confident are usually more prepared to take risks, which shape the way they face the unknown and enable them to believe that their world is controllable (Claxton 1999).

Play is a common childhood experience. Most children have opportunities to play in ways that have been shown to influence learning from social competence to cognitive benefits, including the development of language, imagination and pretence, to supporting children's emotional well-being, and gaining physical benefits, as we have seen in many other chapters in this book. Highly competent children usually bring their curiosity, creativity, enquiry, zest for learning (Whitehead 1929) and interest in others with them to school, and demonstrate such dispositions in their play (see Broadhead, Chapter 14). Children who are socially deprived (Smilansky 1968, 1990; Frede and Barnett 1992; Weikart 2000) and those with difficulties in social interaction and understanding, such as children on the autistic spectrum

(Jordan 2003), however, may experience play differently from the typically developing and supported child (see Georgeson and Payler, Chapter 2).

Building relationships

Supporting children in transition also implies a need to work with parents in order to frame children's educational transitions in positive, playful ways. Parental/family involvement is known to make a difference to children's transitions experiences (Dunlop 2005; Radtke 2009) and is believed to affect children's educational outcomes in the longer term, with parents' psychological support and the child's own disposition identified as having considerable influence on first-grade academic outcomes: 'Children are launched into achievement trajectories when they start formal schooling or even before, and the patterns of these early trajectories are highly stable over childhood and adolescence' (Entwisle *et al.* 2005). The relationships and complementary roles played by parents and educators shift as children move through the education system (see Figure 15.1).

Transitions for children are also transitions for their families: Griebel and Niesel (2002) consider that families co-construct the transition with their child and potentially with their child's educators, and confirm a view that, given differences between families, each child will have a personal experience of transitions that differs from that of any other child. As Alexander (1998) suggests, 'The way in which school treats parents when they first join has a profound influence on their relationship with the school system for the rest of their lives' (p. 128).

Recognising the familiar

Starting at another school frequently accentuates differences, but some things, such as play, remain constant, although cultural differences can be found. By taking part in the activities of the classroom, by watching and listening, children will become familiar with the culture (Bruner 1996) and begin to participate. However, frame play, in which children and practitioners plan and play together, can create a shared classroom culture in which the newly arrived children are developing the culture alongside their more established peers. In frame play, teachers and children plan the play situation and decide the content and context – the frame – for example, if they turn an area of the classroom into an airport or hospital. Supported by this physical frame, children and teachers imagine themes, roles and actions, expressing their decisions verbally, in drawings and through paintings, which serve as models. In other words, they develop a *collective fantasy* (Broström 2007). Rather than

Parents	←———————→	Educators
Home child	Primary educators and nurturers: 'It's my job'	
Starting preschool	Children learning the new; making new adult non-parental relationships	Settling in/ relationships
Co-construction with child	Anticipating school together	Co-construction with one school educator
Preparation for school: physical, practical, intellectual, emotional	Changing identities. Parent of a school child. 'Toughening him up'	Anticipation. Preparation of parent and child
Anticipating change	Playing is over, now it's work when school starts	Valuing play as a continuing activity
No longer a nursery child	Letting go	Child as pupil
Parents as carer and supporter	Collaboration; co-construction; co-educators; cooperation ←———————→	Educator as influential

Figure 15.1 Parental/educator shifts

spontaneous play, much is decided on beforehand and because there is a time interval between the formulation of the plan and realisation of the play, the roles, rules and actions are prepared. This results in frame play being more organised and more purposeful than role play, giving it a clear outcome and creating a common understanding of the imaginary play situation.

In these play contexts children need a wide repertoire of social skills in order to become successful players. For example:

- knowledge about rules and conventions
- empathy with others' needs and feelings
- understanding about rules of interaction, turn taking and negotiation
- ability to compromise and synthesise ideas.

Most children know what play looks like and are familiar with rules, albeit with other children, in other schools, and sometimes in another language. While they are likely to understand these skills they might not understand how their new classroom works or fully recognise the activities taking place. By being involved in frame play situations, children are listened to and empowered to participate in the classroom, which can help them mediate between the old and the new. In addition, this 'meaningful participation is essential to raising standards and achieving positive outcomes' (Garnett 2009: 23).

A high degree of contextual support is usually required to help second-language learners access the curriculum and understand the classroom. One project that did just this involved the use of a computer program, designed to help support new children as they made the transition. A digital camera was used to take photographs of play activities in the classroom. A computer program was then used to present these, together with a written and spoken commentary in English and voice recordings in other home languages, which were made with the help of parents, children and staff.

Personalising transitions

Successful personalised transitions have been recognised as having a huge positive impact (Birmingham City Council 2008). However, we cannot assume that there is a 'universal child' as children are socially constructed and, as we have seen, each will arrive at their school with different experiences. A constructed world is developed in relationship to others and has a number of 'truths'. The way children feel about themselves is learned, and 'positive self-esteem depends upon whether children feel others accept them and see them as competent and worthwhile' (Siraj-Blatchford 1996: 24). For children to gain a positive view of school and feel confident they need:

- a good knowledge of their classroom and some knowledge of the building
- a knowledge of their teacher and the way s/he thinks
- an understanding of the language of the school
- an idea of the nature of the activities that take place in school
- strategies to make friends
- a sense of the classroom culture.

In helping children to build up a picture of themselves and their place in the world, Hurst and Joseph (1998: 9) state, 'it is through our own actions and responses that we teach children how to value themselves and each other'. For example, pupils can be involved in relating to newly arrived children by asking about what matters in this school or setting. The teacher could say 'There are some children who are going to start school soon. What do you think is important for them to know about in this school?' From there the established pupils make classroom books to show the play activities available using photos, drawings and writing specific to the school context. In this way teachers can also gain an understanding of what is important to the current pupils; the established pupils begin to have an understanding of the needs of newly arrived children and the incoming children are better accommodated by those already in the class.

Each school needs to ensure that it is ready for each child who arrives, whether that is at the beginning of term or mid-way through the year; on their own or with a group. It is up to schools to make sure that play opportunities are in place to help children explore their feelings, resolve difficult experiences, continue learning and develop friendships. Children are natural anthropologists and investigators, who need to indulge in depth, not just playing with things, but with people. Play and conversation are the main ways by which young children learn about themselves, other people and the world around them, and learn through:

- individualised play activities that build on previous experiences
- emphasis on emotional and social support within the curriculum tasks
- parent–professional collaboration
- play activities where goals are co-constructed.

Conclusion

This chapter recognises that transitions are increasingly a way of life (Brooker 2008), but draws out atypical transitions, and emphasises the importance of play as a vehicle for supporting children and families when access to new educational settings is not straightforward. Through play, transitions may be personalised: children can draw on their own competence, the contributions they can make in playful situations and instigations of friendship that may fail them in more formal situations if they are unable to communicate conventionally on arrival in school. The power of play in children's culture in itself helps in the crossing of cultures they must make when they arrive in school unexpectedly, as a result of huge changes in their lives or because they are members of mobile families. The personalising of transitions is a matter of each school developing social practices that enable schools, children and their parents to understand one another and where the play environment affords equality of opportunity for all children in a learning community in which each child can contribute to an inclusive classroom culture.

All families may be caught up at some point in time in unexpected changes in family circumstances, which may lead to a move during the school year that brings discontinuities for their children. Sometimes these changes are inconvenient; occasionally they are life shattering. Newly arrived children experiencing atypical transitions need tailored approaches attuned to their circumstances, so allowing a supported transitions process. In all transitions for young children, play provides a recognisable medium for expressing oneself, being beside others, watching and absorbing, imitating, approaching new friends and instigating contact that allows those involved in the demands of changed circumstances to ease into the new. Play and playful learning each form a bridge into school, into new relationships, into different teaching and learning approaches and into a new life. Play affords the opportunity for children in transitions to belong.

Questions to set you thinking

1   What types of play might help newly arrived children communicate and make friends with established children? What play activities are set up to help new children integrate with established children?

2   How might play be used to help children develop resilience during the transition to a new school?

3   How can parents from countries where the curriculum is more 'formal' be helped to understand about learning through play? How can teachers inform parents about the use of 'play for learning' in their classrooms?

4   How can teachers become informed about the child's past experiences of learning through play? How do you use this to plan your teaching?

References and further reading

Alexander, T. (1998) Transforming primary education in partnership with parents. In C. Richards and P.H. Taylor (eds) *How Shall we School our Children? Primary Education and its Future*. London: Falmer Press.

Barber, J. (2008) Feeling positive. *Practical Pre-School for the Foundations Stage*, 84: 7–8.

Barratt-Pugh, C. (1994) 'We only speak English here, don't we?': supporting language development in a multilingual context. In L. Abbott and R. Rodger (eds) *Quality Education in the Early Years*. Buckingham: Open University Press.

Birmingham City Council (2008) *Personalising Learning: Learning Journeys for Early Years to Key Stage 4* (DVD), Birmingham Impact, Birmingham Grid for Learning. Available online at: http://www.televisionjunction.co.uk/pdf/personalising-translation.pdf (accessed 26 June 2009).

Brooker, E. (2008) *Supporting Transitions in the Early Years*. Maidenhead: Open University Press.

Broström, S. (2003) Problems and barriers in children's learning when they transit from kindergarten to kindergarten class in school. *European Early Childhood Education Research Journal, Transitions*. Themed monograph, 1: 51–66.

Broström, S. (2007) Transitions in children's thinking. In A.-W.A. Dunlop and H. Fabian (eds) *Informing Transitions in the Early Years: Research Policy and Practice*. Maidenhead: Open University Press.

Brown, F. (2006) Play theories and the value of play. National Children's Bureau, Library and Information Service, *Highlight*, 223, March.

Bruner, J.S. (1996) *The Culture of Education*. Cambridge, MA: Harvard University Press.

Bruner, J.S., Jolly, A. and Sylva, K. (eds) (1976) *Play – Its Role in Development and Evolution*. New York: Basic Books.

Claxton, G. (1999) *Wise Up: Learning to Live the Learning Life*. Stafford: Network Educational Press.

Curriculum Review Group (2004) *A Curriculum for Excellence*. Edinburgh: Scottish Executive.

Dunlop, A.-W.A. (2005) 'I'd like to be a fly on the wall.' How does children's transition to school affect parents? Paper presented at the EECERA 2005 Annual Conference, Dublin, 31 August–3 September.

Dunlop, A.-W.A. (2009) Transition methodologies – choices and chances. Paper presented at the Scottish Educational Research Annual Conference, Perth, 26–28 November.

Entwisle, D.R., Alexander, K.L. and Olson, L.S. (2005) First grade and educational attainment by age 22: a new story. *American Journal of Sociology*, 110(5): 1458–1502.

Fabian, H. and Dunlop, A.-W.A. (2005) The importance of play in the transition to school. In J. Moyles (ed.) *The Excellence of Play* (2nd edn). Maidenhead: Open University Press.

Frede, E. and Barnett, W.S. (1992) Developmentally appropriate public school pre-school: a study of implementation of the High/Scope Curriculum and its effects on disadvantaged children's skills at first grade. *Early Childhood Research Quarterly*, 7: 483–499.

Garnett, B. (2009) Pupils as partners is the key to personalised learning. *Education Journal*, 112: 23.

Griebel, W. and Niesel, R. (2002) Co-constructing transition into kindergarten and school by children, parents, and teachers. In H. Fabian and A.-W.A. Dunlop (eds) *Transition in the Early Years*. London: RoutledgeFalmer.

Hamilton, P. (2009) *Promoting the Ethnically Diverse Classroom: A Case Study*. Unpublished PhD draft, Wrexham, Wales: Glyndwr University.

Hurst, V. and Joseph, J. (1998) *Supporting Early Learning: The Way Forward*. Buckingham: Open University Press.

Jordan, R. (2003) Social play and autistic spectrum disorders. *Autism*, 7(4): 347–360.

Lave, J. and Wenger, E. (1991) *Situated Learning*. Cambridge: Cambridge University Press.

Misfud, S. (2009) *Starting School, a Case Study into Transition Issues*. Masters thesis, University of Malta, European Masters in Early Childhood Education and Care.

Moyles, J.R. (ed.) (2005) *The Excellence of Play* (2nd edn). Maidenhead: Open University Press/McGraw-Hill.

Moyles, J. (2008) Empowering children and adults: play and child-initiated learning. In S. Featherstone and P. Featherstone (eds) *Like Bees Not Butterflies: Child-initiated Learning in the Early Years*. London: A&C Black.

Office for Standards in Education (OfSTED) (2002) *Managing Pupil Mobility* (reference number HMI 403). Available online at: www.ofsted.gov.uk/public/docs2/managingmobility.pdf (accessed 15 December 2009).

Ostrosky, M.M., Jung, E.Y. and Hemmeter, M.L. (2002) *Helping Children Make Transitions between Activities*. Available online at: http://www.vanderbilt.edu/csefel/briefs/wwb4.html (accessed 4 January 2010).

Radtke, M. (2009) *The Parental Perspective of Involvement or Participation in the Children's Transition Process from Kindergarten to School*. Masters thesis, Martin Luther University, Halle Wittenburg, European Masters in Early Childhood Education and Care.

Siraj-Blatchford, S. (1996) Language, culture and difference: challenging inequality and promoting respect. In C. Nutbrown (ed.) *Respectful Educators – Capable Learners: Children's Rights and Early Education*. London: Paul Chapman.

Smilansky, S. (1968) *The Effects of Sociodramatic Play on Disadvantaged Preschool Children*. New York: Wiley and Sons.

Smilansky, S. (1990) Sociodramatic play: its relevance to behaviour and achievement in school. In E. Klugman and S. Smilansky, *Children's Play and Learning Perspectives and Policy Implications*. New York: Teacher's College Press.

Taylor, G. (1999) Emotional factors affecting learning. *Early Education*, Summer, 28: 11. London: BAECE.

Vygotsky, L.S. (1978) *Mind in Society: The Development of Higher Psychological Processes* (transl. and ed. by Cole, M., John-Steiner, V., Scribner, S. and Souberman, E). Cambridge, MA: Harvard University Press.

Weikart, D.P. (2000) *Early Childhood Education: Need and Opportunity*. Paris: UNESCO: International Institute for Educational Planning.

Whitehead, A.N. (1929) *The Aims of Education and Other Essays*. New York: Macmillan.

16 Play in the early years: the influence of cultural difference

Sacha Powell and Tricia David

Summary

Babies are born with an amazing drive to socialise and to observe, and become a member of the family and community in which they find themselves (Trevarthen 1998). They are active in seeking to participate meaningfully in the life around them – the culture, or cultures, in which they find themselves. This socio-cultural development of young children is the focus of our chapter, particularly the ways in which different socio-cultural contexts afford babies and children opportunities to play – or not – and why.

Introduction

It is always fascinating to observe how young children accept the culture of their particular Early Childhood Education and Care (ECEC) setting. Not only do they quickly adopt behaviours because 'This is what we do here', they also tacitly – and very cleverly – understand what they must not do. When Anthony (3:4 years) started to attend nursery school, he was like a whirlwind, rushing around disrupting the other children's play, pulling paintings and displays off the walls and knocking over furniture. On one occasion he managed to quietly use a time while the other children and the staff concentrated on a birthday celebration to explore the large buckets of powder paint, which every other child accepted as 'off limits', showering it around a screened area of the room. A few weeks later he was called to spend a month attending an assessment centre, booked by the health visitor before his admittance. On his return, nursery staff were dismayed. Anthony now spent his time sitting like a rag doll, rarely moving. Nothing amiss had been detected in Anthony's development but neither had the assessment centre detected what was to become apparent within days. Anthony had been witnessing his father's frequent violent attacks on his mother. Clearly the culture at home was very different from what he experienced in either the nursery or the assessment centre.

Meanwhile, Sheena and Noreen, 4-year-old twins, shared their extended family's love of their Irish heritage, participating in dance classes in their beautiful costumes, enjoying traditional music, often played by family members. Staff at the nursery they attended in the English Midlands knew nothing of this. The girls were immersed in different cultures. Even without the influence of particular customs of ethnic groups' origins, each family develops its own 'family culture', and children endeavour to bring and apply the 'funds of knowledge' (Gonzalez *et al.* 2004) they acquire in one or more of the contexts they encounter.

What do we mean by culture?

Following on from Bruner's (1996) suggestion that culture shapes the minds of individuals, Sanders (2004) considers what we mean by culture particularly in relation to children and their childhoods. He points out that culture is *learned*, *shared* and relies on symbols to convey meaning. He adds that it is also *patterned* – different aspects are linked and each culture is *unique*, while at the same time being part of the *universal* in the sense that human beings are distinguishable from other species because they live within a culture, or cultures. MacNaughton (2003: 14) defines culture as 'what we create beyond our biology. Not given to us, but made by us . . . what we create of the child beyond their biology.'

During the first half of the last century, Russian researchers were keenly interested in human development, both genetically and psychologically. While Vygotsky recognised the affinity between other apes and humans, he saw the huge qualitative differences that separate them. Wersch (1991) cites Vygotsky as arguing that:

> The cultural development of the child is characterized first by the fact that it transpires under conditions of dynamic organic changes. Cultural development is superimposed on the processes of growth, maturation and the organic development of the child. It forms a single whole with these processes. . . . Both planes of development – the natural and the cultural – coincide and mingle with one another.
>
> (p. 22)

Vygotsky (1967) went on to suggest that during play children experiment with the cultural meanings and rules of life, freeing themselves from everyday constraints.

Further, Rogoff (2003: 80–81) states that culture is not a category, like ethnicity or social class. She suggests it is better to focus on the idea that people participate in *communities of practice*, which have 'common and continuing organisation, values, understanding, history, and practices', culture being 'the *common ways* that participants share' (see Bruce, Chapter 18, for further discussion on these concepts).

Ideas about play and learning are being constructed, interpreted or made sense of within each cultural context, and it must be remembered that cultural contexts are not museums – they are dynamic and changing. Thus the ways in which a cultural group understands the place of young children and decides how to provide for them will change over time and place, and will influence the role and status of their play. However, the cultural history of a community or nation will also exert a powerful influence, especially if the values espoused by dominant groups or individuals are embedded in those histories (see also Fabian and Dunlop, Chapter 15).

Research in China (Vong 2005), a country we highlight later in this chapter as illustration, shows how, despite government exhortations to embrace play approaches as a way of fostering entrepreneurial mind-sets, Chinese nursery teachers are disinclined to abandon certain traditional aspects of early years education, such as formally taught Chinese dance. Play approaches and the curricula that depend on them cannot simply be grafted on to one culture from another. Children are *encultured* – they acquire and join in cultural events and practices, learning how to live within their community's culture by participating.

However, especially today with the effects of globalisation, different cultures impinge on one another, and ideas and practices will be absorbed, adapted or rejected according to their perceived relevance. Some members of a cultural group, even young children, may rebel against the 'rules' of their community's culture but most young children are eager to be members of the socio-cultural world around them, adopting a 'this is what we do' attitude.

The cultural ecology of early childhood

During the past ten years, interest in a holistic view of child development – theorising that there is no meaningful boundary between an individual and the context in which they are developing – has resulted in debate about the cultural ecology of young children, with claims that none of us is a member of a single cultural group, for cultures are heterogeneous (Tudge 2008).

Bronfenbrenner's (1979) theory of the ecology of human development was seminal in drawing attention to family, local, national and international contexts, and their congruity or discordance influencing children's development. Throughout his life Bronfenbrenner was concerned about childcare and support for families. He examined the way in which families with young children in the United States, the UK and Canada – with their shared Anglo-Saxon heritage – fared badly compared with those from many other nations in relation to poverty, access to ECEC, and had higher proportions of one-parent families. At that time, he cited negative effects in the USA related to individualism, and a reluctance on the part of more affluent groups to contribute to national systems, such as ECEC, sickness benefits and, topically, health services, which would ensure more positive life experiences for all children.

While the *Cambridge Primary Review*'s (Alexander 2009) advocacy of play approaches to the education of children throughout the early years has been rejected by both the current New Labour government and the Conservative opposition, it is perhaps noteworthy that, within the UK, Wales has taken positive steps to develop play-based educational provision for children from birth to 7. Over a decade ago an analysis of policy documents for Wales and England (David 1998) demonstrated cultural differences that seemed related to the two national histories. The lyricism of the Welsh document contrasted with the managerialism of that for England, and caused one to reflect on the strong cultural attachment to poetry and music in the history of Wales, encouraged in the Welsh-speaking non-conformist Sunday schools, attended by the whole congregation: 'Children were taught more than the Bible in these sessions: they were taught to read, to debate, to sing solfa and to engage in question and answer sessions with the adults' (Hague 2008: 24–25).

Meanwhile, one can see the continued influence of France's history in an underlying urge to ensure young children's identity as citizens, promoted through socio-cultural practices emphasising this. First, the baby's birth is announced by the local mayor, not, as in England, by the parents, and one of the main functions of the écoles maternelles is to enculture young children into citizenship, for example, by subtly immersing them in spoken and written French, displaying posters about local cultural events and encouraging a love of 'la belle France' (David *et al.* 2000).

Play and cultural difference

Since its inception, the *Early Years Foundation Stage* (DfES 2007) in England has been both welcomed and criticised (Bennett 2005; Ellyat 2009), because the emphasis on play and the retention of outcomes (or targets) for the children appear contradictory. Educators are reported to be comfortable but critics suggest they may be setting playful tasks for the children, rather than allowing them sufficient time and space to exercise their own choice and agency. Lambirth and Goouch (2006) suggest some teachers are adopting a 'culture of creative compliance' (where the teacher is skilled in using playful approaches while still fulfilling official demands).

Sutton-Smith (1979) issued a warning that play can be a way of controlling children. In some cultures children share activities with adults rather than being expected to play separately, and clearly young children generally enjoy 'real' experiences, such as baking, sorting clothes for washing, washing-up, cleaning, shopping, using hand tools, gardening, and so on. Sharing in thinking, seeking solutions, discussing and reflecting together about play and learning provides the basis for *dialogic* or *relational pedagogy* (Papatheodorou and Moyles 2009), which means practitioners must create 'an early learning environment that presents opportunities, possibilities for play'. It is the children's intentions that drive adults' roles. Intersubjectivity is fostered (David *et al.* 2010).

In his observational study of culture, class and child rearing, Tudge (2008) reports:

> As was true of all the children . . . by far the most common activity in which they are involved is some sort of play. It's important not to forget that in many ways all three-year-olds are similar, despite my focus . . . on aspects of their daily lives that distinguishes children in one group from those in other groups. The type of play, and the materials with which children play, vary across cultures.
>
> (p. 279)

Tudge goes on to describe the kinds of play engaged in by children in black Greensboro communities, in Korea, and in Russia, Finland, Estonia and Brazil. He urges readers to remember that children's experiences and their play are not only different in different societies, but also in different settings in their own lives – home, ECEC, centres of community gatherings, the homes of other relatives and friends.

Such studies provide welcome knowledge about cultural influences on human development and learning. Much of the research evidence we have to date about young children and play comes from the United States. In her exploration of the role of early childhood in different cultures, Rosenthal (2003) argues that highly individualistic cultures adopt play approaches in ECEC settings and knowledge is co-constructed, whereas in community-orientated cultures adults teach directly to pass on knowledge. She contrasts the USA with China, our next focus.

China: historical background

The People's Republic of China (founded in 1949 by communist revolutionaries) has a relatively short history in relation to 'Chinese civilisation', which is known to have been documented for more than 3000 years. Chinese communist ideologies are built upon long-standing traditions including the teachings of Confucius (551–479 BC) that have dominated the country's philosophies and values for over 2000 years. Therefore, the present political climate that drives for economic reform, modernisation and significant social change in China (especially in urban areas) is underpinned by ancient cultural traditions, layered with more recent socialist principles. Studies within and across China and of Chinese nationals living outside the mainland (including people in Hong Kong and Taiwan) suggest, however, that despite the vast geographical size of the country, the extreme differences in living conditions in some urban and rural areas, and the exposure to change, or to different social systems and philosophies, many Chinese people retain core cultural values (see, for example, Wong 1992; Wu 1996; Li 2002). Pan (1994) identified six key areas:

1 Chinese culture emphasises 'passive acceptance' of fate by seeking harmony with nature
2 Chinese culture emphasises inner experiences of meaning and feeling
3 traditional Chinese culture is typified by a closed world-view, prizing stability and harmony
4 traditional Chinese culture rests on kinship ties and tradition with a historical orientation
5 traditional Chinese culture places more weight on vertical inter-personal relationships
6 traditional Chinese culture weights heavily a person's duties to family, clan and state.

Play and ECEC practices in China

These traditional values, meshed together with more recent ideologies, assumptions and expectations, provide a framework within which to explore what constitutes play in Chinese contexts, and whether/how it is harnessed as a means of 'enculturing' children in a society that is experiencing extensive social and economic change.

Referring to the impact of play, Wood and Attfield (1996: 5) state that play may be 'banned, tolerated, encouraged or indulged'. Translated into a continuum (see Figure 16.1), their words provide a useful tool for thinking about the nature or characteristics of play within particular contexts, about changes over time, and about a culture's motivation for locating play, or specific types of play, at different places along the continuum.

Figure 16.1 Is play . . .?

This model raises numerous questions, as follows.

- What (if any) types of play are banned, tolerated, encouraged or indulged, and why?
- What can we learn about the enculturation of children, and about a culture's values and social systems by asking these questions about the (kinds of) play we see and don't see?
- What can we learn about how (or whether) play is harnessed to serve the purposes of an unwritten socio-political or cultural agenda or, indeed, a 'hidden' curriculum?
- What can we learn about the extent to which children are effecting change through their play, and contributing to the development of cultures?

During the past five to ten years, early childhood educators and policy makers in China's most politically and economically influential cities, Beijing and Shanghai, have begun to reform the structure of early childhood education (including provision for babies and children under 3 and their families). There have also been moves to improve early years teacher training, and to reformulate early childhood curricula and kindergarten guidelines. In 2001, the state-run news agency, Xinhua, reported that the Chinese government in Beijing was to issue preschool education regulations, which, for the first time, had widened the age bracket from 3 to 6 years to birth to 6 years, so that even the youngest children might 'receive systematic education' (Xinhua News Agency, 31 July 2001). This focus on children from birth to 3 has been instigated partly by recent findings from neuroscience. Another key influence is parental demand for high-quality early years education in settings that provide a 'sound pedagogical foundation' for children whose later education and employment will be in highly competitive contexts (Wei and Ebbeck 1996; Powell 2001).

In early years settings where there is an expectation that children's activities will lead to specific learning outcomes, it is important to consider how play is conceptualised and understood. Fundamentally, there is an underlying question about whether a group of people with shared cultural values believe, for example, in play as an '*ars artis*' activity, in which learning is accepted as inherent (but not predictable), or whether they believe that specific playful activities must be afforded for particular learning outcomes to emerge. In the first instance, children may be afforded greater opportunities to determine when, where and how they play. In the second, adults are more likely to influence the nature of playful activities. Sha (1998) explains that play in China has traditionally been linked to physical development but separated from intellectual development, and that this view stems from Confucian thought (see also Pan 1994). In a study of young children's attitudes to play, and those of their families and teachers in China, Sha (1998) discovered that participants saw play as a recreational (rather than a learning) experience. However, teachers used children's natural tendency to play as a motivator to engage them in playful but teacher-directed class activities.

Stepping back from providing mostly teacher-directed activities is further complicated in China by teaching style. Several observers (Gardner 1989; Jin and Cortazzi 1998) have described Chinese teachers' practices as similar to a polished theatrical performance, which Potts (2003) argues limits the extent to which practice can be modified to encompass new ideas that demand repeated deviation from the performance.

Nevertheless, as neuroscientific evidence about synaptic development during play (for example, Sutton-Smith 1997) is influencing the emphasis on play in Chinese early years practice, there are attempts to include 'free' play and greater choice for children. Early childhood practitioners are now expected to modify their practice, supported by training and ongoing professional development. But traditional attitudes towards play (as non-intellectual), coupled with parents' beliefs that teacher-directed activities are better for their children's learning, and performance-like teaching styles, do not ease the transition or help to raise the status of play that is freely chosen by children.

Photograph 16.1 In China, teachers used children's natural tendency to play as a motivator to engage them in playful but teacher-directed class activities.

References to the importance of play in Chinese early years literature can be found as far back as 1923, when educationalist Chen Heqin developed a 15-point model for the work of kindergartens (Shi 1989). References to play also appeared repeatedly in the first national *Guidelines for Kindergarten Education* (Ministry of Education PRC 1981). The most recent *Guidelines for Kindergarten Education* (Ministry of Education PRC 2001), the Beijing Municipal *Guidelines for Kindergarten Education* (BMEC 2003), and accompanying curriculum notes for teachers (BMEC/British Council 2004: 24) explain that kindergartens should pay attention to 'what society wants and expects children to grow up to be, and to children's physical and psychological development and needs'. Within the parameters of society's hopes and expectations of what young Chinese children will become, play is also expected to 'permeate all activities, in each and every aspect of the lives of three and four year olds'. Teachers are advised that play must underpin activities in the work of kindergartens (BMEC 2003: 24).

BMEC, which has responsibility for overseeing early childhood education in the capital, recently advised that:

> One common problem with preschool education in China is that kindergartens do not have activities designed for young children. The educational approach is mostly copied from that used in primary schools. Children are often asked to sit and listen to lessons and do not learn through play.
>
> (BMEC/British Council 2004: 1)

Furthermore, many kindergarten buildings resemble primary schools, catering for hundreds of young children grouped in classrooms housing 30 or more, with few possibilities for flexibility and choice in children's movements and use of spaces. Policy makers, researchers and practitioners are, therefore, enthusiastically working together to develop new ways of providing opportunities for play (including designing new buildings) that reflect the ethos of 'playful everyday life'. Part of their efforts to reform practice involve activities designed to encourage reflection and learning from others' models by, for example, visiting other countries to observe and discuss practice, translating professional books or inviting foreign colleagues to provide training in China (see also Zhu and Zang 2008). Returning to Photograph 16.1, and following our Chinese colleagues' example, we might usefully consider with them why there seems to be a discrepancy between a curriculum that encourages play and provision that we are told excludes it. Further, what is it about play, or particular types of play, that are either unacceptable or problematic in Chinese cultural contexts – and in our own?

Cannella (1997) warned that:

> child-centred pedagogy and play, as central tenets within educational practice, have been created in a particular culture with particular values and biases. Applying the notion of play to all peoples in all situations denies the multiple value structures, knowledges, and views of the world which are created by people in diverse contexts.
>
> (p. 135)

Recent calls to early childhood colleagues in the UK and other countries to provide training for early years professionals in China with particular emphasis on 'learning through play' and 'restructuring the physical environment to support young children's physical and psychological development' (BMEC/ British Council 2004) have shown the extent to which imported pedagogies, ideas and curriculum models including High/Scope, Reggio Emilia, Montessori and developmentally appropriate practice are being explored and developed within Chinese settings. But the pedagogical models are adapted to 'fit' Chinese values and expectations. In looking to other cultural contexts for ideas and guidance (perhaps in the form of training or observation) about play or 'learning through play' we can learn much from the critical reflection of our Chinese colleagues about the extent to which non-indigenous, play-based pedagogies and principles are transferable in whole or part.

Reading Chinese early childhood education curriculum documents and literature, carrying out observations in kindergartens and undertaking discussions with early years professionals offers insights into the purposes of EC provision in China. These also help to illustrate why particular types of play or playful activities 'fit' Chinese cultural contexts and others are more problematic. One such example involves 'messy play' activities (see Photograph 16.2).

In October 2004, in discussions between 280 Beijing kindergarten heads and teachers with four English ECEC professionals, the phrase 'messy play area' arose. The Chinese interpreter had great difficulty in directly translating this phrase (and its underlying sense that mess is expected and acceptable). How could provision for play be intentionally messy? Why would a kindergarten have an area in which children might be encouraged to get dirty and equipment become disorganised? What of the health and safety dangers of allowing young children to play virtually (or totally) naked? Some participants explained that parents would be horrified if their child had been allowed or encouraged to play without clothes (for fear of catching cold) or to get so dirty. Beijing kindergartens are expected, they explained, to instil a sense of orderliness, and to maintain high levels of cleanliness and sterility.

Photograph 16.2 Messy play.

Play, participation and democracy

Some cultural practices may be challenged because they do not promote child-ren's well-being. The Articles of the *United Nations Convention on the Rights of the Child* (UN 1989) are international standards with which countries have agreed to comply, but they will be interpreted by each cultural group in ways that make sense according to their own cultural meanings.

In England, research (Siraj-Blatchford *et al.* 2002; Sylva *et al.* 2004) has influenced the development of the *Early Years Foundation Stage* (DfES 2007) so that play is endorsed as the main approach to the curriculum for children from birth to 5. However, practitioners are exhorted to ensure a balance of adult-led and child-led activities, and to ensure children achieve certain prescribed goals (see Anning, Chapter 1). This culture of performativity and surveillance (David *et al.* 2010) is confirmed by the government's reported facile dismissal of the *Cambridge Review* (Alexander 2009), which advocates play-based learning until age 6, as 'backward looking' (Curtis 2009). Surely an early childhood education which affords young children opportunities to negotiate with peers, to be respectful of others, their views and feelings, to make choices and decisions, to comprehend the implications of those decisions, is the basis of living in a democracy?

Rogoff (2003: 366) suggests there are regularities – 'patterns of cultural processes' – and that one of the most striking is the way children's learning opportunities are structured. In some cultures children learn by observing and joining adult activities. In others, in contrast, children are separated from adults and are mainly inducted into the skills and knowledge they will need for adult life by attending ECEC, where adults use play and child-orientated conversations. During play, young children are working out 'the "scripts" of everyday life – adult skills and roles, values and beliefs' (Rogoff 2003: 298):

> Understanding different cultural practices does not require determining which one way is 'right' (which does not mean that all ways are fine). We can be open to possibilities that do not necessarily exclude each other. Learning from other communities does not require giving up one's own ways, but it does require suspending one's assumptions temporarily to consider others carefully ... There is *always* more to learn.
>
> (Rogoff 2003: 368–369, authors' emphasis)

Questions to set you thinking

1   Reflect on your own childhood and identify some features of your home culture which you believe have shaped you.
2   How would you practise so that the children do not experience a gulf between their home, ECEC and school cultures?

References and further reading

Alexander, R. (2009) *Children, their World, their Education: Final Report of the Cambridge Primary Review*. London: Routledge.

Beijing Municipal Education Commission (2003) *Draft Guidelines for Kindergarten Education*. Beijing Municipal Education Commission Publishing House.

Beijing Municipal Education Commission (BMEC)/British Council Beijing (2004) *Terms of Reference for Training Programme for Chinese Early Years Educators*, July. Beijing: The British Council.

Bennett, J. (2005) Curriculum issues in national policy making. *European Early Childhood Research Journal*, 13(2): 5–23.

Bronfenbrenner, U. (1979) *The Ecology of Human Development*. Cambridge, MA: Harvard University Press.

Bruner, J. (1996) *The Culture of Education*. Cambridge, MA: Harvard University Press.

Cannella, G.S. (1997) *Deconstructing Early Childhood Education: Social Justice and Revolution*. New York: Peter Lang.

Curtis, P. (2009) Devastating criticism of primary education dismissed by Ministers. *Guardian*, 16 October. Available online at www.guardian.co.uk (accessed 18 October 2009).

David, T. (1998) Learning properly? Young children and desirable outcomes. *Early Years*, 18(2): 61–66.

David, T., Goouch, K. and Powell, S. (2010) Play and prescription: the impact of national developments in England. In M. Kernan and E. Singer (eds) *Peer Relationships in Early Childhood Education and Care*. London: Routledge.

David, T., Raban, B., Ure, C., Goouch, K., Jago, M., Barrière, I. and Lambirth, A. (2000) *Making Sense of Early Literacy*. Stoke-on-Trent: Trentham Books.

Department for Education and Skills (DfES) (2007) *Early Years Foundation Stage*. London: DfES.

Ellyat, W. (2009) Own goals. *Nursery World*, 16 July: 20–21.

Gardner, H. (1989) *To Open Minds*. New York: Basic Books.

Gonzalez, N., Moll, L.C. and Amanti, C. (2004) *Funds of Knowledge: Theorizing Practices in Households, Communities and Classrooms*. New Jersey: Lawrence Erlbaum Associates.

Hague, F. (2008) *The Pain and the Privilege*. London: Harper.

Jin, L. and Cortazzi, M. (1998): Dimensions of dialogue: large classes in China. *International Journal of Educational Research*, 29: 739–761.

Lambirth, A. and Goouch, K. (2006) Golden times of writing: the creative compliance of writing journals. *Literacy*, 40(3): 146–152.

Li, G. (2002) *'East is East, West is West'? Home Literacy, Culture and Schooling*. New York: Peter Lang Publishing.

MacNaughton, G. (2003) *Shaping Early Childhood*. Maidenhead: Open University Press.

Ministry of Education of the People's Republic of China (1981) *Draft National Curriculum for the Preschool*. Beijing: Ministry of Education. English translation available in Liljeström, R., Néren-Björn, E., Schyl-Bjurman, G., Öhrn, B., Gustafsson, L. and Löfgren, O. (1983) *Young Children in China*. Clevedon, Avon: Multilingual Matters.

Ministry of Education of the People's Republic of China (2001) *You'eryuan Jiaoyu Zhidao Gangyao (shixing) – (Draft) Guidelines (National) for Kindergarten Education*. Beijing: Ministry of Education of the PRC.

Pan, H.L.W. (1994) Children's play in Taiwan. In J.L. Roopnarine, J.E. Johnson and F.H. Hooper (eds) *Children's Play In Diverse Cultures*. Albany, NY: State University of New York Press.

Papatheodorou, T. and Moyles, J. (eds) (2009) *Learning Together in the Early Years: Exploring relational pedagogy*. London: Routledge.

Potts, P. (2003) *Modernising Education in Britain and China*. London: Routledge-Falmer.

Powell, S. (2001) *Constructions of Early Childhood in China: A Case Study of Contemporary Shanghai*. Unpublished doctoral thesis, University of Kent, England.

Rogoff, B. (2003) *The Cultural Nature of Human Development*. Oxford: Oxford University Press.

Rosenthal, M. (2003) Quality in early childhood education and care: a cultural context. *Early Childhood Education Research Journal*, 11(2): 101–116.

Sanders, B. (2004) Childhood in different cultures. In T. Maynard and N. Thomas (eds) *An Introduction to Early Childhood Studies*. London: Sage.

Sha, J. (1998) *Chinese Parents' and Teachers' Perceptions of Preprimary School Children's Play*. Unpublished master's thesis, University of Wyoming, Laramie, WY.

Shi, H. (1989) Young people's care and education in the People's Republic of China. In P. Olmsted and D. Weikart (eds) *How Nations Serve Young Children*. USA: The High/Scope Press.

Siraj-Blatchford, I., Sylva, K., Muttock, S., Gilden, R. and Bell, D. (2002) *Researching Effective Pedagogy in the Early Years*. London: Department for Education and Skills, Research Report 356.

Sutton-Smith, B. (1979) *Play and Learning*. New York: Gardner Press.

Sutton-Smith, B. (1997) *The Ambiguity of Play*. Cambridge, MA: Harvard University Press.

Sylva, K., Melhuish, E., Sammons, P., Siraj-Blatchford, I. and Taggart, B. (2004) *The Effective Provision of Pre-school Education Project*. London: University of London Institute of Education.

Trevarthen, C. (1998) The child's need to learn a culture. In M. Woodhead, D. Faulkner and K. Littleton (eds) *Cultural Worlds of Early Childhood*. London: Routledge/Open University.

Tudge, J. (2008) *The Everyday Lives of Young Children: Culture, Class, and Child Rearing in Diverse Societies*. New York: Cambridge University Press.

United Nations (1989) *United Nations Convention on the Rights of the Child*. New York: UN.

Vong, K.I. (2005) *Towards a Creative Early Childhood Programme in Zhuhai-SER and Macao-SER of the People's Republic of China*. Unpublished doctoral thesis, University of London.

Vygotsky, L.S. (1967) Play and its role in the mental development of the child. *Soviet Psychology*, 5: 6–18.

Wei, Z. and Ebbeck, M. (1996) The importance of preschool education in the People's Republic of China. *Journal of Early Years Education*, 4(1): 27–34.

Wersch, J.V. (1991) *Voices of the Mind*. Cambridge, MA: Harvard University Press.

Wong, L.Y. (1992) *Education of Chinese Children in Britain and the USA*. Avon: Multilingual Matters.

Wood, L. and Attfield, J. (1996) *Play, Learning and the Early Childhood Curriculum*. London: Paul Chapman.

Wu, D.Y.H. (1996) Parental control: psychocultural interpretations of Chinese patterns of socialization. In Sing Lau (ed.) *Growing up the Chinese Way*. Hong Kong: Chinese University Press.

Xinhua News Agency (2001) Beijing issues regulations on pre-schoolers' education. Xinhua News Agency, 31 July.

Zhu, J. and Zang, J. (2008) Contemporary trends and developments in early childhood education in China. *Early Years*, 28(2): 173–182.

17 Play and the achievement of potential

Theodora Papatheodorou

Summary

This chapter aims to discuss the uses of play for the early identification and prevention of factors and conditions that may place young children at risk of achieving their full educational potential. It begins with an overview of current policies and their aspirational outcomes for children, and current thinking and perspectives on concepts such as special educational needs and inclusion. This will be followed by a discussion of ecological and socio-cultural perspectives in understanding early identification of factors that may place children at risk of achieving their full potential. The chapter will then conclude with a discussion of documentation as a means of sharing with parents their child's successes and progress, and demonstrate how documentation and Individual Play Plans can be used for planning contextually appropriate support.

Introduction

In the UK context, since the late 1980s/early 1990s, there has been a rapid policy development in the field of early childhood, mandating that provision should be made for all children independently of what their specific needs might be (Clough and Nutbrown 2004). This mandate has been further reinforced by a number of recent policies, which require that children's individual needs should be identified early and appropriate provision should be offered in order for them to achieve their full potential. The same policies have also signalled a change in thinking and practice by shifting attention from early intervention to prevention (DoH/DfEE/HO 2000; DfES 2001, 2003, 2004, 2007; DfES/DoH 2004; DCSF 2007a, 2007b).

Indeed, the revised *Code of Practice for SEN* required that young children's needs should be identified early in order to provide appropriate support (DfES 2001). It also recognised that there is a continuum of special educational needs that should initially be dealt with by utilising the resources available within the setting before bringing in specialist support. Similarly, the *National Services Framework for Children* stressed the importance of early intervention by pointing out that 'Delaying early intervention can result in irretrievable loss of function or ability . . . or the intervention being less effective . . .' (DfES/DoH 2004: 23). The introduction of *Every Child Matters* – a milestone in policy development – has placed further emphasis on prevention, and has urged universal or additional targeted support for children who might be at risk of developing special or additional needs (DfES 2003).

The ECM agenda, by explicitly urging prevention rather than intervention, has clearly moved away from the notion of the child being the focus of the problem, to the idea that there are contextual/environmental barriers that hamper learning and development (Papatheodorou 2005). As a result, the introduction of personalised learning that responds to the individual child's needs, interests and aspirations – a long philosophical standing of early childhood – followed in a quest of identifying and removing barriers to the development and learning of individual children (DCSF 2007b; see also Georgeson and Payler, Chapter 2).

From special educational needs to inclusion: changing the focus of attention

Such policies have clearly broadened the boundaries of education and increased awareness of the notion of inclusion (Odom *et al.* 2004). Although inclusion is frequently used as an alternative to special educational needs (Glass *et al.* 2008), there are some fundamental philosophical differences between the two terms. The term 'special educational needs' is often associated with the difficulties or problems owned by the individual, and portrays a deficit-based discourse (Macartney 2008). In contrast, inclusion shifts attention from the individual to the environment (Booth and Ainscow 2002). Inclusion draws attention to three interconnected contextual and environmental dimensions: the creation of inclusive cultures; the development of inclusive policies; and the evolution of inclusive practices (Ballard 1999; Booth and Ainscow 2004), underpinned by a social justice and human rights framework (Purdue 2006).

Inclusion, however, should not be seen as a technical matter that deals mainly with structures and systems that need to be in place for young children to realise their potential. Inclusion is a human/child's rights imperative, which requires that young children are enabled to develop their capacities and participate fully in society (OECD 2007). It is an ethical issue for it embodies a society's values and beliefs about young children, social justice and equity, respect and human dignity. Indeed, this kind of thinking permeates the practice and discourse of the renowned Reggio Emilia preschools, where they talk about *special rights* and *declaration of intent*, instead of special needs and *Individual Educational Plan*, used in the English context (Runswick-Cole and Hodge 2009).

Children's development and learning: ecological and socio-cultural perspectives

Changes in policy focus and priorities, and philosophical repositioning on the issues of special needs and inclusion, mirror the theoretical shifts witnessed, at the same time, in the field of early childhood. For most of the twentieth century, developmental and normative models, which focused on expected norms and developmental patterns observed in children at different ages and stages, dominated the field of early childhood (Bredekamp 1987; Penn 2000).

Since the 1980s, ecological systems theory and socio-cultural theories have provided us with new insights and understandings of child development, learning and behaviour (see also Powell and David, Chapter 16). Although not deviating markedly from developmental notions, Bronfenbrenner's (1979, 1995) ecological systems theory offered us contextual understandings of children's development and learning: the ecological system model demonstrated that children develop differently, depending on their context, and the complex and dynamic interrelationships between contextual and environmental variables.

In socio-cultural terms, learning is a social activity, where teachers and early years practitioners have the role of facilitator, while learners take an active role by explaining their ideas to one another and cooperating in finding the solution to complex problems (Van der Veer and Valsiner 1991; Wenger 1998; Kozulin *et al.* 2003). In terms of ecological systems theory and socio-cultural theories, the child's needs become meaningful only within the context in which they are observed, requiring ecological and multi-dimensional assessment and interventions (Meisels and Atkins-Burnett 2000). Most importantly, the notion of children's active participation and agency in the learning process has repositioned the child in the assessment process and the planning of intervention programmes, in that the child's views are actively sought in order to gain a holistic perspective on the issues under consideration and concern, and develop appropriate support (Nutbrown and Clough 2006).

Currently, our thinking has shifted from the notion of the child with special educational needs to factors that may place the child at risk of developing special needs.

Early identification: some challenges

Both policy changes and philosophical and theoretical shifts present a range of challenges that include:

- children's levels of development
- lack of appropriate tools
- labelling effects
- the attitudes of early years practitioners and teachers
- contextual factors that may not be within the reach of early years practitioners and teachers.

There is now a consensus of opinion that not all children develop according to identified normative patterns; neither is their development continuous nor according to predictable stages. Instead, development can be idiographic and discontinuous, consisting of periods of rapid changes and periods where little change is observed. Similarly, not all children develop at the same rate in all areas of development; some may show higher levels of physical and motor development, while others may have better personal or social outcomes (Vasta *et al.* 1999). In addition, at some stages, some children may show particular needs, which present challenges for both the children themselves and the adults looking after them (Sammons *et al.* 2003). For example, physical development and/or a rapidly growing body may require that children constantly change the cognitive schema of their body, acquire spatial awareness, make adjustments and function appropriately in a given space. During this period, clumsiness and awkward movement may be witnessed, especially when the environment provided does not offer children opportunities to experiment with their bodies in the space available. In the same way, transition from home to nursery may make demands upon children's personal and emotional maturity, which they may not yet have gained (see Fabian and Dunlop, Chapter 15).

Therefore, it is far from easy to make predictions as to whether any identified needs are of temporary or transient nature, and to make judgements about contributory factors to such needs. Indeed, early years practitioners are well aware of the effects of labelling, especially if there is little clarity as to what the need is and what is required for support. However, despite these arguments, there is an overwhelming consensus among them that early identification and intervention are important as they can minimise future difficulties (Jones 2004).

The challenges to early identification are also compounded by the lack of appropriate tools, instruments and procedures. Often instruments used are not suitable for young children, as they are adaptations of instruments developed for older children (Vacc and Ritter 1995; Odom *et al.* 2004). Similarly, age-appropriate instruments, used in a formal way, may mean that children's learning can be markedly different from that which would have been demonstrated in naturalistic environments, e.g. home, play activities or early years settings (Meisels and Atkins-Burnett 2000).

Beyond these issues, early years practitioners' knowledge, attitudes, values and expectations are of equal importance for early identification. Similarly, early years practitioners' understanding of the ecological and socio-cultural models and the human/child's rights imperatives will affect their views and expectations about children's potential, influence their pedagogical practice, and determine whether early identification will focus on the child and her/his needs or on factors that place the child at risk.

Early identification through play

Ecological assessment aims to examine the dynamic interrelationships of multiple factors within and between systems (e.g. family, early years setting) over time and the way they affect the development and learning of the child. Multi-dimensional assessment requires the collection of information from multiple sources (e.g. parents, early years professionals, siblings, the child herself/himself) by using multiple methods (e.g. interviews, observations, documentary evidence; samples of the child's work) across social, emotional, cognitive and motor development, language and communication, and academic performance (Neisworth and Bagnato 1988; Meisels and Atkins-Burnett 2000).

The complexity and dynamic interrelationship of multiple risk factors makes ecological, multi-dimensional and multi-domain approaches less than straightforward. Play, however, is the promise of such approaches because, in play, children perform to the best of their abilities, reveal the challenges they may experience, and receive immediate feedback and support from peers and adults to unfold their potential (Sheridan *et al.* 1995; Wilson 1998; Meisels and Atkins-Burnett 2000; Sayeed and Guerin 2000). Play offers the context in which we can identify and determine a child's current level of learning and development; recognise her/his potential for learning and development; identify the skills that the child needs to reach that potential, and determine the support required from adults and/or peers. Indeed, research has shown that children's level of involvement and engagement in play are important indicators of their current development and predictors of their potential. In general, children who experience difficulties and/or have been identified as having special or additional needs, show less complex play behaviours. They interact more with adults and less with other peers and play materials; when social toys are available, cooperative play and peer interaction increases but, in general, children with potential additional needs display low-level play activity

(Sayeed and Guerin 2000; Odom *et al.* 2004). Cameo 17.1 is illustrative of such behaviours.

Cameo 17.1

George, Annie and Jon are sitting in the activity area, 'Healthy Food'. George and John are sitting around a table. Annie is the waitress who is taking the orders.

> *Annie*: Here is today's menu. [She passes a menu catalogue on to each child.] We have vegetable soup with croutons, fish and chips and, for afters, fresh fruits.
>
> *John*: I'll have fish and chips and ice cream, please.
>
> *Annie*: Sorry Sir, we have only fresh fruits. It's healthy . . . you know . . .
>
> *Annie*: [turning on to George, asks] What do you like George? [George does not reply]
>
> *Annie*: Do you like some soup? [George nods, yes]
>
> *Annie*: [insists] George, say: I like to have some soup and, for afters, fresh fruits, please.
>
> [George repeats after Annie]

Annie leaves the two boys, pretending she is going into the kitchen to fetch the orders. It takes some time before she returns. Meanwhile, John is distracted and leaves the table and the restaurant. Annie returns with a tray.

> *Annie*: [asks, clearly disappointed] Where is John? [Then, turning on to George, says] Oh, well, now it is me and you . . . It's your turn to be the waiter.

Annie sits at the table. She instructs George what to say. He responds and clearly repeats what Annie says. He pretends he is bringing some food for Annie. He seems to be relaxed, enjoying the play. They both now sit at the table. They pretend to eat.

(Adapted from an early years practitioner's observation record. All names in the case studies mentioned in this chapter are pseudonyms)

The observation above has been revealing for George's teacher, who had been concerned about his participation in play. It was almost mid-term and, instead of becoming more involved in play, he became withdrawn. His monosyllabic or non-verbal responses were mainly to adult direct requests. Mrs Nabb (his teacher) wondered whether George had any undiagnosed hearing loss and/or speech and language difficulties that undermined his confidence. This observation seemed to defuse initial concerns about hearing loss and speech and language difficulties.

George's case study exemplifies the potential of play as a platform and tool for early identification of children's needs and possible factors that may be associated with such needs. It also demonstrates how initial concerns may be either supported or refuted on the basis of evidence that is systematically gathered. Furthermore it illustrates that often what is considered to be the child's need is an issue of pedagogical and environmental adjustments. It took the insightful observation and careful planning of the early years practitioner to give George a head start for his involvement and engagement with play.

However, they are not always specific concerns that may prohibit children from achieving their potential. As Cameo 17.2 shows, children's potential is often determined by early years practitioners' and teachers' interest in and engagement with children's play, efforts and endeavours; the level of sustained shared thinking that they establish and the immediate responses and feedback they offer.

Cameo 17.2

Angelica showed special interest in a beautiful lilac butterfly. I brought the plastic butterfly over to the easel to show her the detailed lines in the wings and the patterns on the body. She began to listen and look closely, and painted the core stem body in red on the paper (see Photograph 17.1). I extended my explanation with paint on the paper depicting one half of its body and wings and adding it on to her red body. It was a quick, one-minute practical demonstration. With each stroke of the brush I would point to which line on the butterfly's veins that I was copying. Without hesitation and over talking my point, I handed the brush to the child. Again, without adding extra instruction, I left her to do her half. Her precision was true, and all the time she was focusing and looking at the details I had spoken about and seemed to take her time. Praise was given and she went off to pick another creature, a caterpillar, to bring to the easel.

(From an artist's notes working in an early years setting)

This cameo demonstrates how reflexive action and instantaneous support may provide the scaffolding required for the child to work beyond her level of development. It also illustrates that skills and knowledge that are offered at the right time and in the right way become a powerful and empowering tool for children: they allow them to cross the threshold of current level of

Photograph 17.1   Angelica's butterfly.

Photograph courtesy of Jacqueline Davies, a visual artist

achievement, and enable them to reach and reveal their potential (Papatheodorou and Loader 2009). As Siraj-Blatchford and Sylva (2004) argue, there is nothing wrong with instruction; it is the balance that matters. It takes, however, observant, sensitive and deeply engaged adults to remove potential barriers to children's learning (see Goouch, Chapter 3).

Children's achievement of their potential may also be undermined by decontextualised and highly technical pedagogical practices, which focus primarily on intended learning outcomes rather than being guided by children's interests. Cameo 17.3 is illustrative of how such pedagogical practices may undermine the further development of children's dispositions to learning and prohibit the unfolding of their potential.

Cameo 17.3

The children are sitting on the carpet of the classroom. Max is sitting up straight with his legs crossed and his arms crossed in his lap.

> *Teacher*: Can everyone see? [The teacher has a counting board in front of her. Max shuffles forward close to the number board.]
> *Teacher*: Which number is less than five?
> [Max holds his hand up. Another child answers the question. Max slumps his head into his hands.]
> *Teacher*: Which number is more than four?
> *Max*: Five [he answers without holding his arm up and before the teacher asks him]
> *Teacher*: That's right, but you should hold your arm up.
> [Max slumps his head down into his hands, again.]

The activity continues. Max has his hands in his mouth; he puts his head into his hands; he rubs his eyes; yawns again.

The teacher explains a new game: the children have to run around the hall and stop when she claps her hands. She will then say a number and the children have to get into groups that have the same number of children. Once they form the group with the right number of children they sit down.

The children start running. The teacher claps her hands. Many children do not stop. Max falls on to the floor. The teacher explains the rules again. The children start running. The teacher claps her hands. Max stops and stands still. The teacher calls out: two. Everyone finds a pair and sits down. Due to an uneven number of children in the class Max is left out. The teacher pairs with him. He sits down, smiling. The children stand up and start running again. The teacher says: three. Once again Max is left out and stands with the teacher. He says: 'That's OK; my mum says that everyone can't have a go at once.'

(Adapted from an observer's notes)

In the first maths activity, Max had clearly been disappointed with his participation and the teacher's response when he did so. Gradually, his initial enthusiasm diminished and he became disengaged and bored. Similarly, in the numbers game, Max soon resigned himself to the fact that he was not able to join his peers. Had the teacher acknowledged Max's interest and responded positively to his participation, he would not have withdrawn from the initial learning activity. Again, had the teacher actively engaged with the game rather than reacting to the situation created, Max would not have been excluded from his peer groups. Clearly, early years practitioners have an important role and a responsibility in creating 'inclusive, responsive and respectful community in which everybody belongs and is learning' (Macartney 2008: 34). Otherwise their pedagogy itself may become a source of exclusion and a prohibiting factor for children to show their achievements and reach their potential (see also Georgeson and Payler, Chapter 2). To recall Rinaldi (2006: 141), 'There is a constant relational reciprocity between those who educate and those who are educated, between those who teach and those who learn. There is participation, passion, compassion and emotion.'

Documentation: sharing children's successes and challenges

Family circumstances and conditions prevailing in the child's wider environment may impact on learning (as we have seen in other chapters). In such cases, initial play-based insights become the starting point for seeking out further information from different sources.

Parents are and should remain the first point of reference for receiving further information about their children. While informal discussions and invitations to formal meetings are some of the methods of communication with parents, children's portfolios are an important tool for regular communication. Portfolios include individual and generic stories, which illustrate a child's successes and achievements, and document her/his unfolding learning journey. They include exemplars of children's work chosen by them, and they are complemented with observation records and comments from early years practitioners and parents (Carr 2001; Glass *et al.* 2008).

Portfolios give voice to children and form the basis for sharing information, facilitating reflection and documenting future actions between children, parents and practitioners. They constitute, as Rinaldi (2006: 100) argues, 'a visible trace and a procedure that supports learning and teaching, making them reciprocal because they are visible and shareable'.

Considering George's case, his portfolio may be used to document his engagement in role play through photographic evidence. Mrs Nabb may revisit the photographs with George to elicit his perspectives and feelings about the activity. George's views and perspective can also be included in the portfolio, together with Mrs Nabb's observation and comments. Finally, sharing and discussing the portfolio with George's parents can provide additional insights for his behaviour beyond the early years setting and can be utilised as the forum for articulating their aspirations for George and the means by which to achieve them.

Play-based support

Often modifications in the learning environment, content and mode of play may prove enough to prevent or eliminate some of the difficulties that children may experience (Quinn *et al.* 1998). However, some children's ongoing difficulties may call for additional or special support (DfES 2001). In such cases, an Individual Play Plan (IPP) may be drawn up to embed and keep track of specific learning outcomes for an individual child and the support required in achieving them. The IPP is usually drawn up by the early years practitioner and teacher with the support of the special needs coordinator, and is implemented within the Early Years Action of the revised *Code of Practice for Special Educational Needs* (DfES 2001). While the IPP is drawn around specific learning outcomes for the child, its emphasis is on the support and resources required for these outcomes to be realised through play.

An IPP is a document that outlines the short-term objectives and the long-term goals for the child; play materials and resources required; recommended changes in the learning environment; modification and/or simplification of daily and weekly plan to integrate the intended learning outcomes for the child; the use of the child's existing skills to expand and promote her/his learning further; peer and/or adult support and, if relevant, support from specialists; how the child will be supported at home, if required, and information about the monitoring and the evaluation of the progress made, including review dates (ECRII 1999; Odom *et al.* 2004).

Taking George's case, Mrs Nabbs identified short-term objectives in the domains of social interaction and communication, where his difficulties were mainly witnessed (e.g. George to initiate interactions, make requests, make choices of play materials, increase social interaction with other children and adults in whole-class situations). The long-term goal focused on the personal development domain (e.g. to build up George's confidence). For Mrs Nabb, building up George's confidence was the dynamic and transformative goal that was aimed to be achieved through a series of carefully planned short-term objectives.

However, the kind of support identified in an IPP is often determined by the seriousness of children's needs and the complexity of contributing factors (Odom *et al.* 2004). In general, adult-directed intervention is more effective for young children with less serious difficulties, while the more naturalistic, child-directed intervention is more effective for young children who experience more serious difficulties (see Georgeson and Payler, Chapter 2). Direct instruction produces better results for the acquisition of skills, but children show greater generalisation of skills when intervention is activity based. Therefore, meaningful support and intervention is typified by a balance of child-led and adult-directed activities, and a combination of direct instruction and activity-based learning (Raver 2004; Siraj-Blatchford and Sylva 2004; Norwich and Lewis 2005).

Similarly, the introduction of planned activities, the place and time where they are offered, as well as the suggestions provided to the child during the activity, need careful attention. Environmental changes such as the grouping of children and the membership of such groupings are significant decisions, especially when social interaction and communication are pursued (Odom *et al.* 2004). In George's case, for instance, Mrs Nabb identified particular activities in which he participated and how he was introduced to these activities. She also deliberately included Annie, with whom George developed a rapport, in small-group activities and situations (Figure 17.1).

Finally, the IPP should be embedded in the planning of the overall daily and weekly programme of the early years setting (Odom *et al.* 2004) in order to enable the child to access coherent and meaningful activities in naturalistic settings rather than having partial and unrelated input offered outside the early years setting (Gimpel and Holland 2003).

An IPP is incomplete without a monitoring and evaluation system that states when, how, by whom and how often information will be collected against pre-identified criteria to make judgements about its implementation and its impact on the child (Horner *et al.* 2001; Curtiss *et al.* 2002). Often, the short-term objectives broken down into small observable and measurable elements form the criteria for ongoing evaluation, while summative evaluation is reserved against the long-term goal.

Planning for each and all children's learning

Play can be routinely used to identify the individual needs of all children in early years settings and, consequently, plan activities and programmes that address identified needs and risk factors and/or prevent future difficulties. The *Foundation Stage Profile* (DfES/QCA 2003), for example, can be used as a point of reference to form the overall profile of each individual child and build a collective profile for all children in the early years setting.

Raver (2004) proposes a 'group objective matrix' as a tool for facilitating the embedding of individual and group objectives into daily and weekly planning (Figure 17.2). This offers the information required for flexible differentiated support that takes into account the children's previous experience, and extends such experience to achieve high expectations (Mowat 2009).

Name: George S.　　　　　　Date: 25 October 2004

Duration: From 1 November 2004 to December 2004			
Intended learning outcomes	**Long-term goal:** Increase George's confidence		
	Short-term objectives: initiate interactions; make requests; make choices of play materials; increase social interaction with other children and adults in whole-class situations		
Curriculum modifications	**Environmental modifications**	**Teacher/staff support**	**Support and resources required**
Structured play activities to require the engagement of all children in the group; lead to achievable and rewarding outcomes to boost confidence; and practise and expand learned skills	Provide play materials that require social interaction; organise group membership that promotes peer tutoring and support; include Annie in the group membership	To guide and facilitate George to make choices of play materials and activities, initiate requests, be involved in conversations; offer opportunities for engagement with social play materials; acknowledge George's achievements; offer praise/rewards	All staff to be aware of the intended learning outcomes for George, how play materials and activities have been chosen and how to support George; to provide play materials that require social interaction *Family involvement* Discuss with parents the strategies; involve parents and siblings to follow similar strategies at home
Monitoring/recording	George's progress to be observed once a fortnight, by Mrs Nabb, during structured and unstructured play activities		
Evaluation criteria	Initiation of conversation and interaction, sustaining conversation and interactions, interaction with more than one child in group situation, volunteering to participate in group activities		

(Adapted from Papatheodorou 2005)

Figure 17.1 Individual play plan.

Group objective matrix

Developmental domain (linked to Foundation Stage profile)	George	Annie	Jo	John	Jack	Andrea	Zoe	Mo
Personal, social and emotional development • • •								
Communication, language and literacy • • •								
Physical development • • •								
Creative development • • •								
Mathematical development • • •								
Knowledge and understanding of the world • • •								

(Adapted from Raver 2004)

Figure 17.2   Daily and weekly planning.

Conclusion

Policy changes over the past 30 years, and philosophical and theoretical repositioning, have shifted attention from intervention to prevention; from the
child being the source and focus of identified needs to contextual factors
that contribute to such needs; from the discourse of special educational needs
to inclusion and children's rights. At the same time, the questioning of the
validity of developmental and normative models of early identification led to
ecological, multi-dimensional and multiple-domain approaches, undertaken
in naturalistic environments. In early years, such policy and conceptual
frameworks mean that play has become the platform and means of early
identification and for providing appropriate support for children to achieve
their potential. This conceptual and policy shift has made great demands on
skilful and competent early years practitioners and teachers, who embrace and
implement participatory and inclusive play pedagogies.

Questions to set you thinking

1   What is your current practice regarding the identification of young
    children's needs?
2   How can play be used for early identification of children's needs and
    potential contributory factors?
3   Can you identify changes that need to be made in your current play
    practices?
4   What demands do such changes make upon staff time, training,
    play resources and materials?
5   What procedural and structural changes can be made in the short-
    and long-term planning for play to establish a more inclusive culture
    and ethos?

References and further reading

Ballard, K. (1999) Concluding thoughts. In K. Ballard (ed.) *Inclusive Education:
    International Voices on Disability and Justice*. London: Falmer Press.
Booth, T. and Ainscow, M. (2002) *Index for Inclusion: Developing Learning and
    Participation in Schools*. Manchester: Centre for Studies on Inclusive Education.
Booth, T. and Ainscow, M. (2004) *The Index of Inclusion: Developing Learning, Partici-
    pation and Play in Early Years and Childcare*. Manchester: Centre for Studies on
    Inclusive Education.
Bredekamp, S. (ed.) (1987) *Developmentally Appropriate Practice in Early Childhood*

Programmes (rev. edn). Washington, DC: National Association for Early Years Education (NAEYC).

Bronfenbrenner, U. (1979) *The Ecology of Human Development: Experiments by Nature and Design*. Cambridge, MA: Harvard University Press.

Bronfenbrenner, U. (1995) Developmental ecology through space and time: a future perspective. In P. Moen and G.H. Elder, Jr (eds) *Examining Lives in Context: Perspectives on the Ecology of Human Development*. Washington, DC: American Psychological Association.

Carr, M. (2001) *Assessment in Early Childhood Settings: Learning Stories*. London: Paul Chapman.

Clough, P. and Nutbrown, C. (2004) Special educational needs and inclusion: multiple perspectives of preschool educator in the UK. *Journal of Early Childhood Research*, 2(2): 191–211.

Curtiss, V.S., Mathur, S.R. and Rutherford, R.B. (2002) Developing behavioural intervention plans: a step-by-step approach. *Beyond Behavior* (Winter): 28–31. Available online at: www.ccbd.net/documents/bb/developing_a_BIP_winter_02.pdf (accessed 12 April 2009).

Department for Children, Schools and Families (DCSF) (2007a) *The Children's Plan: Building Brighter Futures*. Norwich: The Stationery Office.

DCSF (2007b) *Personalised Learning*. Available online at http://www.everychild matters.gov.uk/ete/personalisedlearning (accessed 22 December 2009).

Department for Education and Skills (DfES) (2001) *Special Educational Needs Code of Practice*. London: DfES.

DfES (2003) *Every Child Matters. Summary*. Nottingham: DfES Publications.

DfES (2004) *Removing Barriers to Achievement: The Government's Strategy for SEN*. Nottingham: DfES Publications.

DfES (2007) *Statutory Framework for the Early Years Foundation Stage*. Nottingham: DfES.

DfES/Department of Health (DoH) (2004) *Disabled Child. National Services Framework for Children, Young People and Maternal Units*. London: DH Stationery Office.

DfES/QCA (2003) *Foundation Stage Profile Handbook*. London: QCA.

Department of Health (DoH)/DfEE/Home Office (HO) (2000) *Framework for the Assessment of Children in Need and their Families*. Norwich: The Stationery Office (published with DfEE and Home Office).

ECRII (1999) *Me, Too! Inside Preschool Inclusion*, Modifications ECRII Brief #13. Available online at: http://www.fpg.unc.edu/#ecrii (accessed 21 December 2009).

Gimpel, G.A. and Holland, M.L. (2003) *Emotional and Behavioral Problems of Young Children. Effective Interventions in the Preschool and Kindergarten Years*. New York: The Guilford Press.

Glass, B., Baker, K. and Ellis R., with Bernstone, H. and Hagan, B. (2008) Documenting for inclusion: how do we create an inclusive environment for all children? *Early Childhood Folio*, 12: 36–40.

Horner, R.H., Sugai, G.A. and Todd, A.W. (2001) 'Data' need not be a four-letter word: using data to improve schoolwide discipline. *Beyond Behavior* (Fall): 20–22. Available online at: www.ccbd.net/documents/bb/datanotbe4letter word.pdf (accessed 12 April 2009).

Jones, C.A. (2004) *Supporting Inclusion in the Early Years*. Maidenhead: Open University Press.

Kozulin, A., Gindis, B., Ageyev, V.S. and Miller, S.M. (2003) Introduction. Socio-cultural theory and education: students, teachers and knowledge. In A. Kozulin, B. Gindis, V.S. Ageyev and S.M. Miller (eds) *Vygotsky's Educational Theory in Cultural Context*. Cambridge: Cambridge University Press.

Macartney, B. (2008) 'If you don't know her, she can't talk': noticing the tensions between deficit discourses and inclusive early childhood education. *Early Childhood Folio*, 12: 31–35.

Meisels, S.J. and Atkins-Burnett, S. (2000) The elements of early childhood assessment. In J.P. Shonkoff and S.J. Meisels (eds) *Handbook of Early Childhood Intervention* (2nd edn) Cambridge: Cambridge University Press.

Mowat, J. (2009) The inclusion of pupils perceived as having social and emotional behavioural difficulties in mainstream schools: a focus upon learning. *Support for Learning*, 24(4): 159–169.

Neisworth, J.T. and Bagnato, S.J. (1988) Assessment in early childhood special education. A typology of dependent measure. In S.L. Odom and M.B. Karnes (eds) *Early Intervention for Infants and Children with Handicaps An Empirical Base.* Baltimore, MD: Paul H. Bookes Publishing Co.

Norwich, B. and Lewis, A. (2005) How specialized is teaching pupils with disabilities and difficulties. In A. Lewis and B. Norwich (eds) *Special Teaching for Special Children? Pedagogies for Inclusion.* Maidenhead: Open University Press.

Nutbrown, C. and Clough, P. (2006) *Inclusion in the Early Years*. Los Angeles: Sage.

Odom, S.L., Vitztum, J., Wolery, R., Lieber, J., Sandall, S., Hanson, M.J., Beckman, P., Schwartz, I. and Horn, E. (2004) Preschool inclusion in the United States: a review of research from an ecological systems perspectives. *Journal of Research in Special Educational Needs*, 4(1): 17–49.

OECD (2007) *No More Failures: Ten Steps to Equity in Education – Executive Summary*. Paris: OECD.

Papatheodorou, T. (2005) *Behaviour Problems in the Early Years*. London: RoutledgeFalmer.

Papatheodorou, T. and Loader, P. (2009) *The Reggio Emilia Artist's Project: Changing Culture – Changing Pedagogy*. Paper presented at the 19th EECERA conference, Strasbourg, France.

Penn, H. (2000) Part one: how do children learn? Early childhood services in a global context. In H. Penn (ed.) *Early Childhood Services: Theory, Policy and Practices*. Buckingham: Open University Press.

Purdue, K. (2006) Children and disability in early childhood education: 'special' or inclusive education? *Early Childhood Folio*, 10: 12–15.

Quinn, M.M., Gable, R.A., Rutherford, R.B., Nelson, C.M. and Howell, K.W. (1998) *Addressing Student Problem Behavior. An IEP's Team Introduction to Functional Behavioral Assessment and Behavior Intervention Plans.* USA: The Center for Effective Collaboration and Practice. Available online at: http://cecp.air.org/fba/problembehavior/funcanal.pdf (accessed 26 February 2009).

Raver, S.A. (2004) Monitoring child progress in early childhood special education settings. *Teaching Exceptional Children*, 36(6): 52–57.

Rinaldi, C. (2006) *In Dialogue with Reggio Emilia: Listening, Researching and Learning.* London: Routledge.

Runswick-Cole, K. and Hodge, N. (2009) Needs or rights? A challenge to the discourse of special education. *British Journal of Special Education*, 36(4): 198–203.

Sammons, P., Taggart, B., Smees, R., Sylva, K., Melhuish, E., Siraj-Blatchford, I. and Elliot, K. (2003) *The Early Years Transition and Special Educational Needs (EYTSEN) Project.* Nottingham: DfES Publications, Research Report RR431.

Sayeed, Z. and Guerin, E. (2000) *Early Years Play: A Happy Medium for Assessment and Intervention.* London: David Fulton.

Sheridan, M.K., Foley, G.M. and Radlinski, S.H. (1995) *Using the Supportive Play Model: Individualized Intervention in Early Childhood Practice.* New York: Teachers College Press.

Siraj-Blatchford, I. and Sylva, K. (2004) Researching pedagogy in English preschools. *British Educational Research Journal*, 30(5): 713–730.

Vacc, N.A. and Ritter, S.H. (1995) *Assessment of Preschool Children.* ERIC Digest (REIC identifier: ED389964).

Van der Veer, R. and Valsiner, J. (1991) *Understanding Vygotsky: A Quest for Synthesis.* Oxford: Blackwell.

Vasta, R., Haith, M.M. and Miller, S.A. (1999) *Child Psychology: the Modern Science* (3rd edn). New York: Wiley.

Wenger, E. (1998) *Communities of Practice. Learning, Meaning and Identity.* Cambridge: Cambridge University Press.

Wilson, R. (1998) *Special Educational Needs in the Early Years.* London: Routledge.

18 Play, the universe and everything!

Tina Bruce

Summary

In this chapter, some of the traditional principles of early learning are outlined, updated in the light of recent developments, and clarified through examples of different-aged children playing. The 12 features of play (Bruce 1991) are linked with these. Diversity and inclusion in play are shown to be of central importance, and the chapter emphasises the value of cross-cultural aspects of play, and the inclusion of children with complex needs, disabilities and special educational needs.

Introduction

When I was a child, I played schools. Erikson (1963) argues that through our childhood play we are partners with our future. Perhaps, after all, there is sense in the traditional saying that we should give sitting babies a box of objects and that, depending on what they select, their future will be divulged! Through observing and becoming part of a child's play, we discover an individual child's personal play style and 'tune in' to what we, as practitioners, can do to help that child develop the dispositions that support active learning through play.

This chapter is about 'tuning in' to the processes of children's play, and how adults are crucial in encouraging children to participate in the social group and culture. Children are active agents in their own play but they need adults who are informed advocates, promoting and protecting free-flow play not only for children but for adults too. The socio-cultural environment is important in establishing individual children's sense of agency in developing their play (see Powell and David, Chapter 16, and Papatheodorou, Chapter 17).

Research into brain development (Damasio 2004) is showing that nurture triggers, shapes and influences nature. Our environments – social, cultural, physical and material – serve as an extension of our brains, it seems. The developing field of *epigenetics*, building on twin studies as one aspect of its studies, is also beginning to demonstrate the way that genes, relationships, culture and environment interact, such that genes can become re-programmed, impacting on human development (as well as medical knowledge) (see Van Tulleken 2009).

Observing free-flow play in action

Tom, aged 2 years, spent an afternoon cracking a bowl of nuts with two types of nutcracker: a corkscrew model and a pincer model. He was involved in forces, holes and broken parts. He shared this experience with his mother, engaging in shared and sustained conversations as he played (Siraj-Blatchford *et al.* 2002). By the age of 3, he was making paper aeroplanes. He was completely fascinated when shown by an older child that he could cut bits off the wing to make flaps, which speed up and slow down flight and vary the direction of the aeroplane. Vygotsky (1978) has emphasised the importance of children spending time with people who are more skilled than they are, if learning is to be effectively developed.

During his play, Tom loved to throw sticks into bushes in the garden and into water. He, in Europe, is doing what a group of three children (aged 2, 4 and 7) are doing on the banks of the River Nile on the African continent. They are making boats that will sail in particular directions and float with cargoes. Tom is playing with forces, crashes and splashes, just as they are as they throw sticks and stones into the Nile around the boats that they have made. This kind of free-flow play is happening all over the world. There are ubiquitous aspects of play that resonate wherever children are growing up. Ubiquity is about the common core of play, which has a universal dimension.

Hannah at 14 is choreographing a solo dance for her GCSE course. This is the culmination of the dance play she has maintained from the age of 10 months, when she began the 'knees-bend' swaying to music indulged in by children in cultures throughout the world (Davies 2003). At 6 she danced for hours on end with her 4-year-old friend, Ming, using dressing-up clothes, music on a tape recorder and home-made instruments, playing at dancing and using everything she knew about dance.

In Cairo, a different mixed-age group comprising three boys (one 12 year old and two 15 year olds) free-flow play-dance on a patch of park between two busy roads. They have brought a ghetto-blaster, play Arabic music and all do their own thing. Gradually, one echoes what another does. For an hour they increasingly coordinate their movements until they are dancing together. One

Photograph 18.1   Children are active agents in their own play.

of the important features of play involving dance or music is that it does not require talking. In free-flow play, one of the features is that the players are sensitive to each other's personal agendas as well as a feeling of group sensitivity emerging.

At an international conference in England, Nigel Kennedy spoke of the way musicians found they could improvise and literally 'play' music together, which was of a high standard and respected the different cultural backgrounds from which they came. They found they could allow one style of music to emerge and subside, letting another form become dominant at different points. This kind of free-flow playing respects individuals and encourages group sensitivity. There are resonances with the processes involved in creativity here, since improvisation and making connections are key aspects of creativity. This is explored in general terms in both Bruce (2004a) and Duffy (Chapter 8 of this book). It is examined through the lens of dance and movement in Davies (2003) and Pound (Chapter 9), and with a focus on drawing, painting and construction in Matthews (2003). Free-flow play is about functioning at a high level, and also leads to quality in the way individuals interact with the sciences (Gura 1992), as is apparent in Cameo 18.1.

Cameo 18.1

Seven-year-old Chris goes to stay for a week on a cabin cruiser boat holiday on the River Thames with William (11) and Ayo (13). It is his first experience of boat life. Here is another mixed-age group, again untypical of those found in formal schools. The older children teach him to work a lock, tie a knot, move safely on to land, light a barbecue, put up a tent, strip a stick, make an arrow, make a bow from willow, fish, swab the deck and sweep the stairs. He is learning in a very practical way key elements of science and technology as well as geography and history. He sees the older children settle to an hour's homework each day, and spends that time choosing to sketch, play, read and practise, becoming, for example, skilled in lighting his own barbecue. As he plays, he wallows in using the bow and arrow, and celebrates his skill in shooting at a target of his making.

Different children and different cultural expectations influence the play of children (see Chapter 16 of this book). It is the Hadza boys who play with bows and arrows. Similarly, it is Tom, not Ayo, who initiates this kind of play. Characteristically, if Ayo had played this at age 7, she would probably have 'become' Boudicca or someone like her. Girls seem to be drawn into narrative more easily than boys (Paley 1986; Holland 2003; Kalliala 2005).

Chris, like William, loves to 'play' scientifically. His imagined world is to do with alternative hypotheses for what will happen to the arrow when he does this, that or the other (Howe and Davies explore further examples of science, technology and play in Chapter 10). Adults are around, but he can take responsibility and control, and is proud of himself. When he needs help, he asks, or an adult notices and comes to offer help. He is told (or read) a story each evening sitting by the camp fire. In particular he loves King Arthur stories. There is no competition with other 7 year olds. He goes at his own speed and sets himself high standards, encouraged by the admiration of others but influenced to learn by the leadership of the older children.

Play is a concept that embraces diversity, but it is also inclusive.

Both adults and children have the propensity for play in any culture or community. Children with special educational needs, disabilities and complex requirements are now seen as participators in their communities and the encouragement of their play development is now recognised as being of great importance (Ockelford 2008; see also Chapters 2 and 17).

Cameo 18.2

Daniel, from the age of 3, thoroughly enjoyed dressing-up clothes. It was a tradition at family gatherings to play charades, which involved one group acting out words – titles of books, films or famous names – while the others tried to guess who/what they were. Because of his disabilities, Daniel had great difficulty in reading, writing and breaking words down into components. For years, the joy of charades for him was in choosing his dressing-up clothes and trying to get the group to act a story he told. The rest of the family group worked gently around his play agenda. By the time he was about 12, he was thinking about the costumes others would wear, rather than simply planning his own. He began to join in thinking what roles they would adopt, although the storyline and characters still revolved around him. Everyone felt the effort was for him and respected his hard work in trying to do this.

Suddenly, at the age of about 14, he made a huge step forward. He saw that a phrase like 'Footballers' Wives' could be acted out in four parts, according to the number of syllables. He realised, in a quantum leap forward in his thinking, that the group could then make a story out of the whole phrase. He no longer needed to be the centre of attention. The first syllable had a hospital operating theatre with people with bad feet having surgery. The second was a football match with the ball going into the goal. The third had children in a lesson at school not knowing the answer to a teacher's questions, saying 'Erh' all the time. Then came a party and he needed to introduce his wife. The whole word was then acted out, echoing a scene from the programme on television. He was now participating in a group event without needing to dominate the play.

The years from 3 to 14, of dressing-up in imitation of characters, leading into the becoming of characters, with gentle but sustained and relentless encouragement to think of other people's parts in stories and themes acted out, and in what makes a storyline that helps the audience to see the point of the acting, had helped Daniel to develop part–whole relationships (Piaget 1947; Clay 1975; Ferreiro and Teberosky 1983). Play in a social context has made a huge contribution to his development. We often see a slower development in children with special educational needs and disabilities, but this helps to illuminate and show clearly why play is so important in developing learning as a whole person (Papatheodorou, Chapter 17).

The bedrock principles of early childhood practice

We need to reflect further on the experience Chris has on the boat trip, and to consider what schools ought to be like for children at least until the end of the English Key Stages.

Chris helps with chores that are essential to living on a boat. Not all the tasks are pleasant or exciting, but he does them willingly and dutifully and is proud of his contribution. He can see the point of doing them (Whiting and Edwards 1992). He is involved in a little formal learning relating to shopping (number and money) and literacy (stories, reading and writing). He plays for nearly half his day, sometimes alone, but also with William and Ayo. He socialises a great deal, participating in ball games with William. He is with adults who are able to give him attention when he seeks or needs it, or just to be around them watching as they work. He is encouraged to use what is essential and universal to being a human – his possibility to relate to others and to act symbolically and through narrative in a number of ways (see Whitehead, Chapter 5). He can represent experiences through number, language and free-flow play. He is also encouraged to be himself and to develop his free-flow play according to his own temperament. As Brazelton (1969: 281) points out, young children 'show a resistance to being pushed into habits that are not sympathetic to their style, a resistance backed up by all the strength inherent in an well-organized personality, infant or adult'.

The great pioneer educators were aware of the delicate balance between what is universal to being human and the unique way in which every individual is human. For example, the nineteenth-century educator, Froebel, was constantly aware of certain aspects that human beings have in common, which bind them together as a species across the world. He considered free-flow play to be an important one of these, seeing every child as a unique individual who needs sensitive and appropriate help in order to develop and learn optimally. In this way, we can see that play is an integrating mechanism in a child's development, and perhaps into adulthood too. He also valued play because it encourages and supports reflection about living in and participating in community and cultural life.

In Bruce (1987), ten principles were extrapolated from the literature and philosophy of the heritage left by pioneers such as Friedrich Froebel (1782–1852), Rudolf Steiner (1861–1925) and Maria Montessori (1869–1952). These are as follows.

1 Childhood is seen as valid in itself, as part of life and not simply as preparation for adulthood.
2 The whole child is considered to be important. Health, and physical and mental well-being, are emphasised, together with the importance of feelings, having ideas, thoughts and spiritual aspects.
3 Learning is not compartmentalised, because everything is linked.
4 Intrinsic motivation, resulting in child-initiated self-directed activity, is valued.
5 Self-discipline is emphasised (4 and 5 lead to autonomy).
6 There are especially receptive periods of learning at different stages of development.
7 What children can do (rather than what they cannot do) is the starting point in the child's education.
8 There is an inner structure in the child that includes the imagination and that emerges especially under favourable conditions.
9 The people (both adults and children) with whom the child interacts are of central importance.
10 The child's education is seen as an interaction between the child and the environment the child is in – including, in particular, other people and knowledge itself.

While in the UK there is considerable agreement about the principles that guide early childhood education, which are now enshrined in law as the *Early Years Foundation Stage* (DfES 2008), there is also great variation in the way principles are interpreted in practice by those working with young children and their families. There are those who choose to package them into an identifiable method (Montessori, High/Scope, Reggio Emilia) and those who, instead, emphasise the importance of quality training, embedded in sound general principles, as the most effective long-term strategy to encourage reflective practice (Pascal and Bertram 2001; Moyles *et al.* 2002; Bennett 2004).

It is not possible for people to step outside their culture, society or upbringing, but examining commonalities between human beings is useful. It brings together what we know of how children develop according to brain research in biological terms and the socio-cultural dimension of development (Bruce 2004b, 2010). We know that humans have the potential to function symbolically (Athey 1990). They do this in many ways – for example, through language and literacy (see Whitehead, Chapter 5), visual representation (Matthews 2003), dance and movement (Davies 2003), mathematically (Worthington and Carruthers 2003; Griffiths, Chapter 11 of this book), and through play (Moyles 1989; Bruce 1991).

Because there is widespread confusion about what play is, 'free-flow play' (Bruce 1991) was adopted as a term because it expresses a view of play supported by 12 features extrapolated from the literature, as follows.

Twelve features of free-flow play

1 It is an active process without a product.
2 It is intrinsically motivated: children cannot be made to play.
3 It exerts no external pressure to conform to rules, pressures, goals, tasks or definite direction. It gives the player control.
4 It is about possible, alternative worlds, that lift players to their highest levels of functioning, freeing them from the here and now. This involves being imaginative, creative, original and innovative.
5 It is about participants wallowing in ideas, feelings and relationships. It involves reflecting on, and becoming aware of, what we know: meta-cognition.
6 It actively uses previous first-hand experiences, including struggle, manipulation, exploration, discovery and practice.
7 It is sustained and, when in full flow, helps us to function in advance of what we can actually do in our real lives.
8 During free-flow play, we use technical prowess, mastery and competence we have previously developed, and so can be in control. Play is not so much about learning new things as it is about applying and reflecting on what has been learned.
9 It can be initiated by a child or an adult, but if by an adult he/she must pay particular attention to 3, 5 and 11 of the features.
10 Play can be solitary.
11 It can be in partnership or groups, with adults and/or children who will be sensitive to each other.
12 It is an integrating mechanism, which brings together everything we learn, know, feel and understand.

The features are increasingly used by practitioners to inform their observations, and to identify and locate play in the child's learning. They also assist analysis and reflection in keeping formative and summative records.

Commonalities and differences in free-flow play across cultures

It is helpful to begin studying how play develops in children (and adults) by looking at the ubiquitous aspects such as the features common to play. It is also important to look at socio-cultural differences in the way that children play in different families and communities transglobally, if we are to respond to and value the uniqueness of each human being and the rich diversity of different cultures.

Free-flow play is found among children in all parts of the world, as well as in ancient civilisations. It is part of being human. However, those who study play view it through a variety of different lenses, which result in it being encouraged, discouraged, constrained or valued in widely differing ways, which have a great impact on the child's access and opportunities for free-flow playing.

There is a tendency among some to see free-flow play as a privilege enjoyed mainly by middle-class children in Europe and North America and yet, in reality, this is unlikely to be so. It is 'misguided to characterize the middle classes as historical pinnacles of indulgent concern for children's needs' (Konner 1991: 196). It may even be that those in the 'fast lane' of complex industrialised societies are in danger of losing, or at least damaging and seriously eroding, aspects of traditional childhood that are in fact central to being truly successful human adults. 'More haste and less speed' is the dilemma (Alexander 2009; see also Anning, Chapter 1). In complex industrial-ised life there is so much that children need to know. In the UK since the late 1980s there has been slippage into the earlier introduction of formal schooling with an emphasis on direct teaching and the transmitting of a particular cul-ture (Brooker 2002). This is typically presented to children through highly pre-structured experiences in a predominantly 'tell and write' mode. However, this may not produce the kind of adult who can survive the future nearly so well as the adaptive intelligence, imagination and creativity required of children brought up to actively experience and learn in real-life situations, with opportunity and access to free-flow play (Blakemore 2000).

It is not a question of those in complex industrialised societies trying to return to a romantically perceived view of the hunting and gathering or agri-cultural community, where children play, socialise and learn from being with adults as they work each day. It is much more a question of not discarding what is central to humanity (Huizunga 1949) by throwing the baby out with the bath water in an attempt to keep a place in the 'fast lane'. Those who study children free-flow playing do not see romance but a highly effective mechanism giving access to symbolic and physical functioning of a high level.

Children's play is sometimes used and taken over by adults as a way of gaining access to guiding and structuring children's learning so that they are, it is argued, adequately prepared for adult life and helped to learn in ways that are appropriate to childhood. This 'preparation for life' view of play is sup-ported by modern theorists such as Bruner, and has gained great influence in England and North America, although not so much in the Nordic countries and other countries of western Europe (see Moyles 2010).

It is interesting to examine figures produced by Whiting and Whiting's Six Cultures Project (Konner 1991). Five agricultural societies in Kenya, Mexico, the Philippines, Japan and India were studied together with a town called 'Orchardtown' in Pennsylvania, New England, USA. The children in Orchardtown were involved in household and garden chores for 2 per cent of their time. They were engaged in casual social interactions, watching adults, chatting, and so on, for about 52 per cent of the time. Formal school-type learning took up 16 per cent of the time. From these figures, we could perhaps argue that these urban children are playing for a healthy and appropriate part of their day. However, there is more to this, as we shall see later.

We know from Donaldson's (1978) pioneering studies that children perform better on embedded tasks, which make what she calls 'human sense' to them. When the tasks are in the context of their own everyday lives and have purpose and function, and when children are able to learn through their senses with freedom of movement, they learn with more breadth, depth and permanence. Their well-being and sense of self is stronger. They are more confident and engaged, and take pride in what they do. They want to participate and make a good contribution and have the dispositions needed for life-long learning.

Konner (1991: 309) suggests that we have seen a massive switch in developed industrial societies so that children are now in compulsory schooling in contrast to performing compulsory chores or labour. Using figures from the Six Cultures Project, he shows that in agricultural societies children tend to work at chores for their parents for 17 per cent of the time in fields or in the home. They play for 44 per cent of their time. They are involved in casual social interactions, chatting, watching adults, and so on, for 34 per cent of their time, and in formal learning for only 5 per cent of the time.

When we speak of child labour being an abuse of children's rights, we need to be clear what we are talking about. Putting children to work in coalmines and factories with the growth of industrialisation is not the same as children helping in the home or on the family farm. Konner argues (1991: 309) that 'Despite their hardships, chores give children skills they are proud of all their lives, and can bring parents and children closer together.'

In hunting and gathering societies, such as the Kung or Hadza (BBC 1999), children learn through watching, socialising, playing and slowly doing, with virtually no formal teaching. In agricultural societies children are required to do more of the essential chores that arise through living in one place rather than moving on. Pretty Shield (in Niethammer 1977: 27), a member of the Crow tribe, remembering her childhood in the early 1900s, describes the 'chores' element in her education:

> Indian girls were gently led into the art of motherhood, and their
> introduction to other womanly tasks was gradual, too, at least for the
> littlest girls. They accompanied their mothers and big sister while
> they gathered foods, weeded gardens, and went for water and wood.
> As the girls grew older more was expected of them. A Fox woman,
> living in the area of what is now Wisconsin and Illinois, told how she
> was encouraged when she was about nine to plant a few things and to

hoe the weeds. Then she was taught to cook what she had raised, and was lavishly praised for her efforts.

Pretty Shield also remembers the importance of free-flow play during her childhood (Niethammer 1977: 25):

> Learning the role of woman by playing was the pervading method of education for young girls, and mothers often took pains to see that their daughters had accurate miniatures of real household equipment to use in playing house. In some of the Plains tribes such as the Cheyenne, Omaha, Arapaho and Crow, daughters of the more well-to-do families even had their own skin tents as play-houses, and when time came to pack up camp to follow the buffalo, the girls got their own household – tipe, toys and clothes – packed and ready to move.

Kalliala (2005) discusses gender issues in young children's play today and the changes since the 1950s. Her research resonates with the reminiscences of Pretty Shield from the 1900s.

Children in both hunting and gathering societies and agricultural societies learn through watching, playing, socialising and slowly doing, according to an apprenticeship model. Children do not have to tell or write what they learn. They have to show their learning by doing (for example, weaving in the context of everyday life). In their play, they reflect on these active experiences and wallow in them, demonstrating the technical prowess they have been struggling to master. Play is about wallowing in what has been experienced, and dealing with mastering, facing and controlling what is experienced emotionally, socially, bodily, in movement and in thoughts and ideas (Tovey 2007). It is, in the main, about the application of what is known, using the skill and competence that has been developed.

This contrasts with industrial societies, in which household chores are replaced with child labour in factories and mines, or with formal schooling with children following adult-set and led tasks for long hours of the day. Konner argues (1991: 310) that school 'attempts to turn children into a workforce with skills that society needs. In these senses it exploits children just as much as work does.'

Conclusion

All these developments mean that play has been re-established on an official level at the heart of the way practitioners need to work with children in setting up and working in appropriate learning environments indoors and outdoors for children from birth to at least the age of 6. Both the traditional philosophical principles supporting play, with its emphasis on experienced intuition and practice wisdom handed down from generation to generation (Bruce 1987, 2004c) and the theories giving high value to childhood play and beyond into adulthood, remain important. These are confirmed through research evidence from major research projects such as *Effective Provision of Preschool Education (EPPE)* (Sylva *et al.* 2003) and the *Study of Pedagogical Effectiveness in Early Learning (SPEEL)* (Moyles *et al.* 2002), which give clear evidence of the importance of play in the development and learning of young children.

This is not to argue that young children do not benefit from education. It does suggest that it is crucial for parents and practitioners to help children to develop and learn effectively and appropriately according to the way the young brain develops. Practitioners working with groups of other people's children need to be educated, mature, highly trained and qualified so that they can support and extend children's play in an informed way, with the sophistication and sensitivity required to do so. Play needs committed adult advocates.

Societies that neglect their infrastructure are likely to hit problems, producing adults who are not able to problem solve, persevere, concentrate, be imaginative or creative, make connections, improvise, be flexible and adaptive, read the body movements and language of others, see things from different points of view, or tune in to the thoughts and feelings of other people or situations. Free-flow play is part of the infrastructure of any civilisation (Huizinga 1949; Kalliala 2005; Bruce and Ockelford 2009).

Play is, it seems, about the universe and everything. It often has to function in a hostile environment, but when it is encouraged, supported and extended, it makes a major contribution to, and sophisticated impact on, the development of individuals and humanity as a whole.

Questions to set you thinking

1   Describe your own childhood play. Did you play? If you did, how does this resonate with the 12 features of free-flow play outlined in this chapter?
2   What are the commonalities of play, and how do you help children with different cultural experiences to play, alone and/or together?
3   How can you use the 12 features of free-flow play to help you observe, support and plan in developing the play of individual children, or groups of children?
4   How can you use the 12 features of free-flow play to support parents to enjoy play with their children and to encourage children in their own play in the home setting? The case studies of children in the family situation will help you to reflect on this.

References and further reading

Alexander, R. (2009) *Children, their World, their Education: Final Report of the Cambridge Primary Review.* London: Routledge.

Athey, C. (1990) *Extending Thought in Young Children: A Parent–Teacher Partnership.* London: Paul Chapman.

Bennett, J. (2004) Curriculum issues in national policymaking. Keynote address, European Early Childhood Education Research Association International Conference, Malta, September.

Blakemore, S.J. (2000) *Early Years Learning*, Report No. 140 (June). London: Parliamentary Office of Science and Technology.

Brazelton, T.B. (1969) *Infants and Mothers: Differences in Development.* New York: Delacorte Press.

Brooker, L. (2002) *Starting School: Young Children Learning Cultures.* Buckingham: Open University Press.

Bruce, T. (1987) *Early Childhood Education.* Sevenoaks: Hodder and Stoughton.

Bruce, T. (1991) *Time to Play in Early Childhood Education.* London: Hodder and Stoughton.

Bruce, T. (2004a) *Cultivating Creativity in Early Childhood.* London: Hodder Arnold.

Bruce, T. (2004b) *Developing Learning in Early Childhood.* London: Paul Chapman Publishing.

Bruce, T. (2010) Froebel today. In L. Millar (ed.) *Critical Issues in the Early Years.* London: Sage.

Bruce, T. and Ockelford, A. (2009) Understanding symbolic development. In T. Bruce (ed.) *Early Childhood: A Guide for Students* (2nd edn). London: Sage.

Clay, M. (1975) *What Did I Write?* London: Heinemann.

Damasio, A. (2004) *Looking for Spinoza.* London: Vintage, Random House Press.

Davies, M. (2003) *Movement and Dance in Early Childhood* (2nd edn). London: Paul Chapman Publishing.

Department for Education and Skills (DfES) (2008) *Early Years Foundation Stage.* London: DfES.

Donaldson, M. (1978) *Children's Minds.* London: Fontana.

Erikson, E. (1963) *Childhood and Society* (2nd edn). London: Routledge and Kegan Paul.

Ferreiro, E. and Teberosky, A. (1983) *Literacy before Schooling* (K. Goodman Castro). London: Heinemann.

Gura, P. (ed.) (1992) *Exploring Learning: Young Children and Blockplay.* London: Paul Chapman Publishing.

Holland, P. (2003) *We Don't Play With Guns Here: War, Weapons and Superhero Play in the Early Years.* Buckingham: Open University Press.

Huizinga, J. (1949) *Homo Ludens: A Study of the Play Element in Culture*. London: Routledge and Kegan Paul.

Kalliala, M. (2005) *Play Culture in a Changing World*. Maidenhead: Open University Press.

Konner, M. (1991) *Childhood*. Boston, MA: Little Brown.

Matthews, J. (2003) *Drawing and Painting: Children and Visual Representation* (2nd edn). London: Paul Chapman Publishing.

Moyles, J. (1989) *Just Playing? The Role and Status of Play in Early Childhood Education*. Buckingham: Open University Press.

Moyles, J. (ed.) (2010) *Thinking About Play: Developing a Reflective Approach*. Maidenhead: Open University Press.

Moyles, J., Adams, S. and Musgrove, A. (2002) *SPEEL: Study of Pedagogical Effectiveness in Early Learning*. London: DfES, Research Report 363.

Niethammer, C. (1977) *Daughters of the Earth: The Lives and Legends of American Indian Women*. New York: Collier/Macmillan.

Ockelford, A. (2008) *Music for Children and Young People with Complex Needs*. Oxford: Oxford University Press.

Paley, V.G. (1986) *Mollie is Three*. Chicago, IL: University of Chicago.

Pascal, C. and Bertram, T. (2001) *Effective Early Learning: Case Studies in Improvement*. London: Paul Chapman Ltd.

Piaget, J. (1947) *The Psychology of Intelligence* (trans. M. Piercy and D. Berlyne). London: Routledge and Kegan Paul.

Siraj-Blatchford, I., Sylva, K., Muttock, S., Gilden, R. and Bell, D. (2002) *Researching Effective Pedagogy in the Early Years*. London: DfES, Research Report No. 356.

Sylva, K., Melhuish, E., Sammons, P., Siraj-Blatchford, I., Taggart, B. and Elliot, K. (2003) *The Effective Provision of Preschool Education (EPPE) Project: Findings from the Preschool Period*. London: Institute of Education.

Tovey, H. (2007) *Playing Outdoors: Spaces and Places, Risk and Challenge*. Maidenhead: Open University Press.

Van Tulleken, A. (2009) *The Secret Life of Twins: Why am I the Fat One?* BBC1, 30 September.

Vygotsky, L. (1978) *Mind in Society: The Development of Higher Psychological Processes* (trans. M. Cole, V. John-Steiner, S. Scribner and E. Souberman). Cambridge, MA: Harvard University Press.

Whiting, B. and Edwards, C.P. (1992) *Children in Different Worlds: The Formation of Social Behaviour*. Cambridge, MA: Harvard University Press.

Worthington, M. and Carruthers, E. (2003) *Children's Mathematics: Making Marks, Making Meaning*. London: Paul Chapman.

Afterword

Janet Moyles

The arguments for the 'excellence of play' have now been expressed. From practitioners' statements about the value, and the lack, of play-based learning for young children, we have moved forward ever more convincingly, I believe, to end with the concept of full free-flowing play – and covered a whole world of play in education and care in between, all of it based within children's development, learning and natural dispositions.

No one can deny that children (and many adults!) have a natural inclination to play, alongside natural instincts to learn and to be curious and inventive, which are characteristics of the human race in general (Elkind 2008). In a way, these are what make children, children! Perhaps this is one of our adult problems, especially in fast-developing societies: we don't appear to have time for childhood and its incumbent challenges and demands (see Layard and Dunn 2009). Childhood is a very special time in all our lives and one that is worthy of its own concepts and breathing space (see House and Loewenthal 2009).

As I have said elsewhere (Moyles 2009):

> . . . play in all its forms is a powerful scaffold for children's learning: it enables metacognition (learning about how to understand one's own learning and play). It allows children to cope with not knowing something long enough in order to know – they can rehearse, practise, revise, replay and re-learn . . . It frees them from worrying about doing things wrong and gives them confidence to try out alternatives. Children learn to establish their own identity and their place in the order of things through play . . . Play enables children to interrogate the world in which they find themselves without loss of self-esteem and, above all, play enables children to learn that learning is – and should always be – enjoyable, personally profitable and challenging. This is the vital feature if we are to have happy and well-balanced, flexible learners and citizens of the future.
>
> (p. 28)

Playful pedagogies are better able to support children's learning and development, and lead to higher-quality interactions between practitioners and children. Similarly, a curriculum that sanctions and utilises play and child-initiated experience is more likely, as several contributors have argued, to produce well-balanced, happier, more self-confident, self-sufficient children who are more rounded and successful citizens (see Gallinsky 2006). The latter also argues the cost-benefit to society of high-quality, play-based preschool programmes based on the High/Scope and other studies in the USA, which is clearly important in all societies.

Play is what all of us, the contributors to this book, are advocating and offering as the way forward in the education of children, at least those under 7. We can be certain if we observe children's play that much learning is happening. But it is practitioners who are in the position daily of observing how much value there is in children's play and how it can be focused into a very powerful, meaningful and child-initiated learning medium (Moyles 2009). It takes courage and confidence in oneself as a practitioner, as we have seen in many chapters. But we have never had such a well-educated workforce as we are now developing, so surely this is the time to grasp play and make learning through play a success for adults and children?

Those teaching and caring for birth to 6 year olds in England have the support of the play-based EYFS and its related play document (DCSF 2009). Practitioners should now take these (or whatever other curriculum and policies they are working within) and evaluate them in relation to how children are actually *internalising* the learning that is intended, not just *performing* within prescribed boundaries. Having information in itself is not enough: it has to be *used* in meaningful ways to become 'knowledge', both by children and by practitioners. Instead of sidelining play practices in order to 'deliver' a curriculum, we should be taking the best playful pedagogies and raising their profile to implement the best possible quality learning experiences for children. If this is done, children and adults can learn together through play, to the benefit of both (e.g. Moyles and Adams 2001).

Playing and responding playfully means taking some risks both for adults and for children. Whereas children's risks tend to be physical, the risks for practitioners require deep reflection and analysis on currently held values and practices (Brock 2010). Both children and adults have, in the recent past, succumbed to working and playing in 'safe' conditions: adults to working within perceived boundaries of curriculum and policy prescriptions, and children to being cosseted in front of television screens and computer monitors where parents feel they are 'safe'. We know, however, that adults who feel autonomous, 'in control' (of their own lives) and knowledgeable are happier, more self-confident and motivated in their work (see Chapter 15 of this book). There is evidence that children who have the freedom to develop their own ideas and learning through play are known to be more motivated and more competent in cognitive and social skills (Singer *et al.* 2006).

There is a danger, however, that policy makers' intentions might amount to 'hijacking' play for their own purposes (Moyles 2009) – practitioners need to resist this at all costs as they are the ones in day-to-day contact with children, who observe the excellence of play from the children's perspectives. The lack of play training of practitioners is potentially a huge stumbling block for many practitioners, where emphasis on 'delivering' curriculum intentions and outputs is often more heavily stressed than learning through play. This particularly applies to early years teacher training and, to a certain extent, on Early Years Practitioner (EYP) courses where the emphasis on the latter is often on issues only loosely related to playful pedagogy.

Everyone needs to recognise and value play in children's learning: it is not sufficient only that early years practitioners themselves do so. As we saw in the Introduction, practitioners find the justification of play difficult because of pressures of local authority personnel, heads and leaders, other teachers in the school, and parents, many of whom do not equate play with learning, only with recreation. This means a huge role for everyone in the multi-professional teams which are such a large part of early years practices. The education and training of all those who work with or who are responsible for children under 7 should include a goodly proportion of time spent on understanding the value of play and playful pedagogies so that everyone can work together to benefit children and their education. This includes all those who support early years partnerships and those who communicate with parents.

This lack of deeper understanding was brought home to me recently in discussion on UK's Radio 4 over the new *Cambridge Primary Review* (Alexander 2009); it showed that many parents still believe that the earlier children do something like read and write, the quicker they will master the skills – this, despite significant evidence from European and international contexts that learning of such skills is retained only when sufficient time has been spent on allowing children's maturation, language and brain development. It is definitely *not* the case that the earlier the better. Practitioners and the multi-professional team members with whom they interact will be able to support parental understanding and justify their pedagogy only when they themselves have a thorough grasp of play and learning. The issue of professional judgement is also one that should be considered on courses, as much government policy in relation to early years relies on practitioners' judgements of what is appropriate for each unique child in their setting or class.

While there are many international communities from which we can gain knowledge in relation to play and children's learning, such as the Scandinavian systems and the Reggio Emilia and Te Whāriki practices, the picture in other parts of the world is mixed. In all the systems that seem to 'work' for children, the one common denominator is that children do not start school until they are at least 6 years of age. The one very clear message that emerges is that there is no benefit to children in the longer term in starting 'formal' schooling early and, in fact, there is evidence to suggest quite the contrary (e.g. Elkind and Whitehurst 2001; Sharp 2002). Sharp (2002) states 'The arguments in favour of children being taught academic skills earlier do not appear to be borne out by the evidence' (p. 15). On p. 18, she goes on to say, 'There are some suggestions that an early introduction to a formal curriculum may increase anxiety and have a negative impact on children's self esteem and motivation to learn.'

A frequently expressed political vision is for a 'learning society', yet it seems unlikely that this will be a reality unless the earlier play-based learning engenders in children the idea that learning and understanding is something exciting, with which they can cope and that has some meaning for them as unique individuals. All the writers in this book are firmly committed to such a learning society. We all want our children to achieve, recognising that every child does matter and that their well-being is paramount to our future (*Every Child Matters*, HM Treasury 2004). This requires practitioners who are committed to adult engagement and interaction in children's play, be it as models, providers, enhancers, initiators, advocates or contributors, as a way of ensuring quality provision, greater understanding and, above all, a well-conceived and justifiable commitment to creating the most 'excellent' play and learning environments.

References and further reading

Alexander, R. (2009) *The Cambridge Primary Review Research Surveys*. London: Routledge (reports are also available at www.primaryreview.org.uk).

Brock, A. (2010) The nature of practitioners' reflection on their reflections about play. In J. Moyles (ed.) *Thinking About Play: Developing a Reflective Approach*. Maidenhead: Open University Press.

Department for Children, Families and Schools (DCFS)/Qualifications and Curriculum Development Agency (QCDA) (2009) *Learning, Playing and Interacting: Good Practice in the Early Years Foundation Stage*. London: DCFS/QCDA. Available for download at http://downloads.nationalstrategies.co.uk.s3.amazonaws.com/pdf/85679136be4953413879dc59eab23ce0.pdf.

Elkind, D. (2008) *The Power of Play: How Spontaneous, Imaginative Activities Lead to Happier, Healthier Children*. Cambridge, MA: De Capo Lifelong.

Elkind, D. and Whitehurst, G.J. (2001) Young Einsteins. Much too early: much too late. *Education Matters*, 1(2): 8–21.

Gallinsky, E. (2006) *Economic Benefits of High Quality Early Childhood Programs*. Washington: Committee for Economic Development.

HM Treasury (2004) *Every Child Matters*. London: HM Stationery Office.

House, R. and Loewenthal, D. (eds) (2009) *Childhood, Well-being and a Therapeutic Ethos*. London: Karnac Books.

Layard, R. and Dunn, J. (2009) *A Good Childhood: Searching for Values in a Competitive Age*. London: Penguin.

Moyles, J. (2009) Play – the powerful means of learning in the early years. In S. Smidt (ed.) *Key Issues in Early Years Education* (2nd edn). London: Routledge.

Moyles, J. and Adams, S. (2001) *StEPs: Statements of Entitlement to Play*. Buckingham: Open University Press.

Sharp, C. (2002) *School Starting Age: European Policy and Recent Research*. Paper presented at the LGA Seminar, When Should Our Children Start School, London: November.

Singer, D., Golinkoff, R. and Hirsh-Pasek, K. (eds) (2006) *Play = Learning: How Play Motivates and Enhances Children's Cognitive and Social-emotional Growth*. New York: Oxford University Press.

Author index

Subject index